LEARNING PSYCHOTHERAPY

A Time-efficient, Research-based, and Outcome-measured Training Program

LEARNING PSYCHOTHERAPY

A Time-efficient, Research-based, and Outcome-measured Training Program

BERNARD D. BEITMAN, M.D.
and
DONGMEI YUE, M.D.

W. W. Norton & Company
New York   London

For information about permission to reproduce selections
from this book, write to
Permissions, W. W. Norton & Company, Inc., 500 Fifth Avenue,
New York, NY 10110

Composition by The PRD Group
Manufacturing by Hamilton Printing

Library of Congress Cataloging-in-Publication Data

Beitman, Bernard D.
    Learning psychotherapy : a time-efficient, research-based, and
outcome-measured psychotherapy training program / Bernard D. Beitman
and Dongmei Yue.
        p.   cm.
    Includes bibliographical references and index.
    ISBN 0–393–70296–0 (pbk.)
    1. Psychotherapy—Study and teaching.   2. Psychotherapists—
Training of.   I. Yue, Dongmei.   II. Title.
RC459.B45   1999
616.89′14′071—dc21   98–50157   CIP

W. W. Norton & Company, Inc., 500 Fifth Avenue, New York, N. Y. 10110
                    http://www.wwnorton.com

W. W. Norton & Company Ltd., 10 Coptic Street, London WC1A 1PU

1 2 3 4 5 6 7 8 9 0

Contents

Forms

Preface

In 1989, I published a paper on psychotherapy integration that caught the attention of Dongmei Yue of China Medical University in Shenyang, China, who requested a reprint. I sent the reprint and also a copy of my book *The Structure of Individual Psychotherapy*. Dr. Yue found this work consistent with her thinking about psychotherapy and decided to translate it into Chinese.

We developed a correspondence through which she expressed her deep love and appreciation of psychotherapy. In 1993 she visited Columbia, Missouri, for two weeks with two colleagues, Professor Li and Professor Ding. When I reciprocated by visiting Shenyang in 1994 with Drs. Jim Slaughter and Danny Wedding, Dr. Yue and I agreed that she would return to Columbia to develop a psychotherapy training program for China. She arrived in Columbia at the end of 1994.

Three and a half years later, in April 1998, we convened a conference in Columbia to train representatives of five different training programs in the psychotherapy modules described in this book. It had been successfully shaped by our experience with three groups of residents in the Division of Psychiatry at the University of Missouri.

This book grew out of a deep commitment by two people to the strengthening of psychotherapy practice in a time of conflict both within the psychotherapy professions and from without. It is intended to provide the opportunity to grasp the basics for use not only in formal psychotherapy itself but also in the many different helping formats in which one person listens and tries to understand and to further the self-change of another. It introduces not only content but also a new way to teach psychotherapy that we hope will lead to the development of other modules.

There are many people to thank for their contributions to this effort. They include: Mehrunissa Ali, Sohail Ajmal, Richard Bowers, Richard Burch, Deborah Burnley, Mohammad Imran Chishti, Lilian Casupang, Jonathan Colen, Tina Drury, Richard Erwin, David Goldberg, George Gulevich, Marcia Goin, James Griffth, Marcia Hashimoto, John Hall, Cheryl Hemme, Joe Himle, Tod Hutton, Stephen Jarvis, Alok Jain, Joseph Lamberti, Robin Lin, Ruben Mendoza, Lisa Pierce, Jyotsna Ranga, Anusha Ranganathan, Muniza Shah, Daniel Strode, Nigar Sultana,

Ahmed Taranissi, Barr Taylor, Alicia Thompson, Laine Young-Walker, and Ulmar Wadood.

Susan Munro at Norton read the manuscript one day and wanted to publish it the next. She excels in brief, incisive comments. Her broad view of potential readership fits with our view that psychotherapy training programs need a solid foundation that is time-efficient, research-based, and outcome-measured.

BERNARD D. BEITMAN
Columbia, Missouri
January, 1999

LEARNING PSYCHOTHERAPY

A Time-efficient, Research-based, and Outcome-measured Training Program

Introduction

The revolution in the delivery of and payment for medical care in the United States is dramatically transforming the theory and practice of psychotherapy. Psychotherapists, like their physician counterparts, are being asked to become cost-effective, and therefore time-efficient, in the delivery of their services. In addition, they are being asked to generate outcome data to substantiate their clinical effectiveness. There is little doubt that many physicians, health-care personnel, and psychotherapists will find economic survival more difficult, if not impossible, in their current roles. Training programs must respond to these changing demands on practitioners in order to increase the likelihood of their surviving in these tumultuous times.

For much of this century of psychotherapy, psychotherapists have enjoyed the luxury of theoretical debate. In what has been amusingly described as a "dogma eats dogma" environment, various therapists have proclaimed the superiority of their theoretical approaches. Although meta-analytic studies have demonstrated the relative equivalence of several approaches (Lambert & Bergin, 1994), and well-designed comparisons of several schools in the treatment of depression (Klerman, Weissman, Markowitz, Glick, Wilner, Mason, & Shear, 1994) have yielded little difference in the aggregate, psychotherapy debates continue, but with lessening fervor.

Over the past quarter-century, the movement to integrate the psychotherapies has accelerated (Norcross & Goldfried, 1992). Clinicians drawn more by patient needs than by theoretical allegiance have attempted to assimilate potential concepts and techniques from a variety of different schools in order to provide efficient treatment for their patients. Eclecticism has given way to several different integrative approaches, which hold the promise of providing a practical framework of decision points associated with a limited number of potentially effective strategies and techniques applicable to varying patient needs.

Among psychotherapy researchers debates abound between those who support experimentally validated therapies (EVTs) and those who emphasize process variables, particularly those variables that the patient brings to therapy. This training program builds upon the process research paradigm by emphasizing the capabilities of the trainees as they proceed through the learning curve. Instead of claiming that trainees are trained or indoctrinated into a specific orientation, this approach tries to build on trainee strengths and experiences by evoking and sharpening already present psychotherapeutic skills and knowledge. Like their patients, trainees vary in the critical processes related to being successful in therapy, such as readiness to change, social network strengths, and ability to form therapeutic alliances.

There are currently three existing categories of training in psychotherapy. Most training programs fall in the first category. These programs appear to be rather disorganized in their conceptual presentation of psychotherapy, allowing different teachers and professors to present their own perspectives on psychotherapy through supervision and didactic seminars, and implicitly suggesting that trainees should put the ideas and techniques together in a way that suits them personally.

A growing number of training programs fall into the second category. These programs rely on manual-based approaches where trainees are expected to learn the specific techniques, attitudes, and skills associated with a certain approach, for example, cognitive therapy for depression (Beck, Rush, Shaw, & Emery, 1979), or exposure and response prevention for obsessive-compulsive disorder, or interpersonal psychotherapy for depression (Klerman, Weissman, Rounsaville, & Chevron, 1984), or psychodynamic psychotherapy for disturbed interpersonal relationships (Strupp & Binder, 1984). There is much merit in such manual-guided training programs, including the relatively easy provision of outcome criteria and the confidence trainees acquire in their knowledge base. However, reasonable questions arise about the generalizability to clinical practice of manual-based therapies that have been shown to be effective in controlled experimental trials. Controlled studies screen out diverse patients in order to adhere to the uniformity demanded of research protocols (Goldfried & Wolfe, 1996). A manual-focused training program limits understanding of other possible approaches for those patients who have more complicated presentations than those addressed by protocol-prescribed approaches. In addition, trainees are not shown what is fundamental to all these approaches—the basics of psychotherapy that draw them together, making each school a variation on a basic theme. These disadvantages have given rise to a third category of training programs, those in psychotherapy integration, where the techniques shared among the major schools of psychotherapy are emphasized. This program falls into this third category.

What are the goals of an effective training program? The designers of an effective training program must select a limited number of skills that, if effectively taught, will lead to effective psychotherapy. This objective requires careful selection from a wide variety of potential alternatives based on research and clinical experience. The selected alternatives should include what are generally considered to be the common factors or pantheoretical element of the psychotherapies. After all, if we apply the term psychotherapy to an entity, there must be elements that define it across the various orientations subsumed under it. It is toward this aim that this training program is developed. In addition, this training program strives to help trainees to master multiple treatment combinations and to adjust their therapeutic approaches to fit the needs of their patients. An additional goal is to educate trainees to think and perhaps to behave integratively—openly and synthetically, but critically—in their clinical pursuits (Andrews, Norcross, & Halgin, 1992). Trainees are encouraged to examine their own thinking and to apply critical research attitudes to what they do and how they do it. They learn to measure their effectiveness and respond to these evaluations with a sharpening of behavior and thinking. Trainees should be informed consumers of research findings and should respect research evidence that can contribute to clinical effectiveness.

As suggested by Robertson (1995), evaluation of training programs is becoming more and more necessary, but current evaluations tend to be impressionistic and tend not to link process or ongoing evaluation to outcomes with quantitative measures that are valid and reliable. This training program takes some steps in that direction.

GOALS OF THIS TRAINING PROGRAM

As mentioned, we focus on common factors across the different approaches, emphasizing research-proven interventions and concepts as well as clinically pragmatic techniques, all of which provide some reasonable method to measure changes in trainees' ability. In addition, we wish to teach trainees to think flexibly at decision points in order to tailor interventions for specific patients at specific points in the process of therapy.

The training program is based upon two generally accepted constructs: *the stages of psychotherapy* and *the observing self.* Psychotherapy is a process, a series of events proceeding through time. This series of events can be divided into stages reasonably well. Each of the stages has goals, which can become mini-objectives within that process (Beitman, l987). The second construct currently lays hidden beneath the descriptions of psychotherapy: the self-observer. Most therapists encourage their patients to "step back" from their disturbing emotions, thoughts, feelings, and/or interpersonal relationships. This "step back" requires the use of the part of oneself that observes oneself (Deikman, 1983). Called by many names (observing ego, witnessing), this basic psychotherapeutic function must be developed in each new therapist. Patients learn to self-observe from therapists who can observe themselves. Therefore, a continuous goal through each of the modules is to encourage trainees to carefully scrutinize how they think, feel, and behave in their role as therapists.

One of the fears associated with the establishment of any new school of psychotherapy, whether it is called integration or not, is the potential for that school to become rigidified and inflexible and cease to be open to innovation. The stages of psychotherapy are not rooted in any fixed theoretical notion, but rather are aligned with that most perplexing of human experiences: the passage of time. With the advent of managed care, time has become more important than theoretical orientation, because it is time for which therapists are paid, and it is time that saves or loses money from the managed care perspective. Any new developments in psychotherapy theory and practice must closely incorporate varying notions of time.

The stages of psychotherapy provide an outline for the development of different modules. The stages are *engagement, pattern search, change,* and *termination* (Beitman, 1987). The objective of the first stage, engagement, is to build a collaborative relationship between therapist and patient. Module 2 of this training program focuses on facilitating the trainee's ability to establish the working alliance.

During the second stage, pattern search, the objective is to define patterns of thoughts, feelings, and/or behaviors that, if changed, would lead to desirable outcomes. In module 3, we try to improve the trainee's ability to induce, recognize, and discern a patient's pattern or set of maladaptive patterns. During the third stage, change, therapists use different strategies to help the patient relinquish old patterns, initiate new patterns, practice new patterns, and maintain and generalize these new patterns. In module 4, we expose the trainee to the range of change strategies contributed by the various schools. During the fourth stage, termination, the patient and therapist attempt to separate from each other and to maintain therapeutic gains.

There are two very important common factors across the four stages: *therapist verbal response modes* and *therapist intentions*. Different stages may call for the use of different verbal response modes and intentions. For example, the verbal response modes commonly used during engagement are approval, reassurance, offering information, reflection, and self-disclosure. Intentions in this stage may include support, catharsis, instilling hope, and giving information. Common verbal response modes during pattern search include open-ended questions, closed questions, and restatements. Intentions during pattern search may include information-gathering, cognitive focus, behavioral focus, feelings focus, and relationship focus. Verbal response modes during change may be interpretation, confrontation, and self-disclosure. Intentions during change may include reinforcement, encouragement to try new behaviors, challenging the patient, offering insight, and focus on resistance.

The verbal response modes and intentions, described first by Hill and colleagues, are pantheoretical, and some of them are correlated with positive outcomes (Hill, 1982, 1986; Hill, Helm, Tichenor, O'Grady, & Perry, 1988; Hill & O'Grady, 1985; Sipps & Sugden, 1988; Tracey, Hays, & Malone, 1988). Module 1 of the training program focuses on training in verbal response modes and intentions. Thus, trainees learn at the beginning the behaviors (verbal response modes) and attitudes (intentions) that are fundamental to psychotherapy.

Transference and countertransference are among the hardest concepts for trainees to grasp and trainers to teach. Although not emphasized in some therapeutic orientations, transference and countertransference are ubiquitous across psychotherapy, as well as outside of psychotherapy. We believe that the ability to handle transference and countertransference can be improved through training. Module 6 focuses on these critical concepts.

The methods used in this training program encompass homework, seminars, reading, and experiential group modeling; our tools include videotapes, rating scales, case conferences, and supervision.

REQUIREMENTS FOR TRAINEES

One of the major characteristics of this training program is that trainees need to actively participate, rather than passively receive information. In parallel to the process of patient change in psychotherapy, trainees' change largely depends on their own motivation and active participation. While the program can be very interesting and fun, specific expectations in the form of requirements seem to increase trainees' motivation and participation. Requirements for trainees focus on completion of homework, group presentations of homework, and open explanations for their answers. They include:

1. Attending at least 75% of sessions.
2. Completion of 90% of homework assignments.
3. Completion of pre-module and post-module evaluation forms, and videotapes or audiotapes of two patients' third sessions in pre-module and the two in post-module.
4. Completion of both evaluation forms—the COSE and Guided Inquiry—after each module.

Several groups of trainees have discovered much about themselves as they have journeyed through these modules. They have learned to look beyond the ordinary surface of human experience to find patterns and emotions in themselves and their families, as well as their patients. They have become increasingly more confident about their ability to do psychotherapy as they have seen the fundamental processes that hold the schools of psychotherapy together.

Flow Chart of the Training Sessions

PRETRAINING	Trainees' Tasks	Homework
Session 1	Learn the information about the 6 modules of the training program, training methods, the goals of the training program and the requirements (described in the introduction to the training program). Complete Form 1 and COSE (Counseling Self-Estimate Inventory, pretraining) within the session.	X
Session 2	Review directions for the third session audiotape or videotape. Learn how to use the following Pretraining Forms: Form 2, Form 3-a, Form 3-b, Form 4-1, Form 4-2, Form 5, Form 6, Form 7, and Patient Consent Forms.	Have two psychotherapy third sessions audiotaped or videotaped and relevant forms completed.
Session 3 (optional)	Trainees provide feedback about their third session experiences.	Preview module 1 text.
MODULE 1		
Session 1	Discuss module 1 text and learn verbal response modes (Form 8).	Complete Form 9.
Session 2	Discuss Form 9.	Complete Form 10.
Session 3	Discuss Form 10.	Read Form 11.
Session 4	Learn intentions (Form 11).	Complete Form 12.
Session 5	Discuss Form 12.	Rate group members' verbal response modes and intentions in transcription excerpts.
Session 6	Trainees discuss their ratings of verbal response modes and intentions.	X
Session 7	Complete COSE (post-module 1) and GI post-module 1 during the session. Trainees continue the discussion of verbal response modes and intentions.	Preview module 2 text.
MODULE 2		
Session 1	Review module 2 text to discuss working alliance. Watch vignette from the videotape of Dr. Rogers' session with Gloria and learn how to rate the working alliance.	Watch Dr. Rogers' session and then use Form 13 to rate his working alliance.

Session 2	Trainees discuss their rating of Dr. Rogers' working alliance. Watch a vignette from the videotape of Dr. Beitman's session with MF. The group choses several items from Form 13 to rate the working alliance of that session.	Watch Dr. Beitman's session and use Form 15 to rate Dr. Beitman's working alliance with MF.
Session 3	Trainees discuss their rating of Dr. Beitman's working alliance.	X
Session 4	Trainees discuss their rating of Dr. Rogers and Dr. Beitman and compare the rating of their own working alliance with their patients' rating.	Read Form 14-1 and Form 14-2.
Session 5	Complete COSE (post-module 2) and GI (post-module 2) during the session. Discuss Form 14-1 and Form 14-2.	Preview module 3 text.
MODULE 3		
Session 1	Go through module 3 text to discuss inductive reasoning to define patterns. Learn how to do the homework of Form 15-1.	Complete Form 15-1. Read Appendix I.
Session 2	Discuss Form 15-1.	Complete Form 16-1.
Session 3	Discuss Form 16-1. Learn how to do the homework of Form 18.	Complete Form 17.
Session 4	Discuss Form 17.	X
Session 5	Watch Dr. Beitman's videotapes with MF and MC (or use tapes of your own faculty) and discuss the patients' patterns.	Complete Form 15-2.
Session 6	Session 6 is optional depending on whether or not trainees want to see additional psychotherapy sessions from therapists at your sites.	X
Session 7	Discuss Form 15-2.	Complete Form 16-2.
Session 8	Complete COSE (post-module 3) and GI (post-module 3) during the session. Discuss Form 16-2.	Preview module 4 text.
MODULE 4		
Session 1	Go through the module 4 text.	Read module 4 introduction, Appendix II and III.
Session 2	Continue to discuss module 4 text. Learn how to do Form 18-1.	Complete Form 18-1.
Session 3	Discuss Form 18-1.	Complete Form 19-1.

Session 4	Discuss Form 19-1.	X
Session 5	Watch the videotape of ECBIS strategies and discuss them after each videotape vignette.	X
Session 6	Continue to watch and discuss videotapes.	Complete Form 18-2.
Session 7	Discuss Form 18-2.	Complete Form 19-2.
Session 8	Complete COSE (post-module 4) and GI (post-module 4) in the session. Discuss Form 19-2.	Preview module 5 text.
MODULE 5		
Session 1	Go through the module 5 text.	Complete Form 20
Session 2	Discuss Form 20.	Complete Form 21.
Session 3	Complete COSE (post-module 5) and GI (post-module 5) in the session. Discuss Form 21.	Preview module 6 text.
MODULE 6		
Session 1	Go through module 6 text.	Read module 6 text.
Session 2	Continue to go through module 6 text.	Read module 6 text.
Session 3	Learn CCRT method. Go through Form 22. Learn how to use CCRT to rate transference (Form 23).	Complete Form 24.
Session 4	Discuss Form 24.	Read Appendix IV and complete Form 26.
Session 5	Discuss Appendix IV and Form 25.	X
Session 6	Watch Dr. Beitman's videotapes with patients J and the videotape of Dr. Beitman's self-description of his reaction to W. Watch videotapes and discuss transference and countertransference.	Complete Form 26.
Session 7	Discuss Form 26.	Complete Form 27.
Session 8	Discuss Form 27.	Complete Form 28.
Session 9	Discuss Form 28.	Complete Form 29.
Session 10	Discuss Form 29.	
Session 11	Complete COSE (post-module 6) and GI (post-module 6) during the session. Discuss post-module and review the training program.	X

POSTTRAINING	Trainees' Tasks	Homework
Session 1	Trainees learn how to have their third session audiotaped or videotaped and how to use following posttraining forms: Form 2, Form 3-a, Form 3-b, Form 4-1, Form 4-2, Form 5, Form 6, Form 7, Patient Consent Forms (for your site).	Have the third psychotherapy session audiotaped or videotaped with two patients and complete the forms.
Session 2	Discuss the differences between trainees' pretraining and posttraining psychotherapy sessions and the impact on them of this training program.	X

Pretraining

Just who are the trainees and what do they know about psychotherapy? These are the major questions of the pretraining. During the pretraining period, trainees are asked to provide information concerning their personal and professional background and to produce an audiotape from the third session of each of two psychotherapy relationships to serve as a baseline comparison to two post-training psychotherapy relationships. As sometimes problematic as the gathering of the pretraining materials can be, taken together they provide a highly informative view of trainee competence useful as a comparison with the similar postmodule materials.

Session 1

In the first session, the modules of the training program, the training methods, and the goals of the training program are described. Trainees complete the following forms:

- Therapist Training Background (Form 1).
- Counseling Self-Estimate Inventory (COSE-Pretraining) (Larson, Suzuki, Gillepsie, Potenza, Bechtel, & Toulouse, 1992).

Session 2

1. Trainees learn the measures which are to be completed when they see the two psychotherapy patients.

2. Trainees complete the following forms for each patient:

- One Patient Profile (Form 2, pretraining).
- One Working Alliance Inventory-WAI (Form 4-1, therapist version) (Horvath & Greenberg, 1989; Tracey, Glindden, & Kokotovic, 1988).
- One Rating the Therapist's Intentions Form (Form 6) (Hill & O'Grady, 1985).

Each patient completes:

- Two TOP questionnaires (Forms 3-a and 3-b).
- One Working Alliance Inventory-WAI (Form 4-2, patient version).
- One Session Evaluation Questionnaire (SEQ) (Form 5) (Stiles & Snow, 1984).
- One Patient Reaction System form (Form 7) (Hill, Helm, Spiegel, & Tichenor, 1988).
- One patient consent form (appropriate to each institution) for being audio or videotaped.

3. Homework: In order to enter the formal training program the trainee must see two psychotherapy patients for at least three sessions and complete the baseline measures. Session length may vary from 20 minutes to one hour, with 40–45 minutes being preferable. Sessions may be separated by one day, several days, a week, or longer.

Conducting the First Session: Before the first session begins, ask the patient to complete the consent form and the TOP Questionnaire (Form 3-a, pretraining), which measures baseline symptoms, social and work functioning, as well as quality of life. The trainee also completes the Patient Profile (Form 2, pretraining) within the first two sessions.

Third session: The third therapy session is videotaped or audiotaped. (Trainees may find it useful to audiotape or videotape each session so that both trainee and patient become accustomed to the taping process.) The patient should also agree to spend an additional hour reviewing the tape with the therapist after the session or at another time. Before the third session starts the patient should fill out the second TOP questionnaire (Form 3-b, pretraining). Immediately after the session, the patient finishes the WAI (Form 4-2) and SEQ (Form 5). Trainees also complete WAI (Form 4-1). Completing Form 6 (Rating the Therapist Intentions) and Form 7 (Patient Reaction System) generally takes about an hour. We suggest therapist and patient set another hour to review the tape and finish Form 6 and Form 7. Both of them should try to recall what they felt and thought during the session rather than focusing on what they feel at the time of the review. The tape recorder should be stopped after each therapist speaking *turn*. A *turn* is defined as any therapist speech act surrounded by two patient speech acts. At each of these points when the tape is stopped, the therapist uses the Rating Therapist Intentions form (Form 6) to record up to five intentions used in each turn. The patient will use the Patient Reaction System (Form 7) to record reactions that describe feeling-responses to the therapist's interventions.

The same steps are followed with the second patient.

The following forms are to be returned before module 1:

1. Two Patient Profiles (Form 2) and two patient consent forms.
2. Four TOP questionnaires (Form 3-a, Form 3-b) finished before session 1 and session 3.
3. Two WAI (Form 4-1) done by the therapist after session 3.
4. Two WAI (Form 4-2) done by the patient after session 3.
5. Two SEQ (Form 5) completed by the patient after session 3.
6. Two Rating the Therapist's Intentions forms (Form 6) done by the therapist after session 3.
7. Two Patient Reaction System forms (Form 7) completed by the patient after session 3.
8. Two audiotapes or videotapes of session 3.

Session 3 (optional)

This session may be used to gain feedback about trainees' experiences in conducting the third sessions and completing the related forms.

FORM 1

Therapist's Training Background

Name_____   Age_____   Sex_____(M/F)

Marital Status_____   Professional Degree_____

How many children do you have?_____

- -

1. Did you take any courses or seminars in psychotherapy before?_____(Y/N). If yes, please circle the applicable number(s).

   1. Psychoanalysis
   2. Psychodynamic Therapy
   3. Behavior Therapy
   4. Cognitive Therapy
   5. Client-centered Therapy
   6. Family Therapy
   7. Interpersonal Therapy
   8. Eclectic/Integrative Therapy

2. Did you receive supervision before?____(Y/N). If yes, please circle the applicable number(s).

   1. Psychoanalysis
   2. Psychodynamic Therapy
   3. Behavior Therapy
   4. Cognitive Therapy
   5. Client-centered Therapy
   6. Family Therapy
   7. Interpersonal Therapy
   8. Eclectic/Integrative Therapy

3. Did you practice psychotherapy before? _____(Y/N). If yes, what was your psychotherapeutic orientation(s)?

   1. Psychoanalysis
   2. Psychodynamic Therapy
   3. Behavior Therapy
   4. Cognitive Therapy
   5. Client-centered Therapy
   6. Family Therapy
   7. Interpersonal Therapy
   8. Eclectic/Integrative Therapy

4. Did you receive any systematic training in psychotherapy before?____(Y/N). If yes, what was the orientation(s) of the training program?

   1. Psychoanalysis
   2. Psychodynamic Therapy
   3. Behavior Therapy
   4. Cognitive Therapy
   5. Client-centered Therapy
   6. Family Therapy
   7. Interpersonal Therapy
   8. Eclectic/Integrative Therapy

5. Have you been in psychotherapy yourself?___(Y/N). If yes, What was your therapist's orientation(s)?

   1. Psychoanalysis
   2. Psychodynamic Therapy
   3. Behavior Therapy
   4. Cognitive Therapy
   5. Client-centered Therapy
   6. Family Therapy
   6. Interpersonal Therapy
   7. Eclectic/Integrative Therapy

Counseling Self-Estimate Inventory
(Pretraining)

Name (optional)_____   Date_____

This is not a test. There are no right and wrong answers. Rather, it is an inventory that attempts to measure how you feel you will behave as a therapist in a therapy situation. Please respond to the items as honestly as you can so as to most accurately portray how you think you will behave as a therapist. Do not respond with how you wish you could perform each item; rather, answer in a way that reflects your actual estimate of how you will perform as a therapist at the present time.

	Strong Disagree	Some Disagree	Little Disagree	Little Agree	Some Agree	Strong Agree
1. When using responses like reflection of feeling, active listening, clarifying, and probing, I am confident I will be concise and to the point.	1	2	3	4	5	6
2. I am likely to impose my values on the patient during the interview.	1	2	3	4	5	6
3. When I initiate the end of a session, I am positive it will be in a manner that is not abrupt or brusque and that I will end the session on time.	1	2	3	4	5	6
4. I am confident that I will respond appropriately to the patient in view of what the patient will express (e.g., my questions will be meaningful and not concerned with trivia and minutiae).	1	2	3	4	5	6
5. I am certain that my interpretation and confrontation responses will be concise and to the point.	1	2	3	4	5	6
6. I am worried that the wording of my responses like reflection of feeling, clarification, and probing may be confusing and hard to understand.	1	2	3	4	5	6
7. I feel that I will not be able to respond to the patient in a non-judgmental way with respect to the patient's values, beliefs, etc.	1	2	3	4	5	6
8. I feel I will respond to the patient in an appropriate length of time (neither interrupting the patient or waiting too long to respond).	1	2	3	4	5	6
9. I am worried that the type of responses I use at a particular time, i.e., reflection of feeling, interpretation, etc., may not be the appropriate response.	1	2	3	4	5	6

	Strong Disagree	Some Disagree	Little Disagree	Little Agree	Some Agree	Strong Agree
10. I am sure that the content of my responses, i.e., reflection of feeling, clarifying, and probing, will be consistent with and not discrepant from what the patient is saying.	1	2	3	4	5	6
11. I feel confident that I will appear confident and earn the respect of my patient.	1	2	3	4	5	6
12. I am confident that my interpretation and confrontation responses will be effective in that they will be validated by the patient's immediate response.	1	2	3	4	5	6
13. I feel confident that I have resolved conflicts in my personal life so that they will not interfere with my therapy abilities.	1	2	3	4	5	6
14. I feel that the content of my interpretation and confrontation responses will be consistent with and not discrepant from what the patient is saying.	1	2	3	4	5	6
15. I feel that I have enough fundamental knowledge to do effective psychotherapy.	1	2	3	4	5	6
16. I may not be able to maintain the intensity and energy level needed to produce patient confidence and active participation.	1	2	3	4	5	6
17. I am confident that the wording of my interpretation and confrontation responses will be clear and easy to understand.	1	2	3	4	5	6
18. I am not sure that in a therapeutic relationship I will express myself in a way that is natural without deliberating over every response or action.	1	2	3	4	5	6
19. I am afraid that I may not understand and properly determine probable meanings of the patient's nonverbal behaviors.	1	2	3	4	5	6
20. I am confident that I will know when to use open or close ended probes, and that these probes will reflect the concerns of the patient and not be trivial.	1	2	3	4	5	6
21. My assessment of patient problems may not be as accurate as I would like it to be.	1	2	3	4	5	6

	Strong Disagree	Some Disagree	Little Disagree	Little Agree	Some Agree	Strong Agree
22. I am uncertain as to whether I will be able to appropriately confront and challenge my patient in therapy.	1	2	3	4	5	6
23. When giving responses, i.e., reflection of feeling, active listening, clarifying, and probing, I am afraid that they may not be effective in that they won't be validated by the patient's immediate response.	1	2	3	4	5	6
24. I don't feel I possess a large enough repertoire of techniques to deal with the different problems my patient may present.	1	2	3	4	5	6
25. I feel competent regarding my abilities to deal with crisis situations which may arise during the therapy sessions—e.g., suicide, alcoholism, abuse, etc.	1	2	3	4	5	6
26. I am uncomfortable about dealing with patients who appear unmotivated to work toward mutually determined goals.	1	2	3	4	5	6
27. I may have difficulty dealing with patients who don't verbalize their thoughts during the therapy session.	1	2	3	4	5	6
28. I am unsure as to how to deal with patients who appear noncommittal and indecisive.	1	2	3	4	5	6
29. When working with ethnic minority patients I am confident that I will be able to bridge cultural differences in the therapy process.	1	2	3	4	5	6
30. I will be an effective therapist with patients of a different social class.	1	2	3	4	5	6
31. I am worried that my interpretation and confrontation responses may not over time assist the patient to be more specific in defining and clarifying the problem.	1	2	3	4	5	6
32. I am confident that I will be able to conceptualize my patient's problems.	1	2	3	4	5	6
33. I am unsure as to how I will lead my patient toward the development and selection of concrete goals to work toward.	1	2	3	4	5	6
34. I am confident that I can assess my patient's readiness and commitment to change.	1	2	3	4	5	6

	Strong Disagree	Some Disagree	Little Disagree	Little Agree	Some Agree	Strong Agree
35. I feel I may give advice.	1	2	3	4	5	6
36. In working with culturally different patients I may have a difficult time viewing situations from their perspective.	1	2	3	4	5	6
37. I am afraid that I may not be able to effectively relate to someone of lower socioeconomic status than me.	1	2	3	4	5	6

FORM 2 (PRETRAINING)
Patient Profile

Name_____ Sex_____(F/M)   Age_____

Date_____(Month/Day/Yr.)   Therapist Name_____

- -

Diagnosis:

Axis I _____

Axis II _____

Axis III _____

Axis IV _____

Axis V _____

Please have your patient complete this form at the beginning of Session 1

FORM 3–a (PRETRAINING)
Treatment Outcome Profile (TOP)

Patient Name_____ Date_____ (Month/Day/Yr.)

Your opinion counts in helping us evaluate mental health services. Please take a few moments to complete this short survey about how you have been doing during the last month and about the treatment you received. Just check the appropriate circle.

- -

(The following items concern how you feel about your life in general.)

	Strongly Disagree	Disagree	Neutral	Agree	Strongly Agree
1. I am satisfied with my life.	O	O	O	O	O
2. I feel good about myself.	O	O	O	O	O
3. I am happy with the way I look.	O	O	O	O	O
4. I have a good relationship with my family.	O	O	O	O	O
5. I have supportive friends.	O	O	O	O	O
6. My health is good.	O	O	O	O	O
7. I experience little physical pain.	O	O	O	O	O
8. I have adequate physical strength.	O	O	O	O	O
9. I enjoy my leisure time.	O	O	O	O	O
10. I am happy with my job/work.	O	O	O	O	O

(The following items concern feeling you may have had during the last month)

	Strongly Disagree	Disagree	Neutral	Agree	Strongly Agree
11. I have feelings of hopelessness about the future.	O	O	O	O	O
12. I feel worthless.	O	O	O	O	O
13. I feel blue.	O	O	O	O	O
14. I feel weak in part of my body.	O	O	O	O	O
15. My heart pounds and races.	O	O	O	O	O
16. I have to avoid certain things, places, or situations because they frighten me.	O	O	O	O	O
17. I feel that people, in general, are unfriendly and dislike me.	O	O	O	O	O
18. I have urges to beat, injure, or harm someone.	O	O	O	O	O
19. I feel that I am being watched or talked about by others.	O	O	O	O	O

(The following items describe difficult or stressful situations you may have experienced during the last month)

	Strongly Disagree	Disagree	Neutral	Agree	Strongly Agree
20. I have recently had a physical fight with someone.	O	O	O	O	O
21. I have recently tried to harm myself or had a plan to do so.	O	O	O	O	O

	Strongly Disagree	Disagree	Neutral	Agree	Strongly Agree
22. I have recently become upset or angry.	○	○	○	○	○
23. I have recently broken things or destroyed property.	○	○	○	○	○
24. I am able to get around in the community on my own.	○	○	○	○	○
25. I can get help when I need it.	○	○	○	○	○
26. I take care of my home and living space.	○	○	○	○	○
27. I am functioning well at my work/school.	○	○	○	○	○

Please have your patient complete this form at the beginning of Session 3

FORM 3–b (PRETRAINING)
Treatment Outcome Profile (TOP)

Patient Name_____ Date_____ (Month/Day/Yr.)

Your opinion counts in helping us evaluate mental health services. Please take a few moments to complete this short survey about how you have been doing during the last month and about the treatment you received. Just check the appropriate circle.

- -

(The following items concern how you feel about your life in general.)

	Strongly Disagree	Disagree	Neutral	Agree	Strongly Agree
1. I am satisfied with my life.	O	O	O	O	O
2. I feel good about myself.	O	O	O	O	O
3. I am happy with the way I look.	O	O	O	O	O
4. I have a good relationship with my family.	O	O	O	O	O
5. I have supportive friends.	O	O	O	O	O
6. My health is good.	O	O	O	O	O
7. I experience little physical pain.	O	O	O	O	O
8. I have adequate physical strength.	O	O	O	O	O
9. I enjoy my leisure time.	O	O	O	O	O
10. I am happy with my job/work.	O	O	O	O	O

(The following items concern feelings you may have had during the last month.)

11. I have feelings of hopelessness about the future.	O	O	O	O	O
12. I feel worthless.	O	O	O	O	O
13. I feel blue.	O	O	O	O	O
14. I feel weak in part of my body.	O	O	O	O	O
15. My heart pounds and races.	O	O	O	O	O
16. I have to avoid certain things, places, or situations because they frighten me.	O	O	O	O	O
17. I feel that people, in general, are unfriendly and dislike me.	O	O	O	O	O
18. I have urges to beat, injure, or harm someone.	O	O	O	O	O
19. I feel that I am being watched or talked about by others.	O	O	O	O	O

(The following items describe difficult or stressful situations you may have experienced during the last month)

20. I have recently had a physical fight with someone.	O	O	O	O	O
21. I have recently tried to harm myself or had a plan to do so.	O	O	O	O	O

	Strongly Disagree	Disagree	Neutral	Agree	Strongly Agree
22. I have recently become upset or angry.	O	O	O	O	O
23. I have recently broken things or destroyed property.	O	O	O	O	O
24. I am able to get around in the community on my own.	O	O	O	O	O
25. I can get help when I need it.	O	O	O	O	O
26. I take care of my home and living space.	O	O	O	O	O
27. I am functioning well at my work/school.	O	O	O	O	O

(The following items ask your opinion about the treatment you received)

	Strongly Disagree	Disagree	Neutral	Agree	Strongly Agree
28. I feel better after receiving treatment.	O	O	O	O	O
29. I am satisfied withe services I received.	O	O	O	O	O
30. I would return for treatment if I needed help.	O	O	O	O	O
31. My diagnosis and treatment were explained to me.	O	O	O	O	O
32. Treatment staff spent enough time with me.	O	O	O	O	O
33. Treatment staff were understanding of my needs.	O	O	O	O	O
34. Rules and procedures were reasonable.	O	O	O	O	O
35. My privacy was respected.	O	O	O	O	O
36. The facilities were comfortable and pleasant in appearance.	O	O	O	O	O

Reprinted with the permission from Holcomb, W. R., Parker, J. C., & Leong, G. B. (1997). Outcomes of inpatients treated on a VA psychiatry unit and a substance abuse treatment unit. *Psychiatric Services, 48,* 699–704.

You (the therapist) need to complete this form immediately after your third session

FORM 4-1 (PRETRAINING)

Working Alliance Inventory–Form T

Patient's Name_____ Sex_____(F/M) Age_____ Session Number_____

Therapist's Name_____ Date_____(Month/Day/Yr.)

The following sentences describe some of the different ways a person might think or feel about a patient. As you read the sentences, mentally insert the name of your patient in place of _____ in the text. If the statement describes the way you always feel (or think), circle the number 7. If it never applies to you, circle the number 1. Use the numbers in between to describe the variations between these extremes. Work fast; your first impressions are the best. (Please respond to every item.)

	Never	Rarely	Occasionally	Sometimes	Often	Very Often	Always
1. _____ believes the way we are working with his/her problem is correct.	1	2	3	4	5	6	7
2. We agree on what is important for _____ to work on.	1	2	3	4	5	6	7
3. _____ and I agree about the steps to be taken to improve his/her situation.	1	2	3	4	5	6	7
4. My patient and I both feel confident about the usefulness of our current activity in therapy.	1	2	3	4	5	6	7
5. I believe _____ likes me.	1	2	3	4	5	6	7
6. I am confident in my ability to help _____.	1	2	3	4	5	6	7
7. I appreciate _____ as a person.	1	2	3	4	5	6	7
8. _____ and I have built a mutual trust.	1	2	3	4	5	6	7
9. I have doubts about what we are trying to accomplish in therapy.	1	2	3	4	5	6	7
10. We are working toward mutually agreed upon goals.	1	2	3	4	5	6	7
11. _____ and I have different ideas on what his/her real problems are.	1	2	3	4	5	6	7
12. We have established a good understanding between us of the kind of changes that would be good for _____.	1	2	3	4	5	6	7

Please name three things you did that helped your patient in this session:

1. _____

2. _____

3. _____

Name three things you did that were unhelpful to your patient in this session:

1. _____

2. _____

3. _____

Reprinted with permission from Anna Marie Kokotovic.

Please have your patient complete this form immediately after your third session

FORM 4–2 (PRETRAINING)
Working Alliance Inventory–Form P

Patient's Name_____   Sex_____(F/M)   Age_____   Session Number_____

Therapist's Name_____   Date_____(Month/Day/Yr.)

The following sentences describe some of the different ways a person might think or feel about his or her therapist. As you read the sentences, mentally insert the name of your therapist in place of _____ in the text. If the statement describes the way you always feel (or think), circle the number 7. If it never applies to you, circle the number 1. Use the numbers in between to describe the variations between these extremes. Work fast; your first impressions are the best. (Please respond to every item.)

		Never	Rarely	Occasionally	Sometimes	Often	Very Often	Always
1.	I believe the way we are working with my problem is correct.	1	2	3	4	5	6	7
2.	We agree on what is important for me to work on.	1	2	3	4	5	6	7
3.	_____ and I agree about the things I will need to do in therapy to help Improve my situation.	1	2	3	4	5	6	7
4.	What I am doing in therapy gives me new ways of looking at my problems.	1	2	3	4	5	6	7
5.	I believe _____ likes me.	1	2	3	4	5	6	7
6.	I am confident in _____'s ability to help.	1	2	3	4	5	6	7
7.	I feel that _____ appreciates me.	1	2	3	4	5	6	7
8.	_____ and I trust one another.	1	2	3	4	5	6	7
9.	_____ does not understand what I am trying to accomplish in therapy.	1	2	3	4	5	6	7
10.	_____ and I are working toward mutually agreed upon the goals.	1	2	3	4	5	6	7
11.	_____ and I have different ideas on what my problems are.	1	2	3	4	5	6	7
12.	We have established a good understanding of the kind of changes that would be good for me.	1	2	3	4	5	6	7

Please name three things the therapist did that helped you in this session:

1. _____

2. _____

3. _____

Name three things the therapist did that were unhelpful in this session:

1. _____

2. _____

3. _____

Reprinted with permission from Anna Marie Kokotovic.

Please have your patient complete this form immediately after your third session

FORM 5 (PRETTRAINING)
Session Evaluation Questionnaire (SEQ)

Patient Name_____   Therapist Name_____

Session Number_____   Date_____ (Month/Day/Yr.)

Rater_____ (Therapist/Patient)

Please circle the number to show how you feel about this session.
- -

This session was:

1. Bad   Good
   1   2   3   4   5   6   7

2. Safe   Dangerous
   1   2   3   4   5   6   7

3. Difficult   Easy
   1   2   3   4   5   6   7

4. Valuable   Worthless
   1   2   3   4   5   6   7

5. Shallow   Deep
   1   2   3   4   5   6   7

6. Relaxed   Tense
   1   2   3   4   5   6   7

7. Unpleasant   Pleasant
   1   2   3   4   5   6   7

8. Full   Empty
   1   2   3   4   5   6   7

9. Weak   Powerful
   1   2   3   4   5   6   7

10. Special   Ordinary
    1   2   3   4   5   6   7

11. Rough   Smooth
    1   2   3   4   5   6   7

12. Comfortable   Uncomfortable
    1   2   3   4   5   6   7

Reprinted with permission from Stiles, W. B., & Snow, J. S. (1984). Counseling session impact as viewed by novice counselors and their clients. *Journal of Counseling Psychology, 31,* 3–12.

You (the therapist) need to complete this form after your third session. Please read the instructions first.

FORM 6 (PRETRAINING)
Rating the Therapist's Intentions

Therapist Name_____   Patient Name_____

Session Number_____   Date_____(Month/Day/Yr.)

To judge intentions, the therapist should review the tape right after the session (if you cannot, try to do it as soon as possible). The therapist should stop the tape after each therapist turn (everything the therapist says between two client speech acts) and indicate as many intentions as apply for that turn. The numbers in the following table indicate the therapist's turn. Put your intention category numbers for each turn in the column titled "the category numbers of therapist intentions." You should strive to remember exactly what was going through your mind right at the time of the intervention and be as honest as possible in reporting what you were actually thinking. Remember that there are no right or wrong answers; the purpose is simply to uncover what you planned to do at that moment. Also remember that you should indicate your intentions only for that immediate intervention, rather than report global strategies for the entire session. In general, the therapist should choose those intentions that best apply, even if all the phrasing is not exactly applicable to the current situation.

List of Therapist Intentions

1. *Set limits:* To structure, make arrangements, establish goals and objectives of treatment, outline methods to attain goals, correct expectations about treatment, or establish rules or parameters of relationship (e.g., time, fees, cancellation policies, homework).

2. *Get information:* to find out specific facts about history, client functioning, future plans, relationships, work.

3. *Give information:* To educate, give facts, correct misperceptions or misinformation, give reasons for therapist's behavior or procedures.

4. *Support:* To provide a warm supportive, empathic environment; increase trust and rapport and build relationship; help client feel accepted, understood, comfortable, reassured and less anxious; help establish a person-to-person relationship.

5. *Focus:* To help client get back on track, change a subject, channel or structure the discussion if he or she is unable to begin or has been diffuse or rambling.

6. *Clarify:* To provide or solicit more elaboration, emphasis or specification when client or therapist has been vague, incomplete, confusing, contradictory or inaudible.

7. *Hope:* To convey the expectation that change is possible and likely to occur, convey that the therapist will be able to help the client, restore morale, build up the client's confidence to make changes.

8. *Cathart:* To promote relief from unwanted feelings, allow the client a chance to talk through feelings and problems.

9. *Cognitions:* To identify maladaptive, illogical, or irrational thoughts, self-talk, automatic thoughts, attitudes or beliefs.

10. *Behaviors:* To identify and describe the client's inappropriate or dysfunctional behaviors and/or their consequences, analyze the stimulus-response sequences of dysfunctional behavior, describe dysfunctional interpersonal patterns.

11. *Self-control:* To encourage client to take responsibility or gain a sense of mastery or control over dysfunctional thoughts, feelings, behaviors, or impulses; help client become more responsible for interpersonal effects rather than blaming others.

12. *Feelings:* To identify intense feelings and/or enable acceptance of feelings; encourage or provoke the client to become aware of underlying or hidden feelings and experience feelings at a deeper level.

13. *Insight:* To encourage understanding of the underlying reasons, dynamics, assumptions, motivations, history or meaning of cognition, behaviors, attitudes or feelings; may include an understanding of client's reactions to others' behavior.

14. *Change:* To encourage the development of new and more adaptive skills, behaviors, or cognition in dealing with self and others; to offer new, more adaptive assumptive models, frameworks, explanations, views or conceptualizations; to offer new options for behavior or self-view.

15. *Reinforce change:* To offer positive reinforcement or positive feedback about behavioral, cognitive, interpersonal, or affective attempts at change to enhance the probability that change will continue or be maintained; encourage risk-taking and new ways of behaving. To review new changes to understand the reasons for them in order to increase the likelihood that new changes will be maintained.

16. *Resistance:* To overcome obstacles to change or progress by discussing them. May also discuss failure to adhere to therapeutic procedures in the past to prevent possibility of such failure in the future.

17. *Challenge:* To jolt the client out of a present state; shake up current beliefs or feelings; test validity, reality, or accurateness of beliefs, thoughts, feelings, or behaviors; help client question the necessity of maintaining old patterns.

18. *Relationship:* To resolve problems as they arise in the relationship in order to build or maintain a smooth working alliance; to heal ruptures in the alliance; deal with issues appropriate to stage in treatment; identify and resolve distortions in client's thinking about the relationship that are based on past experiences and patterns rather than on current reality.

19. *Therapist needs:* To protect, relieve, or defend the person of the therapist; to alleviate therapist's anxiety. May try excessively to persuade, argue, or feel good or superior at the expense of the client. May be done more in the service of the therapist's needs than the client's.

20. *Interpersonal:* To clarify the patient's reactions, attitudes, thoughts, behaviors, and feelings toward another person and sometimes the other person's reactions to the patient in order to understand the patient's interpersonal schema.

Modified from Hill, C. E., & O'Grady, K. E. (1985). List of therapist intentions illustrated in a case study and with therapists of varying theoretical orientations. *Journal of Counseling Psychology, 32,* 3–22.

The number of therapist speaking turn	The category number(s) of therapist intentions	The number of therapist speaking turn	The category number(s) of therapist intentions	The number of therapist speaking turn	The category number(s) of therapist intentions
1		27		53	
2		28		54	
3		29		55	
4		30		56	
5		31		57	
6		32		58	
7		33		59	
8		34		60	
9		35		61	
10		36		62	
11		37		63	
12		38		64	
13		39		65	
14		40		66	
15		41		67	
16		42		68	
17		43		69	
18		44		70	
19		45		71	
20		46		72	
21		47		73	
22		48		74	
23		49		75	
24		50		76	
25		51		77	
26		52		78	

The number of therapist speaking turn	The category number(s) of therapist intentions	The number of therapist speaking turn	The category number(s) of therapist intentions	The number of therapist speaking turn	The category number(s) of therapist intentions
79		105		131	
80		106		132	
81		107		133	
82		108		134	
83		109		135	
84		110		136	
85		111		137	
86		112		138	
87		113		139	
88		114		140	
89		115		141	
90		116		142	
91		117		143	
92		118		144	
93		119		145	
94		120		146	
95		121		147	
96		122		148	
97		123		149	
98		124		150	
99		125		151	
100		126		152	
101		127		153	
102		128		154	
103		129		155	
104		130		156	

Please have your patient complete this form after your third session

FORM 7 (PRETRAINING)
Patient Reaction System

Therapist Name_____ Patient Name_____

Session Number_____ Date_____(Month/Day/Yr.)

(To the therapist: The patient rates each therapist turn using this "patient reaction system" while you rate the same turn using Form 6, Rating the Therapist's Intentions)

To the patient: Review the tape immediately after the session. Try to remember what you were experiencing during the session. Stop the tape after each therapist speaking turn and list the numbers of the reactions that you felt when you first heard what the therapist said. Choose those reactions that best describe your experiences, even if every part of the definition does not apply or the phrasing is not exactly accurate.

List of Patient Reactions

Positive Reactions:

1. *Understood:* I felt that my therapist really understood me and knew what I was saying or what was going on with me.

2. *Supported:* I felt accepted, reassured, liked, cared for, or safe. I felt like my therapist was on my side or I came to trust, like, respect, or admire my therapist more. This may have involved a change in my relationship with my therapist, such that we resolved a problem between us.

3. *Hopeful:* I felt confident, encouraged, optimistic, strong, pleased, or happy, and felt like I could change.

4. *Relief:* I felt less depressed, anxious, guilty, angry, or had fewer uncomfortable or painful feelings.

5. *Negative thoughts or behaviors:* I became aware of specific negative thoughts or painful feelings.

6. *Better self-understanding:* I gained new insight about myself, saw new connections, or began to understand why I behaved or felt a certain way. This new understanding helped me accept and like myself.

7. *Clear:* I got more focused about what I was really trying to say, what areas I need to change in my life, what my goals are, or what I want to work on in therapy.

8. *Feelings:* I felt a greater awareness or deepening of feelings or could express my emotion better.

9. *Responsibility:* I accepted my role in events and blamed others less.

10. *Unstuck:* I overcame a block and felt freed up and more involved in what I have to do in therapy.

11. *New perspective:* I gained a new understanding of another person, situation, or the world. I understand why people or things are as they are.

12. *Educated:* I gained greater knowledge or information. I learned something I had not known.

13. *New ways to behave:* I learned specific ideas about what I can do differently to cope with particularly situations or problems. I solved a problem, made a choice or decision, or decided to take a risk.

14. *Challenged:* I felt shook up, forced to question myself, or to look at issues I had been avoiding.

Negative Reactions:

15. *Scared:* I felt overwhelmed, afraid, or wanted to avoid or not admit to having some feeling or problem. I may have felt that my therapist was too pushy or would disapprove of me or would not like me.

16. *Worse:* I felt less hopeful, sicker, out of control, dumb, incompetent, ashamed, or like giving up. Perhaps my therapist ignored me, criticized me, hurt me, pitied me, or treated me as weak and helpless. I may have felt jealous of or competitive with my therapist.

17. *Stuck:* I felt blocked, impatient, or bored. I did not know what to do next or how to get out of the situation. I felt dissatisfied with the progress of therapy or having to go over the same things again.

18. *Lack of direction:* I felt angry or upset that my therapist didn't give me enough guidance or direction.

19. *Confused:* I did not know how I was feeling or felt distracted from what I wanted to say. I was puzzled or could not understand what my therapist was trying to say. I was not sure I agreed with my therapist.

20. *Misunderstood:* I felt that my therapist did not really hear what I was trying to say, misjudged me, or made assumptions about me that were incorrect.

21. *No reaction:* I had no particular reaction. My therapist may have been making social conversation, gathering information, or was unclear.

Reprinted with permission from Hill, C. E., Helm, J. E., Spiegel, S.B., & Tichenor, V. (1988). Development of a system for categorizing client reactions to therapist interventions. *Journal of Counseling Psychology, 35,* 27–36.

The number of therapist speaking turn	The category number(s) of patient reaction system	The number of therapist speaking turn	The category number(s) of patient reaction system	The number of therapist speaking turn	The category number(s) of patient reaction system
1		26		51	
2		27		52	
3		28		53	
4		29		54	
5		30		55	
6		31		56	
7		32		57	
8		33		58	
9		34		59	
10		35		60	
11		36		61	
12		37		62	
13		38		63	
14		39		64	
15		40		65	
16		41		66	
17		42		67	
18		43		68	
19		44		69	
20		45		70	
21		46		71	
22		47		72	
23		48		73	
24		49		74	
25		50		75	

The number of therapist speaking turn	The category number(s) of patient reaction system	The number of therapist speaking turn	The category number(s) of patient reaction system	The number of therapist speaking turn	The category number(s) of patient reaction system
76		101		126	
77		102		127	
78		103		128	
79		104		129	
80		105		130	
81		106		131	
82		107		132	
83		108		133	
84		109		134	
85		110		135	
86		111		136	
87		112		137	
88		113		138	
89		114		139	
90		115		140	
91		116		141	
92		117		142	
93		118		143	
94		119		144	
95		120		145	
96		121		146	
97		122		147	
98		123		148	
99		124		149	
100		125		150	

Verbal Response Modes and Intentions

Module 1 focuses on the therapist's verbal response modes and intentions. *Verbal response modes* refer to the grammatical structure of the therapist's verbal response, independent of the topic or content of the speech (Hill, 1982). Verbal response modes are very important because they reflect communication styles or patterns. The specific choice of type of response indicates the relationship between two people (Hill, 1986). Hill and O'Grady (1985) developed a pantheoretical verbal response category system to evaluate therapists' verbal responses. This system consists of 14 nominal, mutually exclusive categories for judging verbal behaviors. These include: *minimal encouragement, silence, approval-reassurance, information, direct guidance, closed question, open question, restatement, reflection, interpretation, confrontation, nonverbal referent, self-disclosure,* and *other.* The revised verbal response modes category system (Hill, 1986) includes nine pantheoretical, nominal, mutually exclusive therapist verbal response modes: *approval, information, direct guidance, closed question, open question, paraphrase* (which includes restatement, reflection, summary, and nonverbal referent), *interpretation, confrontation,* and *self-disclosure.* The 14 verbal response category system is used in this training program because it requires more careful discrimination among the responses.

Research has shown that verbal response modes affect outcomes, especially, as might be expected, the patient's immediate response to the therapist's intervention. Different verbal response modes are perceived to offer different degrees of help by both patients and therapists (Hill, Helm, Spiegel, & Tichenor, 1988). For example, interpretation received a quite helpful rating from both therapists and patients; paraphrase was rated as moderately helpful by patients and therapists; self-disclosure received the highest patient helpfulness rating of all response modes but very different ratings by therapists (some therapists rated it as the most helpful response mode, whereas others rated it as one of the least helpful); approval was rated moderately helpful by patients and less helpful by therapists; open question and confrontation were rated moderately helpful by therapists and less so by patients; and direct guidance was rated least helpful by patients and moderately helpful by therapists. Although we found no studies that have examined the relationship between the immediate outcome of an intervention and the therapeutic outcome, we assume a therapeutic outcome is probably determined by the cumulative effect of immediate outcomes. The training should foster an increase in those verbal response modes that have highly effective immediate outcomes and decrease the frequency of those that have proven less helpful. In order to increase the rate of highly effective verbal response modes, therapists are asked to observe the number and types offered and compare these results with the more ideal combinations.

While the verbal response modes help trainees answer the question "What do I do in the session?", intentions help them answer "What do I want to accomplish in the session?" Hill and O'Grady (1985) defined an *intention* as a therapist's rationale for selecting a specific behavior, response mode, technique, or intervention to use with a patient at any given moment within the session. Intentions refer to *why*, whereas interventions and techniques refer to *what* the therapist does (Hill & O'Grady, 1985). Hill and O'Grady originally described 19 therapist intention categories. Later, Hill, Helm, Tichenor et al. (1988) suggested that only seven intentions occur frequently enough to be used in future research.

We prefer to use 19 intention categories because they force greater discrimination among intentions. The Therapist Intention List includes the following: *set limits, get information, give information, support, focus, clarify, hope, cathart, cognition, behaviors, self-control, feelings, insight, change, reinforce change, resistance, challenge, relationship,* and *therapist needs.* Hill, Helm, Spiegel, and Tichenor (1988) demonstrated that therapist intentions provide a more adequate description of therapist interventions than do therapist response modes. This finding highlights the importance of training therapists in the careful consideration of therapeutic intentions.

In Hill, Helm, Spiegel, and Tichenor's (1988) research, therapists and clients concurred that the most helpful interventions were those in which the therapist helped the client explore feelings and behaviors. Both therapists and clients gave moderately helpful ratings to interventions intended to support, instill hope, and reinforce change, as well as to interventions with intentions concerning cognition, insight, challenge, and resistance. Both participants gave low helpful ratings to interventions with intentions to set limits, give information, address therapist needs, get information, focus, and clarify. In other research (Fuller & Hill, 1985), helpees' ratings of helpfulness were highest for counselors' intentions involving resistance, cognition, and relationships, and lowest for setting limits, getting information, supporting, and focusing.

When Hill, Helm, Spiegel, and Tichenor (1988) explored clients' reaction to therapist intentions, they found that, when therapists intended to *support* and *instill hope,* the clients indeed reported reactions of *support.* When therapists intended to *get information and clarify,* clients reported *no reaction,* which indicated that they felt nothing in particular. When therapists intended to *get information,* clients also reported fewer feelings of being *understood* and *supported.* Thus, when therapists did a lot of data-gathering, clients felt it was not helpful. Although the research showed inconsistent results, it still gives us some hints about how clients perceive therapist intentions. By knowing the range of possible intentions, therapists can attempt to predict probable and desired client response.

You will recall that there are four stages of therapy: engagement, pattern search, change, and termination. Some intentions, such as support, can be seen in every stage of psychotherapy. However, because each stage of psychotherapy has specific goals, some therapist intentions may be used more frequently in a specific stage. Awareness of some association between intentions and stages of psychotherapy helps the therapist decide what he or she intends to do in a specific stage. Establishing a good working alliance is the goal in engagement stage; therefore, frequently used intentions might include *set limits, get information, hope,* and *cathart.* The goal of pattern search is to find the patient's dysfunctional patterns; *focus, clarify, cognitions, behaviors, feelings,* and *interpersonal* will used frequently in this stage. *Change, self-control, reinforce change,* and *relationship* are the intentions seen frequently in the stage of change.

Since therapist intentions account for more outcome variance than response modes (Hill, Helm, Spiegel, & Tichenor, 1988), increasing trainees' awareness of "what I want to accomplish" within the session is crucial for effective training. In other words, augmenting therapists' ability to self-observe their intentions increases the probability that they will carefully evaluate the actual outcome of each intervention and compare it with the outcome that they expected or intended.

Some programs regard changes in verbal response modes and intentions as important outcome variables of their training (Kivlighan, 1989; Sipps & Sugden, 1988; Thompson, 1986). Because we believe verbal response modes and intentions are common factors across theoretical orientations and are related to therapeutic outcomes, we go beyond this, training therapists both to apply these factors and to use them as measures of effective training.

SESSIONS

The goals of module 1 are (a) learning the various verbal response modes and (b) learning the various psychotherapeutic intentions. To accomplish these goals, we use these tools:

1. Hill Counselor Verbal Response Category System (HCVRCS) (Form 8).
2. A transcript for rating Dr. Beitman's verbal response modes (Form 9: the third session with patient known as MF) (Beitman, 1995) and answers to Form 9.
3. Hill's sample transcript (Hill, 1986) (Form 10) and answers to Form 10.
4. The List of Therapist Intentions (Form 11).
5. The same transcript for rating Dr. Beitman's intentions (Form 12: the third session with patient known as MF) (Beitman, 1995) and answers to Form 12.
6. The collection of 1–2 page extracts from the transcripts of one of trainees' third pretraining session. These extracts are gathered together for analysis in sessions 6 and 7.

Session 1

1. The seminar leader goes through the introduction with the group.

2. The training group discusses the definitions of verbal response modes (Form 8) one by one.

3. Homework: The seminar leader assigns the transcript of Dr. Beitman's session with MF (Form 9, the version for rating verbal response modes). Trainees rate Dr. Beitman's verbal response modes, assigning each of Dr. Beitman's response units to one and only one category and writing down the category number to the left of the transcript.

Session 2

1. Trainees bring their ratings of the MF transcript (Form 9) for discussion. They take turns reporting and justifying the category number for each response unit. If there are disagreements, the group attempts to resolve them with the help of the seminar leader.

2. Homework: The seminar leader assigns Hill's (1986) sample transcript (Form 10), asking trainees to assign each therapist response unit to one and only one category, to write down the category number to the left of the transcript, and to bring the transcript to the next training session for discussion.

Session 3

1. The group members discuss their ratings of the Hill transcript, taking turns reporting and justifying the category number for each response unit. If there are disagreements on the category number, the group discusses the item in question until some consensus is reached.

2. Homework: Trainees are asked to study Form 11 (List of Therapist Intentions).

Session 4

1. The training group discusses the 20 intentions one by one.

2. Homework: The group leader assigns the transcript excerpted from Dr. Beitman's session with MF (Form 12, the version for rating intentions). Trainees are asked to imagine Dr. Beitman's intentions at each speech turn and to write the corresponding category number to the left of the transcript. Although ratings are inevitably inaccurate, the exercise encourages trainees to imagine the ongoing intentions of an experienced therapist.

Session 5

1. Trainees proceed through the transcript reporting and justifying their ratings. As they proceed, the seminar leader gives the intentions reported by Dr. Beitman (answers to Form 12), so that trainees can compare their ratings with Dr. Beitman's. This encourages them to examine their own thinking.

2. Homework: The leader assigns extracts (about 1–2 pages) from the third pretraining sessions. Trainees are asked to rate the other group members' verbal response modes and intentions from these excerpts.

Session 6

The seminar leader asks each trainee to pick one or two speech turns from his or her transcript for discussion. The trainees (aside from the therapist) categorize the verbal response modes and guess the intentions in that speech turn. Then the therapist reports his/her intentions to the group. The group members discuss the differences between their ratings and the therapist's.

Session 7

1. The seminar leader assigns COSE (Post-module 1) and Guided Inquiry (Post-module 1) for completion.

2. The group continues to discuss verbal response modes and intentions.

3. Homework: The leader assigns module 2 text to be reviewed before the next session.

FORM 8

Hill Counselor Verbal Response Category System (HCVRCS)

1. Minimal encourager
2. Silence
3. Approval-reassurance
4. Information
5. Direct guidance
6. Closed question
7. Open question

8. Restatement
9. Reflection
10. Interpretation
11. Confrontation
12. Nonverbal referent
13. Self-disclosure
14. Other

1. **Minimal encourager:** A *short* phrase suggesting simple agreement, acknowledgment or understanding. It encourages the client to continue talking but does not request it; it does not imply approval or disapproval. It may be a repetition of a key word, but is not an answer to a question (see *information*).

   a. CL: When I suddenly ran into her, I was lost for words.

      TH: Mmhmm

   b. CL: Whenever I go back there, I feel more depressed.

      TH: Tell me more.

2. **Silence:** A pause of 5 seconds or more is considered silence. Silence may occur between a client's statement and a therapist's statement. It may also occur within a client statement when the client stops talking.

3. **Approval-reassurance:** Provides emotional support, approval, or reinforcement. Helps to normalize a situation or experience. It may imply sympathy or intend to reduce anxiety by minimizing problem.

   a. CL: I feel like a failure. I haven't completed high school, can't go to college, and can't even travel outside of this country because of my illness. I am afraid to try anymore, afraid of failing again.

      TH: Yours is a normal reaction to numerous episodes of severe illness.

   b. CL: I wasn't sure if I should have stood up to her.

      TH: You definitely did the right thing.

4. **Information:** Supplies information (data, facts, resources, theory). It may relate to the psychotherapy process, the therapist's behavior or arrangements (e.g., time, place, fee), but does not include directions for what the client should do (see *direct guidance*).

   a. CL: What triggers panic attacks?

      TH: Some people have phobic responses to their own physical sensations. For example, they fear having a heart attack when they experience a rapid heart rate. Their fear increases their heart rate and scares them more. Some are reacting to separation from people they care about, some are afraid of their own anger and some are reacting to grief and traumatic memories.

   b. CL: How does psychotherapy work?

      TH: First we develop a relationship. Then we define patterns to change. Then I help you to change. Then we separate.

5. **Direct guidance:**   Directions or advice that the counselor suggests for the client or for the client and counselor together, either within or outside of the session. It is not aimed at soliciting more verbal information from the client (see *closed or open question*)

   a. CL: Several different situations seem to trigger my panic attacks.

      TH: Keep a diary in which you record your situation (where you are and what is happening), your panic symptoms, and what you are thinking at the time the panic begins.

   b. CL: I am afraid you will abandon me like everyone else. I know that's irrational but I feel it anyway.

      TH: Since you are reacting to me as you have to others, let us study your reactions as if this is a laboratory of human behavior to see if we can understand and help you change this reaction.

6. **Closed question:**   An inquiry asking for a one- or two-word answer, "yes" or "no," or confirmation of the therapist's previous statement. The client responses to this type of inquiry are typically *limited* and *specific*.

   a. CL: I'm looking for jobs still but had no luck.

      TH: Have you signed up for the computer class?

   b. CL: I'd like to return for another session in a few weeks.

      TH: How many weeks?

7. **Open question:**   A request for clarification of feelings, exploration of a situation, or more details of thinking *without purposely limiting* the response to "yes" or "no" or a response of a few words.

   a. CL: I feel anxious about being here today.

      TH: What seems to be bothering you?

   b. CL: I don't want to ask my grandfather for the plane ticket to visit him.

      TH: Why not?

8. **Restatement:**   A simple repeating or rephrasing of the client's statement(s) (not necessarily the most recent statements). It typically contains fewer but *similar words* and is *more concrete* and *clear* than the client's message.

   a. CL: I gradually remembered a scene in an alley when I was nine when a man, I could not see his face, was forcing my head toward his zipper.

      TH: You began remembering being sexually abused when you were a child.

   b. CL: The personnel manager was trying to force me to retire with an absurd offer.

      TH: The money was not sufficient for you to take early retirement.

9. **Reflection:**   A repeating or rephrasing of the client's statement(s) (not necessarily the most recent statements). It *must contain* reference to stated or implied *feelings*. It may be based upon previous statements, nonverbal behavior, or knowledge of the total situation.

   a. CL: My best friend went out with a person I was dating.

      TH: You feel hurt that she did that.

   b. CL: I love my husband but I hate being with his children.

      TH: Your stepchildren frustrate and anger you.

10. **Interpretation:**   *Goes beyond* what the client has overtly or consciously recognized. It may take several forms: It might establish connections between seemingly isolated statements or events, offer alternative meanings for old or current behaviors or themes, or explain the meaning or cause of feelings, resistance, defensive reactions, or transference (client distortions of the relationship to the therapist).

a. CL: My boss tells me all her problems, asks me to give her rides to work, and never listens to what I say.

TH: As you described your relationship to your mother, you seemed also to listen to all her problems, run many different errands for her and seemed bothered that she rarely listened to your difficulties. That was one of the reasons you moved here from Kansas City. Your relationship to your boss seems quite similar to your relationship to your mother.

b. CL: Almost every time my husband leaves for work in the morning, I start to have a panic attack.

TH: Perhaps the separation from him is a trigger.

11. **Confrontation:**   Contains two parts: The first refers to a usually implied aspect of the client's message or behavior (usually looks like a *restatement*); the second begins with a "but" and presents a contradiction or discrepancy between words and behavior, two things the client has stated, behavior and action, real and ideal self, verbal and nonverbal behavior, fantasy and reality, or the therapist's and the client's perception. Confrontation holds up a verbal mirror to demonstrate the discrepancy that is being ignored.

a. CL: Everything is fine in my family.

TH: You say everything is fine, but your parents criticize you repeatedly, your mother thinks you can never live by yourself, and your parents rarely talk to each other.

b. CL: I think I decided not to go to medical school after all.

TH: You think you won't go to medical school, and yet becoming a physician has been a lifelong dream of yours.

12. **Nonverbal referent:**   Inquires about client's nonverbal behavior, including body posture, voice tone or level, facial expressions, and gestures. No meaning is described.

a. CL: I am not sure what to say.

TH: Your cheeks are very flushed.

b. CL: The whole experience was very educational.

TH: And there are tears in your eyes.

13. **Self-disclosure:** Usually includes an "I." The therapist shares personal experiences and feelings with the client.

a. CL: I question your skill as a therapist. I dislike your approach.

TH: I am confused and surprised by your reaction. Perhaps I am unable to help you.

b. CL: I have trouble understanding my boss. At first I think I know what she wants but then I start doubting myself. I become too suspicious but I can't shake the feeling.

TH: I've had similar problems. My cure was to check my beliefs against reality, to ask the other person, and to ask for the perspective of friends.

14. **Other:**   Statements that are unrelated to client problems, including small talk or greetings, comments about the weather, the news, or events.

a. CL: That explosion that killed those children haunts me.

TH: It was awful.

b. CL: See you next week.

TH: Yeah. See you then.

Modified from Hill, C. E. (1986). An overview of the Hill counselor and client verbal response modes category systems. In L. Greenberg & W. Pinsof (Eds.), *The psychotherapeutic process: A research handbook* (pp. 131–159). New York: Guilford.

FORM 9
Transcript of Dr. Beitman's Session
(Rating Verbal Response Modes)

Name (optional)_____   Date_____

Each response unit is demarcated with a slash mark. When judging, raters should assign each response mode to one and only one category and write down the category numbers on the left of the transcript. Numbers refer to these categories: 1=minimal encourager, 2=silence, 3=approval-reassurance, 4=information, 5=direct guidance, 6=closed question, 7=open question, 8=restatement, 9=reflection, 10=interpretation, 11=confrontation, 12=nonverbal referent, 13=self-disclosure, 14=other.

- -

_____ T: I gave you a homework assignment last time. / How many pages do we have here?/

P: Oh, probably 50.

_____ T: Probably 50. / And the homework assignment was to?/ What was the homework assignment?/

P: Oh, about anger.

_____ T: What about anger?/

P: Describe my feelings about anger.

_____ T: Your feelings about anger. /And, what happened?/

P: As I began writing, I just went ohoooooo, and all these things from my childhood popped out, and I got in touch with my anger (*laughs*).

_____ T: (*Laughs*) You got in touch with your anger./

P: Yeah, I got in touch with my anger.

_____ T: It was my impression last time that you were skating on top of it but never or rarely visiting it. / So this week you got in touch with your anger. / What was that like for you?/

P: Well, at first when I was keeping the anger log, I was surprised, but then as I watched my pattern I noticed anger would arise and immediately I would squash it. (*coughs*) And so, I think it was Thursday when my mother was doing a number on me at the hospital, and I just said that's enough. And so, (*coughs*)

_____ T: Do you want some water?/

P: Yeah, maybe it would be good. I'm sorry. And ah, then I called both my sisters and I said that I was going to take a day or two off from going to the hospital. (*cough, cough*) Mother, she is ill, she is dying, but I never failed to do anything she asked me to do, but she begins demanding (*pounds fist on chair*), throwing fits like a three-year-old, you know, and "You, give me that," and I thought she wanted her tissues so I handed her the tissues. "No, no," but she wanted the lid that went on the hotplate. And so, when I gave her the tissues she threw it and "no, no, no" she says, and she is still pointing.

_____ T: All right./

P: So I stood up to her. I put the tissues back on the tray and I said, "Well, damn Mother, don't wait a minute, that'd be awful." And she looked at me like "what's going on here?"

_____ T: So you told your mother to cool it./ And that's a new experience for you. A relatively new experience for you. / So you at that moment decided not to go after what she was asking you to do. / Now, I'm curious about what that felt like for you, too./

P: Well, at the time I was just angry. I wasn't into evaluating myself. I was just angry.

————— T: Just angry./

P: At that moment, I decided I was doing part of this homework assignment, that I had a right to anger as much as anyone else. If other people are angry, I make excuses for them. They're tired, sick, or something. And then I realized, well, how many of them make excuses for you? How many are willing to say, "Oh, you're angry."

————— T: If you express some kind of irritation?/

P: Um hmm (*yes*).

————— T: You wrote in your diary that when you were growing up you were not permitted to have anger./

————— T: The messages to me in my childhood were that I had no right to my feelings. One time, I was lying on the bed crying, and my mother said, "What's the matter with you?" And I said, "I'm just so lonely." And she said, "Oh hell, you can't be lonely, you're with kids at school all day."

————— T: So she rejected your feelings./

P: Right.

————— T: She said your feelings don't count./

P: I grew up feeling ugly, dumb, lazy, because I couldn't be tired because children don't get tired. I was just lazy. I always figured my father was my buddy because he would sit down and talk to me. But what my father did was philosophize. If I was angry I should understand this person and well, you know, he had a bad marriage, or he was hurt in an accident.

————— T: So, your father gave you a model for how to make excuses for other people's feelings and bad behavior, and then you started being able to apply that way of thinking to yourself./

P: Um hmm (*yes*).

————— T: You've had more feelings in yourself this week than you have for quite a while./ What's that been like for you?/

P: Well, after I stayed up all Friday night writing this, I began to see these patterns and realized that a child comes into the world as a clean slate and then people start writing on it. And so many of these beliefs that had been pounded into my head were not my beliefs. I felt like there was a chance for me to be free of them to think my own thoughts. It felt great!

————— T: You seem to describe feeling liberated from other people's imposed rules and attitudes on you,/ and that was a very wonderful feeling for you./

P: Um hmm (*yes*).

* * *

————— T: And, now you're entering a phase where you're going to be able to express anger differently from before./ Maybe you will need to be able to say something like, "I'm angry," to somebody. Or, " What you said has made me feel angry." / I keep trying to find ways to label your feelings, but I have difficulty./

P: (*coughs*). I'm slippery (*laughs*).

_____ T: You're slippery./ Yeah, there are feelings in there, but it's hard to get to them, and / you're a challenge to try to find what you're feeling at any one moment./ You still will have a tendency, I think, to say something sharp./

_____ T: If you were to express your feelings to that friend of your husband who was talking about "when I was working . . . ," and implying that his wife did nothing equivalent taking care of the children and the household, what feeling would you have . . . how would you have labeled your feeling at that moment?/

P: I knew why his talk bothered me. He sounded so much like my husband Jim. I knew he hit a raw nerve.

_____ T: How did it make you feel? / And this is going to be a challenge for you./

P: Yeah. Right. How did it make me feel?

_____ T: He reminded you of Jim, okay./ This is still intellectual./ How did he make you feel at that moment?/

P: The only thing I can think of is anger.

_____ T: You may have thought, "I feel angry at you for what you're saying."/ Now you don't say words like that? "I feel anger."/

P: No.

_____ T: I mean, you didn't even recognize it before./ But one of the ways that you might safely express the way you feel to someone is to say how you feel./

P: Oh, what a concept. (laughs)

_____ T: (laughs) Yes, what a concept./ So, I want to see if you could practice that a little bit. To put a label on it, because you are slippery around your feelings./ At 48 you've learned a lot of ways to avoid how you feel. There's going to be some work in puncturing through your intellect to get to your emotions./ And, how do you feel about coughing in front of the TV camera?/

P: I don't like it. It'll be a terrible tape. (cough)

_____ T: How does it make you feel?/

P: I don't know. I don't know if I have any feelings about that.

_____ T: If someone else was doing something that would look bad, how do you think that person would feel?/

P: Maybe embarrassed, or ah . . . I basically feel like I'm way on past embarrassment, so (coughs, coughs, coughs) so I don't want to ruin the session by coughing all the way through it, so is that embarrassment? I don't know.

_____ T: Yeah, embarrassment,/ and maybe a little deeper than that./

P: When you come from a deeply dysfunctional family as mine, boy you go farther than that to get embarrassed. (cough) You know . . .

_____ T: No, I don't know. I don't know./ Maybe you don't have to go very far at all to get embarrassed too, which I think is more the case. / If someone was doing something that she couldn't control, that was gonna create embarrassment, how might she feel?/

P: (cough) Embarrassed, I guess. (cough)

_____ T: Frustrated? Helpless?/ These are down a little bit lower because you're not embarrassed yet. / Out of control? / These are words that get to feelings that you're not particularly familiar with. / To be able to struggle with feelings means you have to be able to recognize them./ When you were able to be loving to Jim, how did you feel?/

P: Of course (*laughs*), I first felt loving was that I was going to town and do the shopping and then to the family reunion. I bent down and kissed him and I probably, if anything, felt gratitude that he wasn't going to give me a lot of trouble about it. Because, usually when I leave the house, even though he normally doesn't verbally express anything, he acts as if I am doing something wrong or he'll say, "Yeah, right." He is aware that I read his body language. I'm much better at other people's feelings than my own.

T: What are feelings that other people have?/

P: (*Clears her throat*) Well, I know that Jim feels abandoned when I'm running out of the house and wonders why isn't he enough for me. Why do I have to see friends and family.

T: How does that make him feel, that you have to have other people?/

P: Well, it makes him feel sad and angry and . . . abandoned.

T: Okay, sadness and anger are feelings that people have. You may even have such feelings. / Abandonment can lead to feelings of sadness and anger./ What other feelings do people have?/

P: Oh, everything from joy, hysteria . . .

T: You do hysteria sometimes./

P: Um hmm (*yes*).

T: Joy is a feeling. Sadness, anger, hurt are other ones that people have./ So Jim felt hurt that you need to have other people in your life besides him. / All right./ How good are you at picking up your own sadness?/

P: Oh, pretty good.

T: So, you know that one fairly well?/

P: Um hmm (*yes*).

T: How about telling people that you're sad?/

P: Oh, I don't have too much trouble with that. Ah, with the panic attacks, I have had to talk about my feelings, about feeling sad or hurt or ashamed.

T: So, those feelings are more accessible to you and easier for you to talk about with people. / So anger is the one that you have the most difficulty with then./

P: Um hmm (*yes*).

T: How good are you at recognizing anger in other people?/

P: Oh, yeah. Real good.

T: You're sensitive to that one too, as I might imagine you would be. / What about being able to say to Jim, "I'm angry with you"?/

P: I can do that.

T: Have you done that before?/

P: Oh, yeah. (*laughs*) No more than 10 million times, but it didn't do any good.

T: Now what's the difference between the way you are now about anger and the way you were before?/

P: You mean when I was repressing it?

_____ T: Yes. My impression was that you didn't express anger until it got intense./

P: Um hmm (*yes*).

_____ T: When you came back from Iowa and boom, blew up at him./ If you change, you may be able to say "I'm angry" over smaller things. / You sound like you may be able to say to him, "I care about you," too. / That other feeling may be coming to the surface as you get more comfortable with your own anger. / You're nodding,/ that's what you experienced recently with him./

P: Um hmm (*yes*).

_____ T: Do you care about Jim?/

P: Well, as the semantics go I love Jim, I'm not sure I'm in love with Jim, but yes, I've always known I loved Jim, even when I was angry. But the in love romantic feeling is gone.

_____ T: But you do love him. / How often do you express that feeling to him?/

P: Well, it depends on how big a jerk he is? (*laughs*) Since Jim is negative most of the time, I just talk about whatever's going on, which is what we may have for supper that night or what's goin' on with the kids or mother. So I just stick to daily subjects.

_____ T: I'm curious about how this awareness of your anger is going to influence your relationship to him./

_____ T: I feel the biggest reason I was on such a high as I wrote about anger was because I was able to take a more clinical view and see everyone's patterns and see that I don't have to be controlled by mother or Jim, my grandmother, and my past. I do know it's going to take work, but at this point I don't give a damn what happens with Jim and me, whether we stay together or whether we break up. Because I finally realized that I am okay on my own, and I would rather be free and living in an efficiency apartment somewhere than to live with Jim and feel miserable. So, basically I don't care.

_____ T: Okay. / One final question, and then we will stop for this time. Or two questions really./ What about the spring-summer business and not the winter? / What do you make out of that pattern?/

P: (*coughs*)

_____ T: You had your anxiety in the spring-summer but not during the winter?/ Hard to explain that one still?/

P: Yeah, after Pat her chiropractor did the emotional release thing on me, I started feeling better immediately. I felt better after I was here last time. I felt better as I began to feel like I had a right, if I want to be selfish today. If I want to say, "I'm not going to get out of my nightgown, I'm just gonna lie around, scratch where I want to," you know, then that's okay.

_____ T: And that's where you are now. / And now there is an adventure in front of you./ You're not sure where this is going to take you, but you feel liberated and that feels good./

P: Um hmm (*yes*).

_____ T: What about my role in this?/ What do you need from me in the future in regard to helping you?/

P: I don't know. I guess to keep me from going off the deep end. We still haven't really discussed the safer ways for me to express anger. I can always do the psychologist trick and turn it back around. I'm going to do that on mother the next time she throws one of those fits or demands I do something. I'm going to say, "Mother, I do everything you ask me to, why do you have to be demanding?" Then I'll wait for a reaction. She'll probably throw another fit, but I'll keep asking her that question until maybe she'll say, "Well, that is true. I do get everything I want."

_____ T: Well, you may be able to come up with these safer ways of doing them without much help from me./ So, as you know, I'm going to be on vacation for the next couple of weeks. / During that period of time I'd like you to write down examples of the safer expressions of anger. Let's see what you come up with. / You may come up with more than I could ever come up with because you've been so psychologically clever./ Now that you know that you need to develop safe ways of expressing something you are aware of. /I think you will come up with a lot of good ones. So, I'd like to see what you come up with./ All right?/

FORM 10
Hill's Sample Transcript

Name (optional)_____   Date_____

Each counselor's response unit is demarcated with a slash mark. When judging, raters should assign each response unit to one and only one category and write down the category numbers on the left of the transcript. Numbers refer to the following categories: 1=minimal encourager, 2=silence, 3=approval-reassurance, 4=information, 5=direct guidance, 6=closed question, 7=open question, 8=restatement, 9=reflection, 10=interpretation, 11=confrontation, 12=nonverbal referent, 13=self-disclosure, 14=other.

- -

_____ CO: Hello./ Why don't you start out by telling me what is on your mind?/

CL: I've just been feeling down lately. I'm having a lot of trouble getting motivated and getting stuff done. I haven't felt like going to class. Nothing really interests me.

_____ CO: What is your major?/

CL: I haven't really decided on a major because I haven't found anything that turns me on.

_____ CO: Are you living on campus?/

CL: I'm living at home and I feel a lot of pressure on me. I would like to live in the dorm but my parents won't pay for it and I don't have the money myself.

_____ CO: Mmhmm./

CL: I mean, I live right near campus and they say why should you live in a dorm? You might as well live at home and save us money. It is kind of a stifling feeling just being there.

_____ CO: You would rather live in a dorm than at home right now./

CL: I think I would feel more free in a dorm. I just feel so restricted at home, like they're watching my every move and I don't feel free to come and go as I please. For example, if you want to go out, they always tell me to stay out as late as I want and do what I want, but then the next day they're always asking and checking up on me. I shouldn't have to put up with that anymore at my age.

_____ CO: You're angry because they treat you like a little kid./

CL: Yeah. I'm not sure how to deal with that. They're providing me with a place to sleep and helping me out a little with school so I feel like I can't say anything to them.

_____ CO: It sounds like you think that you have to stay home and do what they want./

CL: Yeah, but it's killing my social life. It's not really what I want to do. It's even having a bad effect on my schoolwork.

_____ CO: I hear you saying that you would feel freer to live your own life if you weren't living at home./

CL: That's true. But the problem with that is money. I'm going to school part-time and working part-time and don't have enough money for a dorm or an apartment. My parents won't give me any more money either. What really burns me up is that my younger brother is not in school and works and they don't give him any of this crap.

_____ CO: I see./

CL: (*pause=8 seconds*) He can do anything he wants, you know, in terms of living at home. They don't bug him at all about what he's doing and where he's going. I guess they think that because I'm the oldest and more responsible, I can handle more than he can. They both had a hard time as kids and they really want me to have what they didn't have. I guess they think I've got a better chance than my brother does to succeed and so they're tougher on me.

_____ CO: Your voice is very loud right now./ You must be very resentful./

CL: Well, I just don't want to live their lives for them. I want to have some fun on my own.

_____ CO: (*silence=5 seconds*)/ You say you want to move out yet you don't./

CL: I guess I don't want to disappoint them. Um, they'd feel real bad if I left.

_____ CO: (*pause=3 seconds*)/ I wonder if you're afraid of making the big step of growing up by moving out?/

CL: I hadn't thought of it that way. I don't know if that's exactly it. I think I'm pretty independent.

_____ CO: Well, let's look at that for a minute./ You say you're independent/ but when your parents tell you to do all these things, you do them./

CL: What else can I do? What choice do you think I have? I'm living there and the rule is that I should do what they say as long as I live under their roof. They might kick me out if I didn't.

_____ CO: You know, when I was your age I had a very difficult time leaving home./ My father had died and my mother was all alone./ I felt guilty for a long time about leaving her./ I wonder if you're feeling some guilt about growing up and leaving them?/

CL: Well, I do feel guilty about leaving but also angry at them for making me feel this way and for treating my brother differently. What do you think I ought to do to resolve this?

_____ CO: Maybe it would be a good idea to drop out of school for awhile, get a job, and make enough money to move into your own apartment./

CL: I've thought about that but feel anxious that I'd never go back to school. But you know, as I think about it, maybe the reason I have so much trouble about motivation in school is because of these conflicts with my parents.

_____ CO: What do you mean?/

CL: Well, if I feel like I'm doing everything for them instead of because I want to do it and if there's always this battle over my future, it's pretty hard for me to figure out what I want.

_____ CO: When you said that, your forehead wrinkled up and you began to look tearful./

CL: (*silence=10 seconds*)

_____ CO: We only have a couple of minutes left./ Where would you like to go from here with this problem?/

CL: Do you think it would be worthwhile to talk to someone again?

_____ CO: What do you think?/

CL: You've made me think about some things. I'm feeling really confused right now. I wasn't sure before this about seeing you because I didn't know what to expect from this counseling but you seem to understand me. Maybe you can help me figure out some of this mess with my parents and school.

_____ CO: Yeah./ It sounds like you have trouble figuring out who you are and what you want out of your life, separate from what your parents want./ That certainly seems like something appropriate to talk about here in counseling./ I think it would be a good idea for you to continue to see me./

CL: I do feel a bit anxious talking to you because it feels like you can see right through me.

_____ CO: I feel somewhat anxious right now too./ I usually feel a little tense until I get to know a person and decide whether we can work together./ I think you did the right thing by coming in at this point in your life./ You'll probably feel better after talking about your concerns./

CL: I hope so. I think I'll go home and think about some of these things. Maybe I'll think about my options about moving out and where I could afford to live. Maybe I'll talk some to my parents about moving out. Does that sound like a good idea to you?

_____ CO: Why don't we talk through that at your next session./ We need to stop now./ I'll see you next week at the same time./

CL: Great. Thank you so much. Have a nice day.

_____ CO: You too./ It's really beautiful weather out./ Feels like spring./

CL: It sure does. Bye now.

Reprinted with permission from Hill, C. E. (1986). An overview of the Hill Counselor and Client Verbal Response Modes Category Systems. In L. S. Greenberg & W. M. Pinsof (Eds.), *The psychotherapeutic process* (pp. 131–159). New York: Guilford.

FORM 11

List of Therapist Intentions

1. Set limits	11. Self-control
2. Get information	12. Feelings
3. Give information	13. Insight
4. Support	14. Change
5. Focus	15. Reinforce change
6. Clarify	16. Resistance
7. Hope	17. Challenge
8. Cathart	18. Relationship
9. Cognitions	19. Therapist needs
10. Behaviors	20. Interpersonal

1. **Set limits:** To structure, make arrangements, establish goals and objectives of treatment, outline methods to attain goals, correct expectations about treatment, or establish rules or parameters of relationship (e.g., time, fees, cancellation policies, homework).

2. **Get information:** To find out specific facts about history, client functioning, future plans, relationships, work.

3. **Give information:** To educate, give facts, correct misperceptions or misinformation, give reasons for therapist's behavior or procedures.

4. **Support:** To provide a warm supportive, empathic environment; increase trust and rapport and build relationship; help client feel accepted, understood, comfortable, reassured, and less anxious; help establish a person-to-person relationship.

5. **Focus:** To help client get back on track, change a subject, channel or structure the discussion if he or she is unable to begin or has been diffuse or rambling.

6. **Clarify:** To provide or solicit more elaboration, emphasis or specification when client or therapist has been vague, incomplete, confusing, contradictory or inaudible.

7. **Hope:** To convey the expectation that change is possible and likely to occur, convey that the therapist will be able to help the client, restore morale, build up the client's confidence to make changes.

8. **Cathart:** To promote relief from unwanted feelings, allow the client a chance to talk through feelings and problems.

9. **Cognitions:** To identify maladaptive, illogical, or irrational thoughts, self-talk, automatic thoughts, attitudes, or beliefs.

10. **Behaviors:** To identify and describe the client's inappropriate or dysfunctional behaviors and/or their consequences, analyze the stimulus-response sequences of dysfunctional behavior, describe dysfunctional interpersonal patterns.

11. **Self-control:** To encourage client to take responsibility or gain a sense of mastery or control over dysfunctional thoughts, feelings, behaviors, or impulses, help client become more responsible for interpersonal effects rather than blaming others.

12. **Feelings:** To identify intense feelings and/or enable acceptance of feelings; encourage or provoke the client to become aware of underlying or hidden feelings and to experience feelings at a deeper level.

13. **Insight:** To encourage understanding of the underlying reasons, dynamics, assumptions, motivations, history or meaning of cognition, behaviors, attitudes or feelings; may include an understanding of client's reactions to others' behavior.

14. **Change:** To encourage the development of new and more adaptive skills, behaviors, or cognition in dealing with self and others; may offer new, more adaptive assumptive models, frameworks, explanations, views or conceptualizations; may offer new options for behavior or self-view.

15. **Reinforce change:** To offer positive reinforcement or positive feedback about behavioral, cognitive, interpersonal or affective attempts at change to enhance the probability that changes will continue or be maintained; encourage risk taking and new ways of behaving. To review new changes to understand the reasons for them in order to increase the likelihood that new change will be maintained.

16. **Resistance:** To overcome obstacles to change or progress by discussing them. May also discuss failure to adhere to therapeutic procedures in the past to prevent possibility of such failure in the future.

17. **Challenge:** To jolt the client out of a present state; shake up current beliefs or feelings; test validity, reality, or accurateness of beliefs, thoughts, feelings or behaviors; help client question the necessity of maintaining old patterns.

18. **Relationship:** To resolve problems as they arise in the relationship in order to build or maintain a smooth working alliance; to heal ruptures in the alliance; deal with issues appropriate to stage in treatment; identify and resolve distortions in client's thinking about the relationship that are based on past experiences and patterns rather than on current reality.

19. **Therapist needs:** To protect, relieve, or defend the person of the therapist; to alleviate therapist's anxiety. May try excessively to persuade, argue, or feel good or superior at the expense of the client. May be done more in the service of the therapist's needs than the client's.

20. **Interpersonal:** To clarify the patient's reactions, attitudes, thoughts, behaviors, and feelings toward another person and sometimes the other person's reactions to the patient in order to understand the patient's interpersonal schema.

Modified from Hill, C. E., & O'Grady, K. E. (1985). List of therapist intentions illustrated in a case study and with therapists of varying theoretical orientations. *Journal of Counseling Psychology, 32,* 3–22.

FORM 12

Transcript of Dr. Beitman's session (Rating Intentions)

Name (optional)_____   Date_____

This is an exercise for understanding the therapist's intentions. You should read each therapist turn and indicate as many intentions as applied for that turn. Then write the category numbers for that turn on the left of the transcript. As you rate, try to think about what the therapist planned to do at that moment and indicate the therapist's intentions only for that immediate intervention, rather than rate global strategies for the entire session. The category numbers are: 1=set limits, 2=get information, 3=give information, 4=support, 5=focus, 6=clarify, 7=hope, 8=cathart, 9=cognitions, 10=behaviors, 11=self-control, 12=feelings, 13=insight, 14=change, 15=reinforce change, 16=resistance, 17=challenge, 18=relationship, 19=therapist needs, 20=interpersonal.

- -

_____ T: I gave you a homework assignment last time. How many pages do we have here?

P: Oh, probably 50.

_____ T: Probably 50. And the homework assignment was to? What was the homework assignment?

P: Oh, about anger.

_____ T: What about anger?

P: Describe my feelings about anger.

_____ T: Your feelings about anger. And, what happened?

P: As I began writing, I just went ohoooooo, and all these things from my childhood popped out, and I got in touch with my anger (*laughs*).

_____ T: (*laughs*) You got in touch with your anger.

P: Yeah, I got in touch with my anger.

_____ T: It was my impression last time that you were skating on top of it but never or rarely visiting it. So this week you got in touch with your anger. What was that like for you?

P: Well, at first when I was keeping the anger log, I was surprised, but then as I watched my pattern I noticed anger would arise and immediately I would squash it. (*coughs*) And so, I think it was Thursday when my mother was doing a number on me at the hospital, and I just said that's enough. And so, (*coughs*)

_____ T: Do you want some water?

P: Yeah, maybe it would be good. I'm sorry. And ah, then I called both my sisters and I said that I was going to take a day or two off from going to the hospital. (*cough, cough*) Mother, she is ill, she is dying, but I never failed to do anything she asked me to do, but she begins demanding (*pounds fist on chair*), throwing fits like a three-year-old, you know, and "You, give me that," and I thought she wanted her tissues so I handed her the tissues. "No, no," but she wanted the lid that went on the hotplate. And so, when I gave her the tissues she threw it and "no, no, no" she says, and she is still pointing.

_____ T: All right.

P: So I stood up to her. I put the tissues back on the tray and I said, "Well, damn Mother, don't wait a minute, that would be awful." And she looked at me like "what's going on here?"

_____ T: So you told your mother to cool it. And that's a new experience for you. A relatively new experience for you. So you at that moment decided not to go after what she was asking you to do. Now, I'm curious about what that felt like for you, too.

P: Well, at the time I was just angry. I wasn't into evaluating myself. I was just angry.

_____ T: Just angry.

P: At that moment, I decided I was doing part of this homework assignment, that I had a right to anger as much as anyone else. If other people are angry, I make excuses for them. They're tired, sick, or something. And then I realized, well, how many of them make excuses for you? How many are willing to say, "Oh, you're angry."

_____ T: If you express some kind of irritation?

P: Um hmm (yes).

_____ T: You wrote in your diary that when you were growing up you were not permitted to have anger.

P: The messages to me in my childhood were that I had no right to my feelings. One time, I was lying on the bed crying, and my mother said, "What's the matter with you?" And I said, "I'm just so lonely." And she said, "Oh hell, you can't be lonely, you're with kids at school all day."

_____ T: So she rejected your feelings.

P: Right.

_____ T: She said your feelings don't count.

P: I grew up feeling ugly, dumb, lazy, because I couldn't be tired because children don't get tired. I was just lazy. I always figured my father was my buddy because he would sit down and talk to me. But what my father did was philosophize. If I was angry I should understand this person and well, you know, he had a bad marriage, or he was hurt in an accident . . .

_____ T: So, your father gave you a model for how to make excuses for other people's feelings and bad behavior, and then you started being able to apply that way of thinking to yourself.

P: Um hmm (yes).

_____ T: You've had more feelings in yourself this week than you have for quite a while. What's that been like for you?

P: Well, after I stayed up all Friday night writing this, I began to see these patterns and realized that a child comes into the world as a clean slate and then people start writing on it. And so many of these beliefs that had been pounded into my head were not my beliefs. I felt like there was a chance for me to be free of them to think my own thoughts. It felt great!

_____ T: You seem to describe feeling liberated from other people's imposed rules and attitudes on you, and that was a very wonderful feeling for you.

P: Um hmm (yes).

* * *

_____ T: And, now you're entering a phase where you're going to be able to express anger differently from before. Maybe you will need to be able to say something like, "I'm angry," to somebody. Or, "What you said has made me feel angry." I keep trying to find ways to label your feelings, but I have difficulty.

P: (coughs) I'm slippery. (laughs)

_____ T: You're slippery. Yeah, there are feelings in there, but it's hard to get to them, and you're a challenge to try to find what you're feeling at any one moment. You still will have a tendency, I think, to say something sharp.

_____ T: If you were to express your feelings to that friend of your husband who was talking about "when I was working . . .," and implying that his wife did nothing equivalent taking care of the children and the household, what feeling would you have . . . how would you have labeled your feeling at that moment?

P: I knew why his talk bothered me. He sounded so much like my husband Jim. I knew he hit a raw nerve.

_____ T: How did it make you feel? And this is going to be a challenge for you.

P: Yeah. Right. How did it make me feel?

_____ T: He reminded you of Jim, okay. This is still intellectual. How did he make you feel at that moment?

P: The only thing I can think of is anger.

_____ T: You may have thought, "I feel angry at you for what you're saying." Now you don't say words like that? "I feel anger."

P: No.

_____ T: I mean, you didn't even recognize it before. But one of the ways that you might safely express the way you feel to someone is to say how you feel.

P: Oh, what a concept. (_laughs_)

_____ T: (_laughs_) Yes, what a concept. So, I want to see if you could practice that a little bit. To put a label on it, because you are slippery around your feelings. At 48 you've learned a lot of ways to avoid how you feel. There's going to be some work in puncturing through your intellect to get to your emotions. And, how do you feel about coughing in front of the TV camera?

P: I don't like it. It'll be a terrible tape. (_cough_)

_____ T: How does it make you feel?

P: I don't know. I don't know if I have any feelings about that.

_____ T: If someone else was doing something that would look bad, how do you think that person would feel?

P: Maybe embarrassed, or ah . . . I basically feel like I'm way on past embarrassment, so (_coughs, coughs, coughs_) so I don't want to ruin the session by coughing all the way through it, so is that embarrassment? I don't know.

_____ T: Yeah, embarrassment, and maybe a little deeper than that.

P: When you come from a deeply dysfunctional family as mine, boy you go farther than that to get embarrassed. (_cough_) You know . . .

_____ T: No, I don't know. I don't know. Maybe you don't have to go very far at all to get embarrassed too, which I think is more the case. If someone was doing something that she couldn't control, that was gonna create embarrassment, how might she feel?

P: (_cough_) Embarrassed, I guess. (_cough_)

_____ T: Frustrated? Helpless? These are down a little bit lower because you're not embarrassed yet. Out of control? These are words that get to feelings that you're not particularly familiar with. To be able to struggle with feelings means you have to be able to recognize them. When you were able to be loving to Jim, how did you feel?

P: Of course (_laughs_), I first felt loving when I was going to town to do the shopping and then to the family reunion. I bent down and kissed him and I probably, if anything, felt gratitude that he wasn't going to give me a lot of trouble about it. Because, usually when I leave the house, even though he normally doesn't verbally express anything, he acts as if I am doing something wrong or he'll say, "Yeah, right." He is aware that I read his body language. I'm much better at other people's feelings than my own.

_____ T: What are feelings that other people have?

P: (*Clears her throat*) Well, I know that Jim feels abandoned when I'm running out of the house and wonders why isn't he enough for me. Why do I have to see friends and family.

_____ T: How does that make him feel, that you have to have other people?

P: Well, it makes him feel sad and angry and . . . abandoned.

_____ T: Okay, sadness and anger are feelings that people have. You may even have such feelings. Abandonment can lead to feelings of sadness and anger. What other feelings do people have?

P: Oh, everything from joy, hysteria . . .

_____ T: You do hysteria sometimes.

P: Um hmm (*yes*).

_____ T: Joy is a feeling. Sadness, anger, hurt are other ones that people have. So Jim felt hurt that you need to have other people in your life besides him. All right. How good are you at picking up your own sadness?

P: Oh, pretty good.

_____ T: So, you know that one fairly well?

P: Um hmm (*yes*).

_____ T: How about telling people that you're sad?

P: Oh, I don't have too much trouble with that. Ah, with the panic attacks, I have had to talk about my feelings, about feeling sad or hurt or ashamed.

_____ T: So, those feelings are more accessible to you and easier for you to talk about with people. So anger is the one that you have the most difficulty with then.

P: Um hmm (*yes*).

_____ T: How good are you at recognizing anger in other people?

P: Oh, yeah. Real good.

_____ T: You're sensitive to that one too, as I might imagine you would be. What about being able to say to Jim, "I'm angry with you"?

P: I can do that.

_____ T: Have you done that before?

P: Oh, yeah. (*laughs*) No more than 10 million times, but it didn't do any good.

_____ T: Now what's the difference between the way you are now about anger and the way you were before?

P: You mean when I was repressing it?

_____ T: Yes. My impression was that you didn't express anger until it got intense.

P: Um hmm (*yes*).

_____ T: When you came back from Iowa and boom, blew up at him. If you change, you may be to say "I'm angry" over smaller things. You sound like you may be able to say to him, "I care about you," too. That other feeling may be coming to the surface as you get more comfortable with your own anger. You're nodding, that's what you experienced recently with him.

P: Um hmm (*yes*).

T: Do you care about Jim?

P: Well, as the semantics go I love Jim, I'm not sure I'm in love with Jim, but yes, I've always known I loved Jim, even when I was angry. But the In love romantic feeling is gone.

T: But you do love him. How often do you express that feeling to him?

P: Well, it depends on how big a jerk he is? (*laughs*) Since Jim is negative most of the time, I just talk about whatever's going on, which is what we may have for supper that night or what's going on with the kids or mother. So I just stick to daily subjects.

T: I'm curious about how this awareness of your anger is going to influence your relationship to him.

P: I feel the biggest reason I was on such a high as I wrote about anger was because I was able to take a more clinical view and see everyone's patterns and see that I don't have to be controlled by mother or Jim, my grandmother, and my past. I do know it's going to take work, but at this point I don't give a damn what happens with Jim and me, whether we stay together or whether we break up. Because I finally realized that I am okay on my own, and I would rather be free and living in an efficiency apartment somewhere than to live with Jim and feel miserable. So, basically I don't care.

T: Okay. One final question, and then we will stop for this time. Or two questions really. What about the spring-summer business and not the winter? What do you make out of that pattern?

P: (*coughs*)

T: You had your anxiety in the spring-summer but not during the winter? Hard to explain that one still?

P: Yeah, after Pat her chiropractor did the emotional release thing on me, I started feeling better immediately. I felt better after I was here last time. I felt better as I began to feel like I had a right, if I want to be selfish today. If I want to say, "I'm not going to get out of my nightgown, I'm just gonna lie around, scratch where I want to," you know, then that's okay.

T: And that's where you are now. And now there is an adventure in front of you. You're not sure where this is going to take you, but you feel liberated and that feels good.

P: Um hmm (*yes*).

T: What about my role in this? What do you need from me in the future in regard to helping you?

P: I don't know. I guess to keep me from going off the deep end. We still haven't really discussed the safer ways for me to express anger. I can always do the psychologist trick and turn it back around. I'm going to do that on mother the next time she throws one of those fits or demands I do something. I'm going to say, "Mother, I do everything you ask me to, why do you have to be demanding?" Then I'll wait for a reaction. She'll probably throw another fit, but I'll keep asking her that question until maybe she'll say, "Well, that is true. I do get everything I want."

T: Well, you may be able to come up with these safer ways of doing them without much help from me. So, as you know, I'm going to be on vacation for the next couple of weeks. During that period of time I'd like you to write down examples of the safer expressions of anger. Let's see what you come up with. You may come up with more than I could ever come up with because you've been so psychologically clever. Now that you know that you need to develop safe ways of expressing something you are aware of. I think you will come up with a lot of good ones. So, I'd like to see what you come up with. All right?

Developing Psychotherapy Competence—A Guided Inquiry
(Post-module 1)

Name (optional)_____   Date_____

1. What was the most important thing that happened in training during past several weeks?

2. What changes are you making in your thinking/feeling about psychotherapy issues as a result of this module?

3. What in this module is *helping you* achieve your desired changes?

4. What aspects/influences *outside* of this module are *helping you* achieve your desired changes?

5. What in this module is *keeping you* from making your desired changes?

6. What aspects/influences *outside* of this module are *keeping you* from making your desired changes?

7. Did you find yourself thinking about topics related to this module between training sessions during past several weeks? If so, what *thoughts have you had?*

8. Are you deriving any *benefits* from this module that you did not expect to happen? If so, what are these benefits?

9. Please state the *most immediate concerns* you are having about your psychotherapy competence.

Reprinted with permission from Heppner, P. P., & O'Brien, K. M. (1994). Multicultural counselor training: Students' perceptions of helpful and hindering events. *Counselor Education and Supervision, 34,* 4–18.

As you answer the following questions, please try to think about how you will behave as a therapist now (after Module 1)

Counseling Self-Estimate Inventory
(Post-module 1)

Name (optional)_____ Date_____

This is not a test. There are no right and wrong answers. Rather, it is an inventory that attempts to measure how you feel you will behave as a therapist in a therapy situation. Please respond to the items as honestly as you can so as to most accurately portray how you think you will behave as a therapist. Do not respond with how you wish you could perform each item, rather answer in a way that reflects your actual estimate of how you will perform as a therapist at the present time.

- -

	Strong Disagree	Some Disagree	Little Disagree	Little Agree	Some Agree	Strong Agree
1. When using responses like reflection of feeling, active listening, clarifying, and probing, I am confident I will be concise and to the point.	1	2	3	4	5	6
2. I am likely to impose my values on the patient during the interview.	1	2	3	4	5	6
3. When I initiate the end of a session, I am positive it will be in a manner that is not abrupt or brusque and that I will end the session on time.	1	2	3	4	5	6
4. I am confident that I will respond appropriately to the patient in view of what the patient will express (e.g., my questions will be meaningful and not concerned with trivia and minutiae).	1	2	3	4	5	6
5. I am certain that my interpretation and confrontation responses will be concise and to the point.	1	2	3	4	5	6
6. I am worried that the wording of my responses like reflection of feeling, clarification, and probing may be confusing and hard to understand.	1	2	3	4	5	6
7. I feel that I will not be able to respond to the patient in a non-judgmental way with respect to the patient's values, beliefs, etc.	1	2	3	4	5	6
8. I feel I will respond to the patient in an appropriate length of time (neither interrupting the patient or waiting too long to respond).	1	2	3	4	5	6
9. I am worried that the type of responses I use at a particular time, i.e., reflection of feeling, interpretation, etc., may not be the appropriate response.	1	2	3	4	5	6

	Strong Disagree	Some Disagree	Little Disagree	Little Agree	Some Agree	Strong Agree
	1	2	3	4	5	6
10. I am sure that the content of my responses, i.e., reflection of feeling, clarifying, and probing, will be consistent with and not discrepant from what the patient is saying.	1	2	3	4	5	6
11. I feel confident that I will appear confident and earn the respect of my patient.	1	2	3	4	5	6
12. I am confident that my interpretation and confrontation responses will be effective in that they will be validated by the patient's immediate response.	1	2	3	4	5	6
13. I feel confident that I have resolved conflicts in my personal life so that they will not interfere with my therapy abilities.	1	2	3	4	5	6
14. I feel that the content of my interpretation and confrontation responses will be consistent with and not discrepant from what the patient is saying.	1	2	3	4	5	6
15. I feel that I have enough fundamental knowledge to do effective psychotherapy.	1	2	3	4	5	6
16. I may not be able to maintain the intensity and energy level needed to produce patient confidence and active participation.	1	2	3	4	5	6
17. I am confident that the wording of my interpretation and confrontation responses will be clear and easy to understand.	1	2	3	4	5	6
18. I am not sure that in a therapeutic relationship I will express myself in a way that is natural without deliberating over every response or action.	1	2	3	4	5	6
19. I am afraid that I may not understand and properly determine probable meanings of the patient's nonverbal behaviors.	1	2	3	4	5	6
20. I am confident that I will know when to use open or close ended probes, and that these probes will reflect the concerns of the patient and not be trivial.	1	2	3	4	5	6
21. My assessment of patient problems may not be as accurate as I would like it to be.	1	2	3	4	5	6

	Strong Disagree	Some Disagree	Little Disagree	Little Agree	Some Agree	Strong Agree
	1	2	3	4	5	6
22. I am uncertain as to whether I will be able to appropriately confront and challenge my patient in therapy.	1	2	3	4	5	6
23. When giving responses, i.e., reflection of feeling, active listening, clarifying, and probing, I am afraid that they may not be effective in that they won't be validated by the patient's immediate response.	1	2	3	4	5	6
24. I don't feel I possess a large enough repertoire of techniques to deal with the different problems my patient may present.	1	2	3	4	5	6
25. I feel competent regarding my abilities to deal with crisis situations which may arise during the therapy sessions—e.g., suicide, alcoholism, abuse, etc.	1	2	3	4	5	6
26. I am uncomfortable about dealing with patients who appear unmotivated to work toward mutually determined goals.	1	2	3	4	5	6
27. I may have difficulty dealing with patients who don't verbalize their thoughts during the therapy session.	1	2	3	4	5	6
28. I am unsure as to how to deal with patients who appear noncommittal and indecisive.	1	2	3	4	5	6
29. When working with ethnic minority patients, I am confident that I will be able to bridge cultural differences in the therapy process.	1	2	3	4	5	6
30. I will be an effective therapist with patients of a different social class.	1	2	3	4	5	6
31. I am worried that my interpretation and confrontation responses may not over time assist the patient to be more specific in defining and clarifying the problem.	1	2	3	4	5	6
32. I am confident that I will be able to conceptualize my patient's problems.	1	2	3	4	5	6
33. I am unsure as to how I will lead my patient toward the development and selection of concrete goals to work toward.	1	2	3	4	5	6
34. I am confident that I can assess my patient's readiness and commitment to change.	1	2	3	4	5	6

	Strong Disagree	Some Disagree	Little Disagree	Little Agree	Some Agree	Strong Agree
35. I feel I may give advice.	1	2	3	4	5	6
36. In working with culturally different patients I may have a difficult time viewing situations from their perspective.	1	2	3	4	5	6
37. I am afraid that I may not be able to effectively relate to someone of lower socioeconomic status than me.	1	2	3	4	5	6

MODULE 2

Working Alliance

Module 2 focuses on the working alliance and on therapeutic boundaries. Much research suggests that the strength of working alliance is highly correlated with various indices of outcomes (Gelso & Carter, 1985; Horvath & Greenberg, 1989; Moras & Strupp, 1982). Different theoretical approaches have given variable emphasis and meanings to the *working alliance*. (Bordin, 1979; Goldfried & Padawer, 1982). Proponents of psychoanalysis address the positive attachment between the patient and the analyst, which provides the latter with authority, strengthens the patient's belief in the analyst's interpretations, and gives the patient the personal strength and confidence to deal with the painful experience. Greenson (1965) defines the working alliance as a relatively nonneurotic, rational rapport the patient has with his therapist. It is essentially realistic and reasonable, more or less synthetic and artificial, and largely based on the patient's acceptance of and agreement with the therapist's approach. Some behavioral therapists perceive the function of the working alliance as creating an environment of safety and trust, conditions that are necessary in order to learn, implement, and practice the techniques that are ultimately responsible for therapeutic change (Horvath, 1995). Rogers (1957) defined the components of the therapeutic relationship: empathy, unconditional positive regard, and congruence. Although these variables appear to play a significant role for client-centered therapists, they do not generalize across therapies (Horvath & Greenberg, 1989). According to Strong (1968), the strength of therapeutic relationship largely depends on the degree to which a patient believes that the therapist is trustworthy and expert.

Bordin's (1979) concept of the working alliance is being increasingly accepted by researchers and practitioners. Bordin emphasized collaboration between the therapist and the patient and defined three components—tasks, goals, and bonds. Horvath and Greenberg (1989) clarified the meaning of these three terms: *Task* refers to the in-therapy behaviors and cognitions that form the substance of the therapy process. In a well-functioning relationship, both persons perceive these tasks as relevant and potentially efficacious; furthermore, each accept the responsibility to perform these acts. A strong working alliance is characterized by the therapist and patient mutually endorsing and valuing the *goals* (outcomes) that are the targets of the intervention. The concept of *bonds* encompasses the complex network of positive personal attachments between the patient and the therapist and includes issues such as mutual trust, acceptance, and confidence.

Bordin's concepts of tasks, goals, and bonds emphasize collaboration between the therapist and the patient. This stance differs from alternative orientations, such as Rogers' (1957) therapist-offered relationship, which relies on the therapist's ability to offer a specific context, and Strong's (1968) patient-determined relationship, which depends on the patient's perception of the therapist's qualities and attitude. Bordin (1979) stated explicitly that the quality of mutuality and collaboration in the working alliance is a primary ingredient in its effectiveness. Another difference between Bordin's notion and others is that Bordin did not regard working alliance as a therapeutic intervention; rather, he perceived it as a vehicle that enables and facilitates therapeutic techniques. In another words, working alliance provides the context for the therapist's strategies and techniques, and both content and interventions may contribute to the outcome separately and together. Bordin's pantheoretical notion of working alliance is used in this training module.

Because the working alliance is a key to the change process, training therapists in the factors that can affect the strength of the working alliance is increasingly important. Theorists argue there are three factors related to the strength of the working alliance: *patient pretherapy characteristics, therapist personal characteristics* (decency, openness, and friendliness), and *therapist technical activity* (Moras & Strupp, 1982). The first two factors go beyond the influence of training. Some studies have explored the therapist's technical contributions to the working alliance. For instance, Horowitz, Marmar, Weiss, Dewitt, and Rosenbaum (1984) found an interaction between therapist technical contributions and client characteristics when assessing measures of the alliance. Specifically, when clients were highly motivated, an examination of negative transference strengthened the alliance; when clients were poorly motivated, however, alliance was strengthened by a consistently positive therapist attitude. Kivlighan (1990) found that increased use of exploration and assessment was negatively related to the strength of the working alliance. Foreman and Marmar (1985) explored therapist technical activities in cases where an initially poor alliance either remained poor or was strengthened over the course of therapy. They found that in cases with improving alliances therapists were more likely to address the client's defenses, address the client's guilt, address the client's problematic feelings in relation to the therapist, and link the problematic feeling with the therapist to the client's defenses. Kivlighan and Schmitz (1992) found that counselors whose working alliance improved were relatively more challenging and here-and-now (rather than there-and-then) oriented, compared to those counselors whose working alliance did not improve. Although more studies are needed to define the relationship between therapist techniques and the strength of working alliance, these findings provide us with some of the information we need to consider in establishing and maintaining the working alliance.

The therapist's intent in engaging a patient in a working alliance may be described in another way: The therapist attempts to grasp both intuitively and objectively the role-relationship model most appealing or most familiar to the patient. In other words, how does the patient conceptualize the role of the other person in a close, trusting, and confiding relationship? For example, patients who are highly reactant (rebel against direction from others) may be best engaged by empathic understanding, therapist self-revelation, and gentle questioning, while nonreactant patients maybe more easily engaged through direct guidance, direct questioning, and possibly confrontation.

Since a good working alliance is characterized by mutual endorsement of tasks, goals, and an interpersonal bond, self-observing behaviors and thoughts that are associated with these three elements can provide useful ongoing feedback. In this module, in order to augment the trainees' ability to self-observe and manage effective behaviors related to the working alliance, we focus on increasing the trainees' awareness of these three elements by giving them the opportunity to rate two experts' working alliance. Self-observing working alliance related behaviors, not only of therapists but also of patients, facilitates establishing and maintaining a good working alliance. For example, perhaps a patient doesn't want to take responsibility for a task that therapist and patient have mutually agreed would be useful. Helping the patient self-observe this discrepancy may lead to a self-evaluation that may produce the agreed upon results, a better task to perform (e.g., a more useful homework assignment), or possibly a new awareness of how this example illustrates a general pattern of behavior (e.g., agreeing but then failing to carry out the agreement).

Managing boundaries and avoiding boundary violations are also crucial to a healthy working alliance, since boundary violations can destroy the working alliance. This is why the Exploitation Index (EI; Epstein & Simon, 1990, 1992) is used here as a systematic training device in understanding boundary crossings. The EI consists of seven somewhat extremely stated subcategories: generalized boundary violation, eroticism, exhibitionism, dependency, power-seeking, greediness, and enabling. Study and discussion of the EI can promote increased awareness of these potential psychotherapeutic pitfalls among the trainees.

SESSIONS

The goals of module 2 are to understand the basic elements of the working alliance and therapeutic boundaries. In pursuit of these goals, we use these tools:

1. The videotapes of Dr. Rogers' session with Gloria (Shostrom, 1966) and Dr. Beitman's third session with MF.
2. Working Alliance Inventory (WAI) (Form 13, observer version).
3. Exploitation Index (Form 14-1).
4. The Description of Exploitation Index (Form 14-2).

Session 1

1. The seminar leader goes through the introduction with the group, describing the concepts behind Bordin's view of the working alliance—tasks, goals, and bonds.

2. The seminar leader distributes Form 13 and plays the tape of Dr. Rogers' session. Trainees are asked to rate items based on what they watched on the tape and to justify the rating.

3. Homework: The seminar leader distributes the videotape of Dr. Rogers' session (they can watch the tape together, in small groups or separately, or rate a session from one of the local faculty if the Rogers tape is not available). Trainees are asked to watch the whole session and then complete Form 13 (WAI) within 30 minutes of viewing the tape without any discussion with other colleagues.

Session 2

1. Trainees return the completed Form 13.

2. The training group discusses feelings and thoughts about Dr. Rogers' session.

3. The seminar leader assigns the WAI (Form 13). After trainees watch 10 minutes of the tape of Dr. Beitman's session, the seminar leader asks them to rate the items they picked from Form 13 based upon what they watched on the tape and to justify the rating.

4. Homework: Trainees are asked to use Form 13 to rate Dr. Beitman's session.

Session 3

1. Trainees bring the videotape and Form 13, which they have used to rate Dr. Beitman's session.

2. The group discusses Dr. Beitman's session.

Session 4

1. The seminar leader shows the group scores of the WAI ratings of the two therapists. Trainees compare their own ratings of Rogers and Beitman with those of other trainees, as well as with the group averages.

2. The seminar leader presents the results of the therapists' and patients' ratings of the working alliance from the third pretraining sessions. This will help trainees to be aware of how patients and therapists perceive the working alliance differently.

4. Homework: The seminar leader assigns the Exploitation Index (Form 14-1) and the Description of Exploitation Index (Form 14-2). Trainees are asked to review them for the next session.

Session 5

1. Trainees complete COSE (Post-module 2) and Guided Inquiry (GI, Post-module 2).

2. Trainees return Forms 14-1 and 14-2. This session focuses on the importance of the therapeutic boundary between the therapist and the patient.

3. The group discusses the subcategories and items on Forms 14-1 and 14-2.

4. Homework: Preview the module 3 introduction.

FORM 13
Working Alliance Inventory–Form O

Patient's Name_____ Sex_____(F/M) Age_____ Session Number_____

Therapist's Name_____ Date_____(Month/Day/Yr.)

The sentences below describe some of the different ways a therapeutic dyad may interact in therapy. Read the sentences. If a statement describes the ways you *always* perceive the dyad, circle the number 7; if it *never* applies to the dyad, circle the number 1. Use the numbers in between to describe the variations between these extremes. Work fast; your first impressions are the ones we would like to see. (Please don't forget to respond to every item.)

- -

	Never	Rarely	Occasionally	Sometimes	Often	Very Often	Always
1. There is a sense of discomfort in the relationship.	1	2	3	4	5	6	7
2. There is agreement about the steps taken to help improve the client's situation.	1	2	3	4	5	6	7
3. There is a concern about the outcome of sessions.	1	2	3	4	5	6	7
4. There is agreement about the usefulness of their current activity in therapy (i.e., the client is seeing new ways to look at his/her problem).	1	2	3	4	5	6	7
5. There is a good understanding between the client and therapist.	1	2	3	4	5	6	7
6. There is a shared perception of the client's goals in therapy.	1	2	3	4	5	6	7
7. There is a sense of confusion between the client and therapist.	1	2	3	4	5	6	7
8. There is a mutual liking between the client and therapist.	1	2	3	4	5	6	7
9. There is a need to clarify the purpose of the session.	1	2	3	4	5	6	7
10. There is disagreement about the goals of the session.	1	2	3	4	5	6	7
11. There is a perception that the time spent in therapy is not spent efficiently.	1	2	3	4	5	6	7
12. There are doubts or a lack understanding about what participants are trying to accomplish in therapy.	1	2	3	4	5	6	7

	Never	Rarely	Occasionally	Sometimes	Often	Very Often	Always
13. There is agreement about what the client's responsibilities are in therapy.	1	2	3	4	5	6	7
14. There is a mutual perception that the goals of the session are important for the client.	1	2	3	4	5	6	7
15. There is the perception that what the therapist and client are doing in therapy is unrelated to the client's current concerns.	1	2	3	4	5	6	7
16. There is agreement that what the client and therapist are doing in therapy will help the client to accomplish the changes he/she wants.	1	2	3	4	5	6	7
17. Both participants perceive that the therapist is genuinely concerned for the client's welfare.	1	2	3	4	5	6	7
18. There is a clarity about what the therapist wants the client to do.	1	2	3	4	5	6	7
19. The client and the therapist respect each other.	1	2	3	4	5	6	7
20. Both participants feel that the therapist is not totally honest about his/her feelings toward the client.	1	2	3	4	5	6	7
21. Both the client and the therapist feel confident in the therapist's ability to help the client.	1	2	3	4	5	6	7
22. The client and therapist are working on mutually agreed upon goals.	1	2	3	4	5	6	7
23. Both participants feel that the therapist appreciates the client as a person.	1	2	3	4	5	6	7
24. There is agreement on what is important for the client to work on.	1	2	3	4	5	6	7
25. As a result of these sessions there is clarity about how the client might be able to change.	1	2	3	4	5	6	7

	Never	Rarely	Occasionally	Sometimes	Often	Very Often	Always
26. There is a mutual trust between the client and therapist.	1	2	3	4	5	6	7
27. The client and therapist have different ideas about what the client's real problems are.	1	2	3	4	5	6	7
28. Both the client and therapist see their relationship as important to the client.	1	2	3	4	5	6	7
29. Both the client and therapist perceive the client as having fears that if he/she says or does wrong things, the therapist will stop working with him/her.	1	2	3	4	5	6	7
30. The client and therapist collaborated on setting the goals for the session.	1	2	3	4	5	6	7
31. There is a mutually perceived sense that the client is frustrated with what he/she is being asked to do in therapy.	1	2	3	4	5	6	7
32. The client and therapist have established a good understanding of the changes that would be good for the client.	1	2	3	4	5	6	7
33. Both the client and therapist perceive that the things they are doing in therapy do not make sense to the client.	1	2	3	4	5	6	7
34. Both the client and therapist think that the client doesn't know what to expect as the result of therapy.	1	2	3	4	5	6	7
35. Both the client and therapist view the client as believing that the way they are working with his/her problem is correct.	1	2	3	4	5	6	7
36. Both participants feel that the therapist respects and cares about the client, even when the client does things the therapist does not approve of.	1	2	3	4	5	6	7

Reprinted with permission from Horvath, A. O., & Greenberg, L. S. (1989). Development and validation of the working alliance. *Journal of Counseling Psychology, 36,* 223–233.

FORM 14–1
Exploitation Index

Name_____ Date_____(Month/Day/Yr.)

Rate yourself according to the frequency with which the following statements reflect your behavior, thoughts, or feelings with regard to any particular patients you have seen in psychotherapy within the past 2 years, by placing a check in the appropriate box. Appropriate frequency as follows: rarely = about once a year or less; sometimes = about once every 3 months; often = once a month or more.

　　If you have seen few or no patients in the past 2 years, use your imagination to rate yourself according to frequency that the following statements would have reflected your behaviors.

	Never	Rarely (yearly)	Sometimes (quarterly)	Often (monthly)
Generalized boundary violations				
1. Do you seek social contact with patients outside of clinically scheduled visits?	☐	☐	☐	☐
2. Do you tell patients personal things about yourself in order to impress them?	☐	☐	☐	☐
3. Do you and your patients address each other on a first-name basis?	☐	☐	☐	☐
4. Do you accept a medium of exchange other than money for your services? (e.g., work on your office or home, trading of professional services)	☐	☐	☐	☐
5. Have you accepted for treatment individuals known to be referred by a current or former patient?	☐	☐	☐	☐
6. Have you accepted for treatment persons with whom you have had social involvement or whom you knew to be in your social or family sphere?	☐	☐	☐	☐
7. Do you find yourself doing any of the following for your family members or social acquaintances: prescribing medication, making diagnoses, offering psychodynamic explanations for their behavior?	☐	☐	☐	☐
Eroticism				
8. Do you find yourself comparing the gratifying qualities you observe in a patient with the less gratifying qualities in your spouse or significant other? (e.g., thinking, "Where have you been all my life?")	☐	☐	☐	☐
9. Do you feel that your patient's problem would be immeasurably helped if only he/she had a positive romantic involvement with you?	☐	☐	☐	☐
10. Do you feel a sense of excitement or longing when you think of a patient or anticipate her/his visit?	☐	☐	☐	☐
11. Do you take pleasure in romantic daydreams about a patient?	☐	☐	☐	☐
12. When a patient has been seductive with you, do you experience this as gratifying sign of your own sex appeal?	☐	☐	☐	☐

	Never	Rarely (yearly)	Sometimes (quarterly)	Often (monthly)
13. Do you touch your patients? (Exclude handshake.)	☐	☐	☐	☐
14. Have you engaged in a personal relationship with patients after treatment was terminated?	☐	☐	☐	☐

Exhibitionism

15. Do you feel that you can obtain personal gratification by helping to develop your patient's great potential for fame or unusual achievement?	☐	☐	☐	☐
16. Do you take great pride in the fact that such an attractive, wealthy, powerful, or important patient is seeking your help?	☐	☐	☐	☐
17. Do you disclose sensational aspects of your patient's life to others (even when you are protecting the patient's identity)?	☐	☐	☐	☐

Dependency

18. Do you find yourself talking about your own personal problems with a patient and expecting her/him to be sympathetic to you?	☐	☐	☐	☐
19. Do you find it painfully difficult to agree to a patient's desire to cut down on the frequency of therapy, or to work on termination?	☐	☐	☐	☐
20. Do you find the chronic silence or tardiness of a patient a satisfying way of getting paid for doing nothing?	☐	☐	☐	☐

Power-seeking

21. Are you gratified by a sense of power when you are able to control a patient's activity through advice, medication, or behavioral restraint? (e.g., hospitalization, seclusion)	☐	☐	☐	☐
22. Do you ask your patient to do personal favors for you? (e.g., get you lunch, mail a letter)	☐	☐	☐	☐
23. Do you find yourself trying to influence your patients to support political causes or positions in which you have a personal interest?	☐	☐	☐	☐

Greediness

24. Do you ever use information learned from patients, such as business tips or political information, for your own financial or career gain?	☐	☐	☐	☐
25. Do you join in any activity with patients that may serve to deceive a third party? (e.g., insurance company)	☐	☐	☐	☐
26. Do you undertake business deals with patients?	☐	☐	☐	☐
27. Do you accept gifts or bequests form patients?	☐	☐	☐	☐
28. Do you recommend treatment procedures or referrals that you do not believe to be necessarily in your patient's best interests, but that may instead be to your direct or indirect financial benefit?	☐	☐	☐	☐

	Never	Rarely (yearly)	Sometimes (quarterly)	Often (monthly)
Enabling				
29. Do you fail to deal with the following patient behavior(s): paying the fee late, missing appointments on short notice and refusing to pay for the time (as agreed), seeking to extend the length of sessions?	☐	☐	☐	☐
30. Do you make exceptions for your patients, such as providing special scheduling or reducing fees, because you find the patient attractive, appealing, or impressive?	☐	☐	☐	☐
31. Do you make exceptions in the conduct of treatment because you feel sorry for your patient, or because you believe he/she is in such distress or so disturbed that you have no other choice?	☐	☐	☐	☐
32. Do you make exceptions for your patient because you are afraid she/he will otherwise become extremely angry or self-destructive?	☐	☐	☐	☐

Reprinted with permission from Epstein R. S. & Simon, R. I. (1990). The Exploitation Index: An early warning indication of boundary violations in psychotherapy. *Bulletin of Menninger Clinic, 54,* 450–465.

FORM 14–2
Description of Exploitation Index

1. **Generalized boundary violations.** Generalized boundary violations focus on therapist and patient addressing each other by first name, participating in social contact outside scheduled visits, accepting mediums of exchange other than money, accepting referrals from previous patients, accepting patients from one's social sphere, and treating one's family members or friends in the same manner as patients. These items address a general problem of adherence to the original task of the therapy.

2. **Eroticism.** Eroticism addresses the issues of whether it is exploitive for a therapist ever to have a personal relationship with a patient, even after the completion of treatment, for example, prolonged fantasizing of, or planning for, a sexual relationship with a patient and the therapist's consciously and unconsciously molding the patient into an ideal sexual partner. This hidden agenda would subvert any original intent to facilitate health and independence. Therapists must accept the stipulation that their fee or salary is the only specific material gratification they can ever receive from any patient.

3. **Exhibitionism.** Exhibitionism here refers to the therapist's bragging about the accomplishments, notoriety, or special qualities of their patients. Therapists often rationalize such exploitive discussion by saying that it takes place only among the colleagues, is adequately disguised, or is already public knowledge. Such overvaluation or envy of patients may be accompanied by covert signals that keep therapists from helping patients with their exhibitionistic defenses.

4. **Dependency.** Dependency addresses the issue of whether the therapist is being gratified by the patient's chronic lateness or silence, a situation in which manifestations of the patient's illness provide a tempting gift that could satisfy the therapist's dependency wishes. Although helping the patient overcome such resistive behavior may not be immediately possible, resolution of the illness may be hampered if the therapist derives too much pleasure from the resistance. Openly acknowledging this potential with the patient may help the therapist elucidate the patient's unconscious desire for unconditional love, which the therapist enjoys vicariously.

5. **Power-seeking.** Power-seeking addresses the therapist's need to feel a sense of mastery and control over the patient. All patients are potentially vulnerable to this need because of the nature of the transference and because of the still-common expectation that doctors order patients around "for their own good." Certain patients, such as those with passive-dependent traits or those who have been abused, are particularly vulnerable. The willingness of patients to be controlled may tempt therapists to deny the significance of their own behavior. Many patients actively encourage and derive a perverse enjoyment from such exploitation, which may be a way to master severe feelings of helplessness associated with victimization.

6. **Greediness.** Contractual fee arrangements are a formal part of the treatment boundary. Devious monetary arrangements will obviously contaminate the foundation of therapy. When a patient seeks help, the overt agreement is that the patient will pay a fee, which is the therapist's only compensation. In return, the patient expects the therapist's best recommendations. Greediness addresses the issue of therapists' getting financial benefit beyond their professional compensation. For example, the clinician refers the patient to Dr. A, with whom the referring clinician has a financial arrangement (or other quid pro quo), while knowing that another available professional, Dr. B, would be more effective for this particular problem. The referring clinician who rationalizes that Dr. A, after all, is also highly competent is denying the betrayal of the patient, whose trust requires the best recommendation, not one that gives the doctor an additional benefit and so violates the original treatment covenant.

7. Enabling. As a way of validating their own self-worth, mental health professionals are vulnerable to the occupational hazard of becoming entwined in attempts to "cure" their patients. The "rescue fantasy" and the high social value placed on helping others can serve as a tenacious defense against recognizing this form of using patients. Ironically, the therapist almost always winds up being victimized in turn. Fear of experiencing the patient's spiteful rage and of losing the "special" admiration of the "rescued" patient forces the therapist into an intimidated and often helpless stance. The patient's victimization of the therapist also represents a violation of the treatment boundary. Common clinical manifestations of such behavior include failing to pay the fee, paying the fee late, attempting to interfere in the therapist's personal life, or threatening the therapist's safety. If the therapist allows such actions to continue, it raises the question of whether the therapist has some inner personal need that may be contrary to the need of the patient. Frequent activity that involves making exceptions for a patient, combined with any romantic feelings for the patient, may be prodromal symptoms of "falling in love." Such episodes can serve as a warning that the therapist may have already become blind to the patient's shortcomings, to say nothing of the patient's psychopathology. For this reason, a healthy self-regard on the therapist's part is essential not only for protective purposes and for demonstrating a proper role model, but also for helping detect and deal with cases of patient exploitiveness.

Reprinted with permission from Epstein R. S. & Simon, R. I. (1990). The Exploitation Index: An early warning indication of boundary violations in psychotherapy. *Bulletin of Menninger Clinic, 54,* 450–465.

Developing Psychotherapy Competence—A Guided Inquiry
(Post-module 2)

Name (optional)_____   Date_____

1. What was the most important thing that happened in training during past several weeks?

2. What changes are you making in your thinking/feeling about psychotherapy issues as a result of this module?

3. What in this module is *helping you* achieve your desired changes?

4. What aspects/influences *outside* of this module are *helping you* achieve your desired change?

5. What in this module is *keeping you* from making your desired changes?

6. What aspects/influences *outside* of this module are *keeping you* from making your desired changes?

7. Did you find yourself thinking about topics related to this module between training sessions during past several weeks? If so, what *thoughts have you had?*

8. Are you deriving any *benefits* from this module that you did not expect to happen? If so, what are these benefits?

9. Please state the *most immediate concerns* you are having about your psychotherapy competence.

Reprinted with permission from Heppner, P. P. & O'Brien, K. M. (1994). Multicultural counselor training: Students' perceptions of helpful and hindering events. *Counselor Education and Supervision, 34,* 4–18.

As you answer the following questions, please try to think about how you will behave as a therapist now (after Module 2)

Counseling Self-Estimate Inventory
(Post-module 2)

Name (optional)_____ Date_____

This is not a test. There are no right and wrong answers. Rather, it is an inventory that attempts to measure how you feel you will behave as a therapist in a therapy situation. Please respond to the items as honestly as you can so as to most accurately portray how you think you will behave as a therapist. Do not respond with how you wish you could perform each item, rather answer in a way that reflects your actual estimate of how you will perform as a therapist at the present time.

	Strong Disagree	Some Disagree	Little Disagree	Little Agree	Some Agree	Strong Agree
1. When using responses like reflection of feeling, active listening, clarifying, and probing, I am confident I will be concise and to the point.	1	2	3	4	5	6
2. I am likely to impose my values on the patient during the interview.	1	2	3	4	5	6
3. When I initiate the end of a session, I am positive it will be in a manner that is not abrupt or brusque and that I will end the session on time.	1	2	3	4	5	6
4. I am confident that I will respond appropriately to the patient in view of what the patient will express (e.g., my questions will be meaningful and not concerned with trivia and minutiae).	1	2	3	4	5	6
5. I am certain that my interpretation and confrontation responses will be concise and to the point.	1	2	3	4	5	6
6. I am worried that the wording of my responses like reflection of feeling, clarification, and probing may be confusing and hard to understand.	1	2	3	4	5	6
7. I feel that I will not be able to respond to the patient in a non-judgmental way with respect to the patient's values, beliefs, etc.	1	2	3	4	5	6
8. I feel I will respond to the patient in an appropriate length of time (neither interrupting the patient or waiting too long to respond).	1	2	3	4	5	6
9. I am worried that the type of responses I use at a particular time, i.e., reflection of feeling, interpretation, etc., may not be the appropriate response.	1	2	3	4	5	6

	Strong Disagree	Some Disagree	Little Disagree	Little Agree	Some Agree	Strong Agree
	1	2	3	4	5	6
10. I am sure that the content of my responses, i.e., reflection of feeling, clarifying, and probing, will be consistent with and not discrepant from what the patient is saying.	1	2	3	4	5	6
11. I feel confident that I will appear confident and earn the respect of my patient.	1	2	3	4	5	6
12. I am confident that my interpretation and confrontation responses will be effective in that they will be validated by the patient's immediate response.	1	2	3	4	5	6
13. I feel confident that I have resolved conflicts in my personal life so that they will not interfere with my therapy abilities.	1	2	3	4	5	6
14. I feel that the content of my interpretation and confrontation responses will be consistent with and not discrepant from what the patient is saying.	1	2	3	4	5	6
15. I feel that I have enough fundamental knowledge to do effective psychotherapy.	1	2	3	4	5	6
16. I may not be able to maintain the intensity and energy level needed to produce patient confidence and active participation.	1	2	3	4	5	6
17. I am confident that the wording of my interpretation and confrontation responses will be clear and easy to understand.	1	2	3	4	5	6
18. I am not sure that in a therapeutic relationship I will express myself in a way that is natural without deliberating over every response or action.	1	2	3	4	5	6
19. I am afraid that I may not understand and properly determine probable meanings of the patient's nonverbal behaviors.	1	2	3	4	5	6
20. I am confident that I will know when to use open or close ended probes, and that these probes will reflect the concerns of the patient and not be trivial.	1	2	3	4	5	6
21. My assessment of patient problems may not be as accurate as I would like it to be.	1	2	3	4	5	6

	Strong Disagree	Some Disagree	Little Disagree	Little Agree	Some Agree	Strong Agree
22. I am uncertain as to whether I will be able to appropriately confront and challenge my patient in therapy.	1	2	3	4	5	6
23. When giving responses, i.e., reflection of feeling, active listening, clarifying, and probing, I am afraid that they may not be effective in that they won't be validated by the patient's immediate response.	1	2	3	4	5	6
24. I don't feel I possess a large enough repertoire of techniques to deal with the different problems my patient may present.	1	2	3	4	5	6
25. I feel competent regarding my abilities to deal with crisis situations which may arise during the therapy sessions—e.g., suicide, alcoholism, abuse, etc.	1	2	3	4	5	6
26. I am uncomfortable about dealing with patients who appear unmotivated to work toward mutually determined goals.	1	2	3	4	5	6
27. I may have difficulty dealing with patients who don't verbalize their thoughts during the therapy session.	1	2	3	4	5	6
28. I am unsure as to how to deal with patients who appear noncommittal and indecisive.	1	2	3	4	5	6
29. When working with ethnic minority patients, I am confident that I will be able to bridge cultural differences in the therapy process.	1	2	3	4	5	6
30. I will be an effective therapist with patients of a different social class.	1	2	3	4	5	6
31. I am worried that my interpretation and confrontation responses may not over time assist the patient to be more specific in defining and clarifying the problem.	1	2	3	4	5	6
32. I am confident that I will be able to conceptualize my patient's problems.	1	2	3	4	5	6
33. I am unsure as to how I will lead my patient toward the development and selection of concrete goals to work toward.	1	2	3	4	5	6
34. I am confident that I can assess my patient's readiness and commitment to change.	1	2	3	4	5	6

	Strong Disagree	Some Disagree	Little Disagree	Little Agree	Some Agree	Strong Agree
35. I feel I may give advice.	1	2	3	4	5	6
36. In working with culturally different patients I may have a difficult time viewing situations from their perspective.	1	2	3	4	5	6
37. I am afraid that I may not be able to effectively relate to someone of lower status than me.	1	2	3	4	5	6

Inductive Reasoning to Determine Patterns

In module 3, we focus on the search for dysfunctional patterns. The goal of pattern search is to define patterns of thought, feeling, and/or behavior that are within the patient's ability to influence, and that, if changed, would lead toward a desirable outcome (Beitman, 1987). Almost every therapeutic approach, no matter how it explores and explains human experience, identifies patients' general dysfunctional patterns from limited samples of information that the patient presents through verbal or nonverbal information during the session. In addition, each school looks at a limited number of general dysfunctional patterns. For example, cognitive therapy focuses on patients' cognitive distortions; interpersonal therapy clarifies patients' interpersonal schemas; psychodynamic therapy emphasizes the influence of childhood experience on current functioning; family therapy examines the manner in which family organization maintains dysfunctional patterns. Inductive reasoning is a common and necessary process across psychotherapy schools, as all therapists must process individual bits of data in order to define general patterns. Discovering these patterns is a prerequisite to helping patients change. Training in the use of inductive reasoning can help trainees develop efficient ways to think about the process of elucidating dysfunctional patterns.

By inductive reasoning therapists generalize from specific pieces of information to patterns that persist across situations. We call these specific pieces of information "inducing points," because therapists induce or infer general patterns from them. By forming tentative generalizations from several inducing points, therapists can develop "well formed" patterns. "Well formed" means that the pattern (1) appears to fit the patient well, (2) is viewed by both the therapist and patient as needing to be changed, (3) includes sufficient details to suggest what needs to be changed, and (4) will, once changed, lead to the desired outcome. The development of a pattern or set of patterns usually requires an iterative process: The therapist infers the broad outlines of a pattern from an inducing point and waits for confirmation or disconfirmation from subsequent data points. Sometimes the hypothetical pattern is presented directly to the patient, who then confirms or disconfirms, sometimes adding nuances. The more experienced the therapist, the more quickly patterns can be defined. (Unfortunately, however, experience may lead to the therapist to select a pattern before the pattern has been clearly supported by data.) As part of this process the patient and therapist reach a consensus about a pattern that seems to underlie many other dysfunctional symptoms and patterns. It is thought that, if the basic pattern is changed, the patient will benefit with symptom reduction and an increase in social and work functioning. (Some may argue that accurate selection of a pattern is less important than agreement that the pattern should be changed, so that the words describing the pattern provide a means, a fulcrum, around which change can take place. The pattern is a metaphor, rather than an accurate and complete depiction of reality.)

If the patient agrees that this pattern should change, the next step would be to help the patient define the reasons he or she has not changed it. This next step leads to change strategies, which will be presented in module 4.

Dysfunctional patterns have been defined at different levels of detail—from very general to very specific. In this section we outline the characteristics and some examples of three levels of pattern abstraction. The first or most general can be labeled the "personality traits level," the second is the "psychotherapy school level," and the third is "personal." The most general patterns encompass the less general ones.

DYSFUNCTIONAL PATTERNS

Level I, General Descriptors

The most general patterns (abstractions) seem to be universally applicable to most mental disorders. They are beyond the influence of any therapeutic theories or orientations. Such patterns provide a general picture of the patient but do not give any suggestion on how to change.

This personality trait level includes the following pattern names:

Submissive	Passive
Perfectionistic	Grandiose
Self-defeating	Hypersensitive
Irresponsible	Obsessive
Overdependent	Unassertive
Aggressive	Impulsive
Paranoid	Indecisive
Self-aggrandizing	Self-depreciating
Low self-esteem	Dysfunctional family
Codependent	Maladaptive family communication

Level II, School-based Patterns

We call the second level of patterns the "psychotherapy school level." Here the patterns come from attempts of various psychotherapeutic approaches, with their respective theoretical perspectives, to describe and understand pathology or dysfunction. Each approach uses specific theoretical terms to describe dysfunctional patterns, such as:

Psychodynamic:
    Reenactment from past to present
    Unconscious conflicts
    The superego vs. the id
    Maladaptive defense mechanisms
    Human developmental stages and crises

Interpersonal Psychotherapy:
    Role transitions
    Interpersonal skill deficits
    Role conflicts
    Unresolved grief
    Core conflictual relationship theme

Behavior Therapy:
    Stimulus control
    Operant conditioning
    Modeling

Cognitive Therapy:
    Automatic thoughts
    Cognitive schemas
    Cognitive distortions

Client-centered Therapy:
    Negative self-concept

Existential Therapy:
    Fear of responsibility and freedom
    Fear of death
    Existential isolation
    Meaninglessness

Experiential Therapy:
    Avoidance of emotional awareness
    Conflict splits
    Unfinished business

Family Therapy:
    Triangles
    Boundary problems
    Disturbed homeostasis
    Circular causality

Level III, Patient Relevant Patterns

At the third level dysfunctional patterns are more concrete and can be observed both clinically and in daily life. They often provide sufficient detail to point the way toward change. This level involves the specific, descriptive patterns of individual patients. These patterns or parts of them usually appear in therapist reflections and restatements of what patients say and differ from patient to patient. For example, Ms. C often felt angry and frustrated in communicating with others because she thought they neglected her needs. The therapist explored the way she communicated with others and found that she always assumed others would know her needs or feelings without her having made herself clear; she expected others to anticipate her wants, to, in effect, read her mind. Her third level pattern might be "she incorrectly assumes that she has already communicated her needs."

Behaviors can be interpreted at all three levels. For example, a husband never confronts his wife's blaming him (the third level), which might be due to a second level pattern, such as a cognitive distortion ("If I confront her, I will lose her"), a reenactment from past to present (he never confronted his mother's controlling behavior because he was afraid of being abandoned by her), or negative reinforcement (his mother left because his father became very angry about his wife's nagging). At the first level we might say that he is passive, submissive, and dependent.

The presentation of a hypothetical pattern provides a stimulus for patients to join in an interactive process. They may agree, add to, or redo a suggested pattern until it feels right. Positive feeling grows as therapist and patient together build the hypothetical pattern that appeals to both of them.

Inducing points can come from many different sources. When a therapist selects a response, such as a thought, a feeling, a behavior, or an interpersonal interaction, as an inducing point, the event should represent a maladaptive response. Although there are rich sources of inducing points, usually the therapist's questions are the most important means of getting enough information to infer patterns. Questions not only allow the therapist to obtain information but also initiate change directly by stimulating insight in the patient. When therapists are aware of the importance of detecting dysfunctional patterns, they ask "good" or "right" questions. The experienced therapist might know more than a beginning therapist about what kind of questions he or she needs to ask. Asking the "right" or "good" questions in psychotherapy will take practice and experience.

Figure 3–1 illustrates the relationship between inducing points and patterns. Taken together inducing points can be developed into well-formed patterns (level 3) that also have characteristics of the other two levels.

Inductive reasoning applies not only to identifying the patient's dysfunctional patterns, but also to the timing of interventions, like knowing when to point out these patterns to the patient and how to help the patient confront and change them. Therapists infer patterns of patient responsiveness by noticing under what conditions they are receptive to therapeutic interventions and under what other conditions they are not. Therapists also attempt to predict the consequences of their interventions, based upon both the previous responses of the current patient and the responses of previous patients. These predictions are, of course, patterns that are also inferred from a variety of data points. In addition, therapists need to avoid "overinducing," that is, prematurely grasping a pattern with too little information or arriving at a well-formed pattern too quickly. Inaccurate pattern definition may cause patients to lose confidence in the therapist's ability to help them. On the other hand, the collaborative presentation of an inaccurate or weakly formed pattern can elicit the patient's help in clarifying and sharpening it. We would like to emphasize that several similar instances of a pattern must be observed, and the patient must confirm the pattern, to establish its existence.

Data

(Inducing Points)

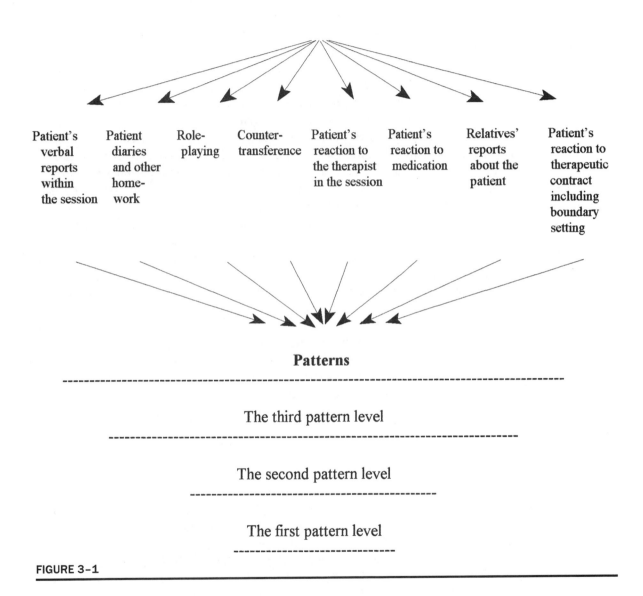

Patient's verbal reports within the session

Patient diaries and other home-work

Role-playing

Counter-transference

Patient's reaction to the therapist in the session

Patient's reaction to medication

Relatives' reports about the patient

Patient's reaction to therapeutic contract including boundary setting

Patterns

The third pattern level

The second pattern level

The first pattern level

FIGURE 3-1

The ability to induce dysfunctional patterns is related to the therapist's knowledge of various patterns from clinical and personal experiences. Experiences with previous patients facilitate discovery of patterns in current patients, while the therapist's personal experiences help him or her anticipate details that would confirm a pattern, especially if the therapist has experienced the pattern personally. For example, a therapist familiar with depression can more quickly grasp the patient's hopelessness about the future, lack of confidence in self, and likely abandonment by others. Therapists who are familiar with patients who are distrustful or paranoid understand feelings of distrust, being overly cautious about the meaning of interpersonal reactions, and being afraid of some unnamed negative consequence.

The training will expand the trainee's knowledge of different dysfunctional patterns and the routes by which inductive thinking can help to establish these patterns. In most cases there is no single "right way" to describe a pattern; there are probably many different words that could convey the same idea. It is crucial that therapists learn to describe patterns in ways that are useful to each patient, using the idiosyncratic words and sentence structures most familiar to the patient. Therefore, therapists must be both flexible and reasonably accurate when they describe patterns. Please note, however, that no psychotherapy research clearly demonstrates that accuracy of pattern definition is highly correlated with the outcome. It seems clear that effective therapists are not restricted to either "one patient—one pattern" or "one pattern fits all patients" strategies. While for certain patients there is a "right" pattern, with others the discussion of several possible patterns may provide the springboard for change. This might explain the apparent equivalence of effect in the treatment of depression by cognitive therapy, behavior therapy, and interpersonal therapy. The self-confidence that emerges from simply naming the problem may in itself suggest avenues for change (the Rumpelstiltskin effect). On the other hand, most therapists agree that for some patients fairly narrow, clearly defined patterns must be presented in order to accomplish specific therapeutic objectives.

Pattern induction is related to but differs from verbal response modes and intentions. Therapists may use open questions, closed questions, restatements, reflections, confrontations, or other verbal response modes to uncover the patient's patterns. The therapist's intentions, such as cognition, behaviors, feelings, interpersonal interactions, and the therapy relationship, are used in the process of inductive reasoning to define patterns associated with these areas. Verbal response modes are the tools by which data points can be defined.

HOMEWORK

Homework allows therapists to obtain more information. The triple-column technique (Beck, Rush, Shaw, & Emery, 1979) is a very useful way to infer patient patterns. The first column describes the situation and context in which the symptom or dysphoric event is taking place. The second describes the type and intensity of the emotion associated with each event. The third column is to record the "automatic thoughts" that link the situation to the consequence. The triple-column technique can help both patient and therapist identify a connection between when and where the symptoms occurred and what thoughts and feelings the patient had at that time. In this module we emphasize the value of training therapists to use homework to induce patterns in the patient.

SESSIONS

The goals of module 3 are (1) to understand the concept of inductive reasoning and how to find the patient's patterns from inducing points, and (2) to learn how to use the triple-column technique. Our tools are:

1. Induction point vignettes (Form 15-1 and Form 15-2)
2. Transcripts for inductive reasoning (Form 16-1, Form 16-2)
3. Triple-column Diary (Form 17)
4. Appendix I. Level II patterns
5. Videotape of Dr. Beitman's fifth session with MC
6. Videotape of Dr. Beitman's second session with MF

Session 1

1. The seminar leader discusses the concept of the inductive reasoning (module 3 introduction).

2. Homework: The seminar leader assigns the 10 inducing point vignettes (Form 15-1). After the leader discusses the introduction to this form, trainees are asked to complete it.

Session 2

1. The group discusses the 10 inducing point vignettes (Form 15-1)

2. Homework: The seminar leader assigns the two transcripts (Form 16-1). Trainees are asked define the patients' maladaptive patterns before the next session.

Session 3

1. Trainees discuss Form 16-1—the patients' patterns induced from the transcripts.

2. Homework: The seminar leader introduces the triple-column techniques (Beck et al., 1979). Trainees are asked to use the triple-column diary sheet (Form 17) to write down their own feelings (e.g., excessive anger), unwanted thoughts (e.g., excessive self-criticism), or maladaptive behaviors (e.g., smoking) associated with specific events.

Session 4

Trainees discuss their own triple-column diaries (Form 17) and attempt to articulate personal patterns. This faciliates learning of the triple-column technique that trainees and their patients will use to define patterns.

Session 5

1. The group members watch segments of Dr. Beitman's sessions with MC and MF and discuss the patients' patterns.

2. Homework: The seminar leader assigns the second 10 inducing points (Form 15-2). Trainees are directed to induce each patient's patterns without discussion with colleagues before the next session.

Session 6 (optional)

The seminar leader may show an additional videotape.

Session 7

1. The group discusses Form 15-2.

2. Homework: The seminar leader assigns the transcripts for inductive reasoning (Form 16-2) and asks trainees to complete this form and bring it to the next session.

Session 8

1. Trainees complete COSE (Post-module 3) and Guided Inquiry (GI, Post-module 3).

2. The group discusses Form 16-2.

3. Homework: The seminar leader assigns module 4 introduction for review before next session.

Level II,
School-based Patterns

PSYCHODYNAMIC

Reenactment from past to present: The psychodynamic approach advocates understanding the patient's present problem in terms of the patient's past experience. Patients' emotional, cognitive, and/or interpersonal patterns are reflections of the past experiences and relationships. Patients will often repeat these patterns in current relationships, including the relationship with the therapist.

Unconscious conflicts: One of Freud's theories—the topographic model—divided a mind into three systems: the unconscious, the preconscious, and the conscious. For Freud, conscious awareness is only a small part of mental functioning. It does not determine people's behaviors. The preconscious consists of experiences, thoughts, and memories that can be easily revived into conscious awareness when needed. The unconscious consists of needs, motivations, and instinctual impulses, and they conflict with those thoughts in the conscious mind. In order to avoid the distress resulting from these conflicts, people repress them into the unconscious. Although these repressed materials are out of awareness, they do influence behaviors and are at the root of neurotic symptoms. Therefore, unconscious conflicts become one of the explanations for the patient's behaviors and symptoms.

The superego vs. the id: In order to describe the dynamic interaction between unconscious and conscious, Freud developed his theory of the structure of personality. He divided "self" into three: id, ego, and superego. The id, which represents instinctual energy and inherited urges, seeks its gratification without considering the constraints of social reality (pleasure principle). Id is modified after birth by the experiences with parents, the social value system, and the culture. Ego is developed during this process of socialization. Ego represents the part of the personality responsible for coordinating internal and external reality. It either allows some drives of the id to be gratified or suppresses the craving of the id. This decision depends on the constraints of external reality (reality principle). The superego is developed as the child becomes socialized and values and taboos of society are internalized into the child's thought processes. Superego is the part of mind that rewards one for being "good" or reproaches one for being "bad" (conscience principle). Guilt is often evoked when values of the superego have been contravened. Because of its asocial nature, the id continuously conflicts with the superego while the superego is attempting to repress the id. Excessive superego development or too little superego development can lead to a variety of symptoms and/or dysfunctional patterns.

Defense mechanisms: Defense mechanisms are generally defined as repetitive, stereotyped, automatic thought patterns used to cope with anxiety and prevent being overwhelmed. Defense mechanisms serve the ego in muting the anxiety generated by conflicts between the id and superego. In many instances defense mechanisms, rather than being pathological, are used in normal adaptation. Since defense mechanisms protect people by keeping the conflicts out of awareness, they can help to perpetuate the psychological disturbance by leaving it unexamined. Following are brief descriptions of some common mechanisms:

- Repression: Most defense mechanisms repress unwanted thoughts and feelings from conscious awareness, much as censorship by repressive governments keeps certain ideas from public awareness. Outside of awareness, the individual removes unwanted thoughts, memories, and feeling from consciousness.
- Denial: Rather than operating outside of awareness, denial may be conscious or preconscious. It simply distorts reality to fit the individual's needs. Denial is useful to the recovering post-heart attack patient while it is harmful to the alcoholic's husband who refuses to see how her drinking is destroying their family.
- Projection: Rather than admitting having a distressing attribute, the patient projects this characteristic onto someone else. The other person becomes a blank screen onto which the attribute is projected like a film strip for a movie. For example, a self-defined highly moralistic person accuses his boss of being dishonest and unethical when he himself was unethical.
- Rationalization: Many people are adept at manufacturing "good" reasons to explain their own attitudes and actions. Rationalization helps to explain away bad decisions, losses, or hurtful behavior. It allows people to reduce their responsibility for what they do and what they think.
- Conversion: A distressing idea or feeling can be turned into a physical disorder. This transformation appears to be more common in less educated persons.
- Regression: Some people under various stresses revert to former behavior that characterized them at an earlier developmental phase. It is as if the newer, more mature levels of development are less well-established so that under duress they are diminished, permitting less adaptive patterns to emerge. For example, a husband, recently able to reduce his physical assaults on his wife, hits her again after being fired from his job and not sleeping for 24 hours.

Source: Corey (1996)

Human development: Several psychoanalytic models address the ever-evolving nature of the human psyche from birth until death. Although most people tend to believe that something constant about themselves remains with them throughout their lifetimes, all of us proceed through predictable stages and challenges that repeatedly reform who we are and what we can do. The developmental models vary in the challenges selected and the names chosen for stages, yet they all hold in common two related principles: (1) The manner in which certain developmental challenges and stages are confronted can have lasting influence on subsequent psychological functioning, and (2) each stage provides a window of opportunity for the creation of specific abilities and functions, which, if not mastered within a relatively specific time frame, can create lingering disabilities later on. Nevertheless, psychotherapists hold strong beliefs in the plasticity of the mind-brain to overcome developmental deficiencies. For example, each of us learns to trust oneself and others, and how to love and feel close to others in the cauldron of our early upbringing. As children, we also learn to recognize and express feelings of rage, anger, hostility, and hate, through which we discover our own autonomy and power as a person. We learn who we are in relationship to others by the way we are treated by parents and siblings. Not only these early experiences but also schooling, work, and later social and family relationships shape our identities in the world. These experiences provide lasting imprints on our lives.

Much has been written on this subject, because developmental challenges and stages can be viewed from many perspectives. One helpful perspective is offered by self-psychology and object-relations approaches and is summarized here. (Trainees should also become acquainted with the work of Erik Erikson (1963) on this subject.)

Individual development can be considered to be the process by which individuals separate and differentiate themselves from others. In describing four stages, we use the terms coined by Mahler (Hedges, 1983). In the first months of life the infant is thought to be responding to physiological rather than psychological states (infantile autism). In this undifferentiated state there is no whole self or whole others; the infant responds to perceived parts of the other—breast, face, hands, mouth—rather than a unified self or other.

From the third to approximately eighth month, the infant is intensely dependent on the primary caregiver. No longer an interchangeable part, the caregiver is expected to provide a high degree of emotional attunement with the infant (symbiosis).

The child then moves through several subphases involving differentiation and separation from the caregiver and then returning for a sense of confirmation and comfort. The toddler who proudly demonstrates self-sufficiency and then runs back to a welcoming parent can be said to illustrate the main issues of this period (separation/individuation). Other significant people are looked to as approving mirrors for the child's sense of self in order to help with the development and maintenance of self-other boundaries.

By the thirty-sixth month the child has usually entered the fourth and final stage by moving toward a sense of self and other constancy. Others are seen more fully as separate from the self because the self has firmer boundaries that protect against being overwhelmed through fusion with others.

But the separation/individuation process does not stop here. Throughout the life span of each individual the twin processes of joining with another in close relationships and pulling back into the sphere of oneself drives the ever-changing process of differentiation from others and clearer definition of the self.
Sources: Corey (1996), Erikson (1963), and Hedges (1983)

INTERPERSONAL PSYCHOTHERAPY

Role transitions: Role transitions occur with the progression through the stages of the human life-cycle. Biological maturation transitions individuals through infancy, childhood, adolescence, early parenting, later parenting, and the decline of physical capacity with aging. Social transitions, which are greatly influenced by social class and historical events, include beginning school, leaving home, graduating from college, joining the military, marriage, divorce, job promotion and/or loss, and retirement. Many life-cycle challenges, such as the death of a child, divorce, major disease, and trauma, are unexpected and catastrophic. Both biologically and socially determined role transitions require people to manage the loss of familiar social supports and attachments and develop new sets of social skills. Problems arise from role transitions bidirectionally; e.g., the transition may trigger depression or depression can lead to an unexpected transition like divorce. Many transitions aptly fit being called "partial deaths," since the person permanently loses a social role that was expected to go on indefinitely. The divorced father who rarely sees his children, the bilateral leg amputee who can no longer run, the 50-year-old forced to retire because of company policy all experience the death of part of themselves.
Source: Klerman, Weissman, Rounsaville, & Chevron (1984)

Interpersonal (skill) deficits: Optimal social functioning requires establishing and maintaining some close relationships with family members and/or intimate friends, less intense friendships and acquaintances, and adequate handling of work and/or school roles. Socially isolated people lack relationships with intimates or friends or may have no work role. Such people may have longstanding or temporary deficiencies in social skills. Those who are severely isolated socially tend to be more severely disturbed.
Source: Klerman, Weissman, Rounsaville, & Chevron (1984)

Role conflicts: Role conflicts refer to situations in which the patient and at least one significant other person have nonreciprocal expectations about their relationship. For example, the wife expects the husband to take care of the children with her, while the husband thinks that is her responsibility, or a husband expects his son to join the family business but the son has other ideas, or a daughter wants to marry someone outside her religion, race, or nationality and her parents threaten to reject her.
Source: Klerman, Weissman, Rounsaville, & Chevron (1984)

Unresolved grief: Grief associated with the death of a loved one can be divided into normal or abnormal. Abnormal grief may be delayed or distorted. In a delayed reaction the grief is experienced long after the loss and so it may not be recognized

as a reaction to the original loss. A distorted grief reaction is devoid of sadness or dysphoric mood but instead manifests with nonaffective symptoms immediately following the loss or possibly years afterward.
Source: Klerman, Weissman, Rounsaville, & Chevron (1984)

Core conflictual relationship theme: Each person develops a set of expectations about his/her relationships to other people. These interpersonal expectations can be analyzed by examining reciprocal interactional sequences and explicating the pattern that emerges. The first step in the sequence asks "What does the patient want from other people?" The second step: "How do other people react to the expression of the patient's wish?" The third step: "How does the patient react to this reaction?" The underlying assumption of this concept is that each person develops a basic set of interactional patterns that emerge from the core conflict.
Source: Luborsky & Christoph (1990)

BEHAVIORAL THERAPY

Stimulus control: We are bombarded each day by stimuli that create a variety of effects on us based upon our previous experiences with them. From some we recoil, to others we are attracted, and the majority we ignore. A stimulus may be more than a single sound or sight. Various contexts, social and physical environments influence our behavior. For example, the recovering heroin addict who visits the neighborhood in which his addicted friends live will be more likely to return to drug use, since the environment brings out in him behaviors associated with that place.

Operant conditioning: Behavior is conditioned by its consequences. In other words, the events that follow a specific behavior influence the probability that this behavior will be repeated. A rewarding event increases the probability that the behavior will be repeated, while a noxious event decreases the likelihood that the behavior will be repeated. The consequence *operates* on the behavior.

The problem in connecting consequences with specific behaviors arises from the differing interpretations human beings might make of the same consequence. For example, being intoxicated might be fun for one person and horrible for another. If an action leads to a desirable, pleasurable outcome, the person or animal is likely to repeat it. Operant conditioning has been extensively researched in animal laboratories. One set of studies examined animal behaviors using a wooden box with a door that could be opened by pulling a loop. When a cat was placed within the box it first made a number of ineffective movements, but eventually it accidentally pulled the loop and escaped. Gradually the animal decreased the length of time before it pulled the loop and escaped. Operant conditioning can explain some patients' maladaptive behaviors or dysfunctional patterns. For example, avoidance of phobic stimuli usually yields a reduction in anxiety. This relief from anxiety reinforces avoidance behavior.
Source: Sullivan (1996)

Modeling: Individuals learn social behavior socially—by watching and imitating how others behave. Attractive, successful models are more likely to be copied than those who are unattractive and unsuccessful.

COGNITIVE THERAPY

Automatic thoughts: Cognitive therapy is based upon the idea that cognitions are "mediating events" between stimulus and response. In yet simpler terms, an activating event (A) triggers a belief (B) which leads to a consequence (C). This is the ABC of cognitive therapy.

The belief (or attitude, construct, schema) emits a brief statement to the self (self-statement) that proceeds quickly through preconscious thinking, rarely reaching consciousness. This "automatic thought" is a reflex thought stimulated by the activating event. It becomes a clue to the content of the underlying cognitive schema that created it. For example, each time she came late to the seminar a resident apologized more than was necessary. The automatic thought she experienced, slightly out of awareness, was that she was offending the others and was about to be criticized. This automatic thought led her to apologize. Her underlying belief contained a fear of not living up to the expectations of others.

Automatic thoughts may be gathered systematically through the use of diaries in which the individual records the activating event, the response, and the intervening automatic thoughts (see the triple column technique).

Negative automatic thoughts associated with depression can be defined as spontaneous self-statements characterized by the cognitive triad of negative views of self, negative interpretation of ongoing experiences, and negative view of the future. Cognitive therapy involves training patients to observe and record these automatic thoughts and helping them learn to discriminate between these thoughts and actual events and understand the relationship between these thoughts, affects, behaviors, and environmental events.

Sources: Beck, Rush, Shaw, & Emery (1979), and Merluzzi & Boltwood (1989)

Cognitive schemas: Many different terms have been used to describe the filters human beings use to interpret their realities: attitudes, beliefs, worldview, maps of reality, constructs, and schemas. Schemas determine the manner in which individuals respond to their world and are in turn altered by these experiences. Psychotherapy is but one way for people to change how they construe, understand, and interpret what they experience both internally (e.g., emotions, body sensations) and externally.

Cognitive distortions: Cognitive distortions refer to misinterpretations of reality that reinforce negative conclusions, that is, dysfunctional cognitive schemas. Beck describes specific kinds of cognitive distortions, including: (1) overgeneralizing (formulating a general rule based on a single or a few isolated instances and applying the rule in a wide range of situations; for example, after his girlfriend left him, a man said, "No one will ever love me"); (2) dichotomous thinking (categorizing experiences in only extreme points of view, either white or black; for example, "I am the most worthless person in the world"); (3) selective abstraction (conceptualizing a situation simply on the basis of negative aspects; for example, "My boss doesn't like me because he didn't ask about my work yesterday"); (4) personalizing (attributing external events to oneself without any causal connection; for example, "She looks unhappy today, I must have done something wrong"); (5) arbitrary inference (drawing a conclusion without evidence or even with contradictory evidence; for

example, after she made a speech, "It must be an awful talk," even though she heard long applause from the audience); (6) catastrophizing and minimizing (emphasizing negative and downplaying positive outcomes; for example, after being separated from her abusive husband, she thought, "I can't survive without someone's support," while ignoring that she is not abused by him anymore).
Sources: Beck & Weishaar (1989), and Allen (1996)

CLIENT-CENTERED THERAPY

Negative self-concept: Self-concept refers to a person's conceptual construction of him- or herself, including perceptions, attitudes, and feelings about self and the perceptions of the relationships of the "I" with others.

Everyone, from earliest infancy, has a strong need for positive regard or approval from others. The self-concept is developed through the process of socialization and is heavily dependent on the attitude and evaluation of those who constitute the individual's significant others. Individuals can internalize significant others' criticism and develop a negative self-concept. In client-centered therapy, the disturbance is conceptualized in terms of the degree of success or failure experienced by the individual in resolving these conflicts. Once caught in negative self-concept, the person is likely to grow more disturbed, because the negative self-concept often induces behaviors that reinforce the image of inadequacy and worthlessness.
Source: Thorne (1996)

EXISTENTIAL THERAPY

Emphasizing the individual alone in the world, existential psychotherapists encourage therapists to ponder the ultimate concerns of individual human existence: fear of death, fear of freedom and responsibility, fear of isolation and the need for meaning in life.

Fear of responsibility and freedom: In answer to the question, *Are we victims of our circumstances or creators of our own lives?* existential therapists insist that our lives are the products of our own decisions, including our own failures to decide. No matter how awful or wonderful the circumstances, we can choose how to respond—positive or negative is every person's choice. Therefore, people should come to realize that they are responsible for their lives, actions, and failure; they direct their lives. Fear of responsibility is evident in the search for causes outside the self for one's situation. Blaming others reduces self-responsibility but also reduces personal freedom.

On the other hand, many patients blame themselves excessively, rather than blaming others. This excessive self-blame contains a hidden and exaggerated sense of power, as if "I can change everyone else's life." Ironically, such excessive power taken to the self leads to paralysis of decision-making and helplessness in being responsible for the self. Freedom to choose is then strongly inhibited.

We experience anxiety when we use our freedom to choose to move out of the known into the realm of the unknown. People try to avoid this anxiety by denying

their creative ideas, by avoiding risk, by failing to learn from mistakes, by being frightened to choose, or by having somebody else decide for them.
Sources: Yalom (1980) and Corey (1996)

Fear of death: Death is the most obvious ultimate concern; nobody can escape it. From the existential point of view, a core inner conflict involves awareness of death and a simultaneous wish for eternal life. People, at the deepest level, respond to death with terror. To cope with this terror, individuals employ defenses against the death awareness. To experience existential anxiety is to confront the emptiness of the universe, helplessness in the face of awesome and impersonal power and the foundational terror of self-annihilation. Some panic attacks are triggered by this terrifying confrontation with nonexistence.
Sources: Corey (1996), and Yalom (1980)

Existential isolation: Each of us is alone in the universe. Our individual uniqueness carries with it the realization that our own consciousness cannot be fully shared with anyone else (except for those rare and special moments, sometimes referred to as "existential encounters," when two individuals seem to share the same space and time). Between the intense existential encounter and the loneliness of an isolated room, individuals achieve different degrees of attachment and involvement with others. For some terror lies in isolation, as if the self will disintegrate into many pieces; this generates intense fear and the desire to attach to others.

Existential therapists believe that no relationship can eliminate isolation, but experience can be shared with another in such a way that the pain of isolation is reduced. Some people, such as borderline patients, may experience existential anxiety when they are alone. They begin to doubt their own existence and believe that they exist only in the presence of another, that they exist only so long as they are responded to or are thought about by another individual. People may attempt to deal with isolation by fusion, such as fusing with a lover ("I" disappears into "we"), a group, or an organization.
Sources: Corey (1996) and Yalom (1980)

Meaninglessness: Human beings struggle for a sense of significance and purpose in life. Without a sense of purpose, life has no pull toward the future. Religious beliefs, political causes, athletics, parenting, learning, and helping others provide some of the many ways that life can be provided meaning. Without meaning people tend to dissolve into hedonistic pursuits or existential despair. Meaninglessness may arise as people disregard the old or traditional value systems without finding or building other, suitable ones to replace them. Some believe that each person has a "mission in life" a "Great Work" to accomplish, that part of life's odyssey is to find the purpose and strive to fulfill it.

Sometimes meaninglessness arises when individuals are "not true to themselves," when what is of utmost significance is ignored in favor of another pursuit more congruent with society's expectation and/or the prized goals of others.

Note: Existential psychotherapy is not a specific technical approach that presents a set of rules for therapy. Rather, it asks deep questions about the nature of the human being and the nature of anxiety, despair, grief, loneliness, isolation, freedom, creativity, and love. It emphasizes that we are not the victims of circumstances;

rather, we are what we choose to be. This view differs from the position of psycho-analysis, in which freedom is determined by the unconscious, and behavioral therapy, in which freedom is mainly influenced by the sociocultural conditioning. Existential therapy is a process of helping patients explore and search for freedom and meaning in life while confronting and accepting humans' isolation and inevitable death.

EXPERIENTIAL (GESTALT) THERAPY

Avoidance of emotional awareness: Awareness is noticing, recognizing, and being in touch with. Avoidance refers to the means people use to keep themselves from awareness of unfinished business and from experiencing the uncomfortable emotions associated with unfinished situations.

In Gestalt therapy, despite the importance of thinking and rationality, emotional awareness is emphasized in maintaining one's health and integration. The avoidance of emotional awareness limits our full experience of internal and external reality, which can be a major impediment to managing ourselves effectively in the world. *Sources:* Corey (1996) and Parlett & Hemming (1996)

Conflict splits: The human condition has often been described as containing conflicts between two alternatives. Gestalt therapy emphasizes the common tension between emotion and cognition, which can be played out in many different ways. Some patients "know" what is right but cannot "believe" it because of their strong emotional investment in the belief. Said in many ways by representatives of other schools (for example, superego vs. id from psychodynamic), conflict splits can also be described as deeply felt emotions in conflict with externally derived standards that oppose desires or needs. For example, "I think that I should be involved more with other people but I want to stay home alone because I hate being around them." Experiential therapists will isolate these splits in order to better define their origins and attempt to resolve them.

Unfinished business: Feelings that arise from painful, overwhelming experiences can be held back from conscious awareness and yet impede full or normal functioning because the needs from which these feelings emerge are blocked. The "working through," resolution, or letting go of these feelings has yet to have taken place.

FAMILY THERAPY

Triangles: As suggested by Murray Bowen, anxiety can easily develop within intimate relationships. Under stressful pressures two people might recruit or discover a third person to whom each can direct their anxious energy. This redirection reduces anxiety within the system and leads to stability. However, triangulation does not necessarily lead to resolution of the conflicts in the dyad and, in the long run, the situation is likely to worsen. For example, a married couple may focus their attention on a problematic child instead of fighting with each other. If the child's problem resolves or the child leaves home, then the couple must confront their unresolved conflict, live with intense anxiety, leave each other, or find another person or subject with which to form a triangle.

Boundary problems: Family structure is maintained by appropriate boundaries between subsystems. A clear and effective boundary indicates that individuals can interact with the subsystem at a regulated and optimal degree. There are two ineffective types of boundaries. Rigid boundaries are overly restrictive and restrain contact to outside systems, resulting in individuals or subsystems being disengaged and isolated from each other. With enmeshed boundaries family members are overly involved with and usually overly responsive to one another. Distances between subsystems are decreased and boundaries are blurred and diffused. A common boundary problem within the family involves an alliance between a parent and a child against another parent or stepparent—the cross-generational alliance—which can stabilize family dynamics but create symptoms or problems.

Disturbed homeostasis: Homeostasis is a term borrowed from biology and systems theory. It refers to a balanced, steady-state equilibrium in a system. Families are described as homeostatic units that maintain relative constancy of their internal functioning. The concept of homeostasis is relevant not only to functional families but also to dysfunctional ones. Family therapists often conceptualize family problems as the tendency to maintain the family's equilibrium in spite of developmental and unexpected events. The "identified patient" in family therapy may be regarded as the person to restore the homeostasis. For example, a child's symptomatic behavior may be a response to parental discord. The child's problem distracts the parents from their interpersonal difficulties as they become concerned about the "identified patient." On the other hand, the tendency toward homeostasis may inhibit a family system from adjusting to developmental events such as a child's beginning school by continuing to treat the child as if he/she were a preschooler.

If one member of a couple changes or improves in some way, perhaps through finding a new job or through psychotherapy, the marital balance could be disrupted, leading the other spouse to become symptomatic or leave—unless that spouse adapts to the new equilibrium by also changing.
Source: Nichols & Schwartz (1991)

Circular causality: In contrast to linear causality, which focuses on how A's response causes B's response, circular causality focuses on the reciprocal influence of A on B and B on A. In a relationship things do not occur necessarily because one partner "causes" them but rather as the result of a complex cycle of interactions in which both partners actively participate. Moreover, a person's actions within a relationship stem not from a single cause, either in the immediate or remote past, but from a continuing chain of causation in which both partners are initiators and recipients. Thus, systems therapists do not focus on one of the protagonists, but pursue, instead, change in which both partners contribute actively to facing and solving the problem.

Circular questioning refers to the therapist's asking one family member about an interaction, and then asking another family member to respond to the first person's answer, and then asking a third person to respond to the second person. This concept relies on the fact that family members reciprocally influence each other; the pattern of responses to these questions provides an example of the manner in which they do that.
Source: Growe (1996)

FORM 15–1
Inductive Reasoning to Determine Patterns

Name (optional)_____   Date_____

This module introduces a critical aspect of psychotherapeutic thinking: deriving a pattern of psychological dysfunction from bits and pieces of information presented by the patient. From these pieces of information, which we will call "inducing points," therapists build patterns to be changed. They are called inducing points because therapists "induce" patterns from them.

This is no cut-and-dried activity. Several different instances of a pattern must be observed to confirm its existence. The following case illustrates the manner in which inducing points can be used to derive a general pattern:

A husband loves cherry pie. One day he bought one for himself and put it in the refrigerator. When he wanted to eat it, he found the pie was not there. His wife had eaten it but he did not confront her about it. What was his interaction pattern?

One answer might be: "He's passive." This answer is right and it describes the first level pattern. But it does not provide sufficient detail upon which to develop a pattern that begins to *suggest what needs to be changed or modified. We recommend you try to induce "well-formed" patterns, at the second and third level. We also recommend that, when you describe the pattern, you think about what you would say to the patient and how it might influence him.* Doing this will help you to induce and describe more specific rather than too general patterns. A better answer for this case, thus, would be: "If she wants something, he gives it to her without question, even if it goes against what he wants for himself."

In this case, other evidence suggested that this pattern described an important part of their relationship. For example, his wife wanted them to build a large and expensive house that was beyond their economic means. He did not want to spend the extra money, but he agreed to do it anyway.

If the patient agrees that this is a pattern to change, the next step would be to help the patient define the reasons he has not changed this pattern. In this example, it seemed that the patient needed to learn how to say "no" to his wife. The question, "What prevented him from doing so?" becomes part of the change sequence. This next step leads to change strategies, which are presented in module 4.

Please read the following vignettes and try to induce "well-formed" or third-level patterns. We recommend that when you describe the patterns, you think about what you would say to the patient and remember that how you say it will influence the patient.

- -

1. A 26-year-old, attractive female patient told her therapist that whenever she goes to parties, nobody pays attention to her. One day, one of her male colleagues said to her, "You look very good." She got mad at him because she thought he was ridiculing her. What was her pattern?

_____

_____

_____

_____

_____

_____

2. A 33-year-old successful bank manager felt very stressed. Several days ago, a woman working with him at the same office seemed unhappy, and he thought it was because of something he had done. He ruminated for several days about this problem. He then discovered that she was unhappy because her daughter was dating someone she did not like. What pattern is he demonstrating?

    _____

    _____

    _____

    _____

    _____

    _____

3. A 45-year-old woman always silently took care of the needs of her two sons and husband. She often felt angry and disappointed with them because they never expressed appreciation for her efforts. She bought several cassettes of her son's favorite music and put them in his book bag. When her son took the bag and was going to leave for school, she cried out to him, "You never check what is in your bag, do you? You never notice how I care for you and love you, do you?" What might be her pattern toward her sons and husband?

    _____

    _____

    _____

    _____

    _____

    _____

4. Ms. C is a 33-year-old secretary. When she communicates with somebody she thinks she should be always chattering and her mouth always has to keep talking. She feels very embarrassed and nervous if there is silence. When she talks to somebody on the phone, it is hard for her to say "goodbye" first, although she wants to. What is (are) the possible reason(s)?

    _____

    _____

    _____

    _____

    _____

    _____

5. A 36-year-old male came to see a psychotherapist for depression. He said his marriage is okay and he rarely quarrels with his wife. When the therapist asked, "How do you deal with disagreements between you and your wife?" He said, "I change my mind and agree with her, so we never fight." What is his pattern in the relationship with his wife?

    _____

    _____

_____

_____

_____

_____

_____

6. A 36-year-old husband complained that his wife was too independent and didn't need him anymore, because she was often ignored by him when he gave her a suggestion, such as which color car she should buy, when she should call him, which restaurant they should go to, or whom they should invite to her birthday party. What is his pattern with his wife?

_____

_____

_____

_____

_____

7. A 33-year-old woman told the therapist that, each time before coming to therapy, she considered over and over what she needed to say and how to say it in order for therapist to understand accurately. However, she still felt she couldn't express herself very well and that made her very anxious. What is the pattern she is demonstrating?

_____

_____

_____

_____

_____

8. The patient saw the therapist for depression. After the first session, the therapist and the patient scheduled the date and time of the next session and then the patient left. Several minutes later, the patient came back and very timidly asked, "I am afraid I can't come on that day, would you mind changing the appointment time?" Next session, the therapist asked the patient why he didn't ask for the more convenient time during the last session instead of afterward. The patient said, "I wanted to ask, but I thought you would be angry at me for that." What might be his pattern?

_____

_____

_____

_____

_____

9. A 63-year-old man reported many continuing fights with his wife of 35 years. Following are two examples of their fights:

a. They decided to move from another town to their current location because he was offered a new job there. They discussed the move in great detail. She agreed to go. After they had been there a few months, she became dissatisfied. She blamed him entirely for the move. He accepted the blame.

b. His wife accused him of having a sexual problem. She said he was impotent. The patient, however, stated that he was able to have an erection if he masturbated. However, if he penetrated his wife, and became "a little soft," she got angry at him and his erection went away. She told him it was all his problem and that he should do something about it. He agreed. What is her pattern, his pattern, and the pattern of the couple?

_____

_____

_____

_____

_____

_____

10. A high school teacher was criticized by one of her colleagues in front of other teachers. Since then she has had trouble sleeping and concentrating at work. She has become depressed. Two years earlier she had been in a car accident that had injured her brain sufficiently to require that she enter a brain injury treatment program lasting three months. She was able to return to work as a teacher; however, she noticed that she required more time to prepare lessons for her class. She also noticed that since the accident criticisms of her work by students, parents, and other teachers bothered her much more than they had before the accident. What was bothering her so much that she reacted so strongly to the criticisms?

_____

_____

_____

_____

_____

_____

11. A 38-year-old hospital laboratory technician came to her first appointment in acute distress. While in the waiting room she cried intensely, sobbing, and sometimes wailing. Her dog Hercules had died suddenly. She loved this dog and relied upon him for comfort and understanding. She calmed down during a session of empathic listening and over time gradually recovered from the grief of the loss. However, she started to turn to her husband for comfort that he had not given her before. He did not change. Her demands escalated. He would not respond with the increasing support and interest she desired. He began divorce proceedings. How would this female patient react to the divorce?

_____

_____

_____

_____

_____

12. A 35-year-old woman described longstanding anxiety and depression. She refused any psychoactive medications. She readily engaged with the therapist, quickly expressing intense anger when condemning her primary care physician, "who never cared about me." She easily acknowledged respect for her therapist, "I wouldn't come back if I didn't think you were helping me." However, she sometimes canceled appointments and occasionally did not call to cancel. Nevertheless, she called the therapist to discuss problems, often attempting to extend the conversation. At work she was convinced that her boss strongly disliked her, despite self-reported efforts to do everything she could to do a good job. Her marriage deteriorated despite efforts at marital therapy; her husband initiated divorce proceedings. "Nobody likes me. I try to please everyone. It doesn't work. I quit trying." How would you characterize her interpersonal relationships?

_____

_____

_____

_____

_____

_____

FORM 16–1

Transcripts for Inductive Reasoning

Name (optional)_____   Date_____

1. The excerpt from a transcript of Dr. Aaron Beck

(Patient is a 40-year-old female who has recently been left by her boyfriend.)

T-1:   Well, how have you been feeling since I talked to you last?

P-1:   Bad.

T-2:   You've been feeling bad . . . well, tell me about it?

P-2:   It started this weekend . . . I just feel like everything is an effort. There's just completely no point to do anything.

T-3:   So, there are two problems; everything is an effort, and you believe there's no point to doing anything.

P-3:   It's because there's no point to doing anything that makes everything too hard to do.

T-4:   Because there's no point and everything feels like an effort. And when you were coming down here today, were you feeling the same way?

P-4:   Well, it doesn't seem as bad when I am working. It's bad on weekends and especially on holidays. I sort of expected that it would happen.

T-5:   You expected to have a hard time on holidays . . . And when you left your office to come over here, how were you feeling then?

P-5:   Kind of the same way. I feel that I can do everything that I have to do, but I don't want to.

T-6:   You don't want to do the things you have to.

P-6:   I don't want to do anything.

T-7:   Right . . . and what kind of feeling did you have? Feel low?

P-7:   I feel that there's no hope for me. I feel my future . . . that everything is futile, that there's no hope.

T-8:   And what idea did you have about today's interview?

P-8:   I thought that it would probably help as it has always happened in the past . . . that I would feel better—temporarily. But that makes it worse because then I know that I am going to feel bad again.

T-9:   That makes it worse in terms of how you feel?

P-9:   Yes.

T-10:   And the reason is that it builds you up and then you get let down again?

P-10:   I feel like it's interminable, it will just go this way forever, and I am not getting any better . . . I don't feel any less inclined to kill myself than I ever did in my life . . . In fact, if anything, I feel like I'm coming closer to it.

T-11:   Perhaps we should talk about that a little bit because we haven't talked about the advantages and disadvantages of killing yourself.

P-11:   (*smiles*) You make everything so logical.

T-12:   (*testing therapeutic alliance*) Is that bad? Remember you once wrote something . . . that reason is your greatest ally. Have you become allergic to reason?

P-12:   But I can't try anymore.

T-13:   Does it take an effort to be reasonable?

P-13:   I know I am being unreasonable; the thoughts seem so real to me . . . that it does take an effort to try to change them.

T-14:   Now, if it came easy to you—to change the thoughts, do you think that they would last as long?

P-14:   No . . . see, I don't say that this wouldn't work with other people. I don't try to say that, but I don't feel that it can work with me.

T-15:   So, do you have any evidence that it did work with you?

P-15:   It works for specific periods of time, and that's like the Real Me comes through.

T-16:   Now, is there anything unusual that happened that might have upset the apple cart?

P-16:   You mean this weekend?

T-17:   Not necessarily this weekend. As you know, you felt you were making good progress in therapy and you decided that you were going to be like the Cowardly Lion that Found His Heart. What happened after that?

P-17:   (*agitated, bows head*) It's too hard . . . it would be easier to die.

T-18:   At the moment, it would be easier to die—as you say. But, let's go back to the history. You're losing sight and losing perspective. Remember when we talked and made a tape of that interview and you liked it. You wrote a letter the next day and you said that you felt you had your heart and it wasn't any great effort to reach that particular point. Now, you went along reasonably well until you got involved. Correct? Then you got involved with Jim. Is that correct? And then very predictably when your relationship ended, you felt terribly let down. Now, what do you conclude from that?

What might be the patient's patterns?

1. _____

2. _____

3. _____

4. _____

Reprinted with permission from Beck, A. T. (1995). An interview with a depressed and suicidal patient. In D. Wedding & R. Corsini (Eds.), *Case studies in psychotherapy* (pp. 120–121). Itasca, IL: Peacock.

2. The excerpt from a transcript of Dr. Peggy Papp (family therapy)

(The patient is the 23-year-old anorectic daughter—Rachel)

T-1:   So you feel you're the bad guy and your father is the bad guy in the family. In what way do you feel you can bring comfort to your father?

Rachel: (daughter)   Because I can understand his viewpoint.

Clare: (daughter)   If there are two bad guys, then you both share the burden?

Rachel: There's company.

T-2:   How do you go about giving him company?

Rachel: We have a lot of common interest, we both like cars and nature and the Bronx Zoo, and we have a good time. We go across the country together.

T-3:	What do you think his life would be like if you weren't around?
Rachel:	I don't know—I guess he'd survive.
T-4:	Do you think he'd be lonely?
Rachel:	Maybe, sometimes—I'm nice company for him.
T-5:	Then who would there be around to really understand him?
Rachel:	(*long pause*) I don't know.
T-6:	You don't think your mother could understand him?
Rachel:	She will never ever. I shouldn't say that, but as far as I can see, it'll be a very tough thing for my mother to ever understand how my father feels about her family. She will never ever see how he feels about her.
Mother:	But who do I think of when I want somebody to make nice to me? I go right back to the womb. On Tuesday I spent the day with my mom and dad and it was a good day. It was a hard day. I took them shopping. They're very old.
T-7:	Do you feel they're the only ones who nurture you?
Mother:	(*nodding*) Who really take care of me. I don't want anyone here to feel bad, but, Sandy [another daughter who is not in the session] also takes care of me.
Rachel:	But you demand too much. You're very hard to give to when you demand.
T-8:	Let's see then. When you feel ganged up on by Rachel and your husband, you then go for nurturing to your parents. And who does your husband go to?
Mother:	There's always been a young man in his life who treats him like God. Now it's Roy.
T-9:	You're saying that he always finds someone who is like a son to him?
Mother:	Yes, Roy is like a son.
T-10:	Was he disappointed he didn't have a son?
Mother:	(*whispers*) Very.
T-11:	You whispered that "very." You don't want the girls to hear that?
Mother:	(*emphatically*) Very displeased that he didn't have a son.
T-12:	Do you think they don't know that?
Rachel:	I am daddy's son.
T-13:	In what way have you been his son?
Rachel:	Just—my interest in things which aren't typically feminine. I'm not scared of bugs, little things like that. Daddy asked me to cook hamburgers on the barbecue pit because I can handle it. (*She imitates a boy.*)
T-14:	What's that like for you to be his son?
Rachel:	I kinda like it. (*She laughs and acts like a boy again.*) I don't mind, but I don't think he thinks of me as a boy.
T-15:	Do you think of yourself as a boy?
Rachel:	No. I was saying that I felt so independent on this move. It always bugs me to be dependent on people.
T-16:	What do you think it's going to be like for him, your moving out?

Rachel: I think it's going to be all right for him. Already they're talking about switching homes with me.

T-17:   Do you think he's going to miss you?

Rachel: Maybe. He said he was going to miss some things but not others.

T-18:   Well, do you think your mother's going to be able to take care of his loneliness?

Rachel: Not unless she starts to look at him from a more objective point of view.

T-19:   Do you think you can teach her?

Rachel: I try, I really try. Then she accuses me of ganging up on her.

Clare: (*defending mother*) Daddy's not nice all the time, either.

What might be the patterns of Rachel?

1. _____

2. _____

3. _____

4. _____

What might be the patterns of mother?

1. _____

2. _____

3. _____

4. _____

What might be the patterns of father?

1. _____

2. _____

3. _____

4. _____

What might be the patterns between the Rachel and father, Rachel and mother, and father and mother?

Rachel and father:

_____

_____

_____

_____

Rachel and mother:

_____

_____

_____

_____

Father and mother:

_____

_____

_____

_____

What might be the patterns among Rachel, father, and mother?

_____

_____

_____

_____

Reprinted with permission from Papp, P. (1995). The daughter who said no. In D. Wedding & R. Corsini (Eds.), _Case studies in psychotherapy_ (pp. 179–180). Itasca, IL: Peacock.

FORM 17
Triple-column Diary

Name_____

Date/Time	Situations	Negative Emotions or Symptoms	Automatic Thoughts

FORM 15–2
Inductive Reasoning to Determine Patterns

Name (optional)_____   Date_____

Please read the following vignettes and try to induce well-formed or third-level patterns. When you describe the patterns, you need to think about what you would say to the patient and how it is going to influence the patient, as you did for Form 15-1.

- -

1. A 23-year-old female student accused her mother of caring more about her sister than she cared about her. For example, her mother bought shoes for both of them, but her sister's shoes were a little more expensive. However, sometimes her mother bought her things that were more expensive than the things she bought for her sister. In fact, the mother appeared to balance the number of times she bought each daughter the more expensive item. Nevertheless, the patient believed that her mother felt guilty about caring so much for her sister and tried to relieve this guilt by buying the patient more expensive things sometimes. What is (are) her pattern(s)?

_____

_____

_____

_____

_____

_____

2. A 45-year-old family practitioner was prescribed antidepressants by a psychiatrist during psychotherapy following his divorce. Shortly after beginning the medication, he went on a two-week vacation, during which he experienced painful urinary retention secondary to the antidepressant. He did not, however, stop taking it. When asked later by his psychiatrist what he would have told one of his patients with this side effect, he replied that he would have suggested stopping it. When asked why he did not stop it, he replied that he preferred to "tough it out." How might the patient react when he has problems with his wife?

_____

_____

_____

_____

_____

_____

3. A 22-year-old student, although in college, was still living with her parents because her parents didn't want her to move out. When her classmates asked her to join them on a trip during spring break, she agreed although she didn't want to go. What might be her response to other people's needs or demands?

_____

_____

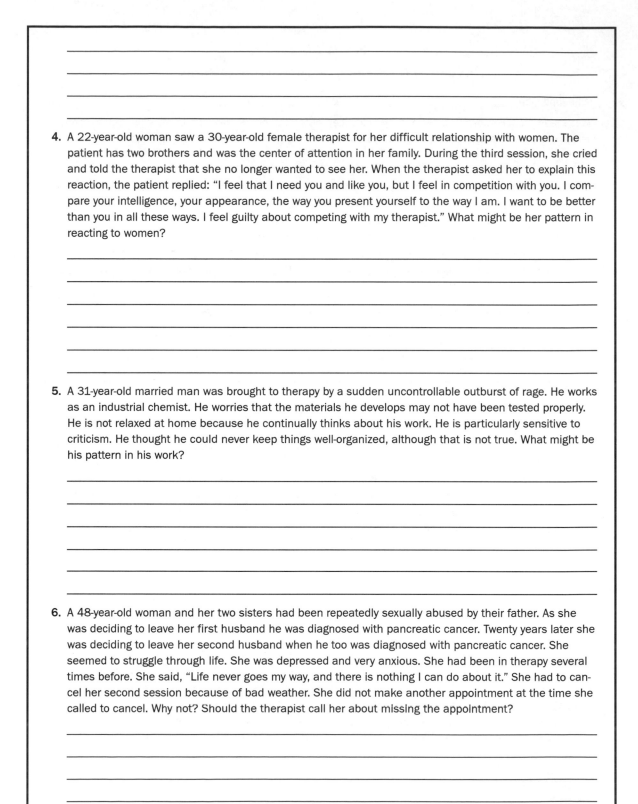

4. A 22-year-old woman saw a 30-year-old female therapist for her difficult relationship with women. The patient has two brothers and was the center of attention in her family. During the third session, she cried and told the therapist that she no longer wanted to see her. When the therapist asked her to explain this reaction, the patient replied: "I feel that I need you and like you, but I feel in competition with you. I compare your intelligence, your appearance, the way you present yourself to the way I am. I want to be better than you in all these ways. I feel guilty about competing with my therapist." What might be her pattern in reacting to women?

5. A 31-year-old married man was brought to therapy by a sudden uncontrollable outburst of rage. He works as an industrial chemist. He worries that the materials he develops may not have been tested properly. He is not relaxed at home because he continually thinks about his work. He is particularly sensitive to criticism. He thought he could never keep things well-organized, although that is not true. What might be his pattern in his work?

6. A 48-year-old woman and her two sisters had been repeatedly sexually abused by their father. As she was deciding to leave her first husband he was diagnosed with pancreatic cancer. Twenty years later she was deciding to leave her second husband when he too was diagnosed with pancreatic cancer. She seemed to struggle through life. She was depressed and very anxious. She had been in therapy several times before. She said, "Life never goes my way, and there is nothing I can do about it." She had to cancel her second session because of bad weather. She did not make another appointment at the time she called to cancel. Why not? Should the therapist call her about missing the appointment?

7. A 28-year-old woman whose husband is addicted to alcohol came for help for depression. Whenever he got drunk, she became furious at him. When he sobered up, she told him she would leave him. He begged her forgiveness and swore he would never drink again. She believed him and did not leave. Describe the pattern between them.

_____

_____

_____

_____

_____

8. A 33-year-old pharmacist reported that she did not want to return to work because she did not trust her supervisors. She was afraid that they would deny her request for pharmacy technicians if she needed the technicians. She had not asked yet, so she did not know whether her request for the technicians would be denied. She recognized her fear as unfounded, yet she could not help feeling intensely anxious. She wanted a new job somewhere else.

Her mother had been diagnosed with schizophrenia when the patient was six years old. Her father became dependent upon her to take care of her younger siblings. She felt an intense loss of adequate parenting. She felt her needs as a child had been ignored.

The feelings about her supervisors had begun when she returned home for Christmas. Six weeks later, when she saw the therapist, she had not been able to shake the intense anxiety about her supervisors. What pattern is she demonstrating?

_____

_____

_____

_____

_____

9. A 24-year-old student entered psychotherapy because she could not maintain intimate relationships with men. When she was 14 years old, a man exposed himself to her in a park where she was reading a book. She was very frightened but never told anybody because she felt very embarrassed and ashamed. She thought that perhaps the way she was sitting had attracted him. She had her first boyfriend when she was 20 years old. Whenever she was with him, however, she tried to avoid any sexually suggestive behaviors because she thought he would think of her as promiscuous. She was very passive in her relationship with her boyfriends. She told the therapist she has already lost several boyfriends. What are her patterns toward men?

_____

_____

_____

10. A 45-year-old divorced psychologist began to reexperience social phobia when his fiancée became emotionally withdrawn from him as her daughter by a previous marriage prepared to return to college. His fiancée usually had difficulty separating from her daughter. The psychologist began to be self-conscious while shopping. Sometimes he began to sweat and feared people were staring at him. He had not had the symptoms for several months. Of what pattern is this likely an example?

11. A 23-year-old student entered therapy for depression. She reported having had four different roommates, but each of them had left her. She worries now that her fifth roommate will also leave her. She complained that none of them cared about her. She reported, "One day I felt a little stomach pain and lay in bed. My roommate should have thought that I was hungry and needed something to eat. But she didn't ask me." As therapy progressed, she continued to ask the therapist to allow her to call and come to see him whenever she needed because she had so much pain and couldn't bear it. When the therapist asked, "What if I am seeing another patient or I am doing other things when you come without an appointment?" The patient replied, "I don't think other patients are in greater pain than I am. Helping me is more important than your 'other things.'" What might be her pattern toward her roommates?

FORM 16–2

Transcripts for Inductive Reasoning

Name (optional)_____ Date_____

1. The excerpt from a transcript of Dr. Albert Ellis

Martha , an attractive 23-year-old woman, came for help because she claimed she was compulsive, afraid of males, had no goals in life and was guilty about her relationship with her parents.

P-1: Well, for about a year and a half since I graduated from college, I've had the feeling that something was the matter with me. I seem to have a tendency toward punishing myself. I'm accident-prone. I'm forever banging myself or falling down stairs, or something like that. And my relationship with my father is causing me a great deal of trouble. I've never been able to figure out where is the responsibility and what my relationship with my parents should be.

T-1: Do you live with them?

P-2: No, I don't. I moved out in March.

T-2: Any other children?

P-3: Yes. I have two younger brothers. One is 20; the other is 16. I'm 23. We never had much money, but we always had the feeling that love and security in life are what count. And the first thing that disturbed me was, when I was about 16 years old, my father began to drink seriously. To me he had been the infallible person. Anything he did was right. And since I moved out and before I moved out, I've wondered where my responsibility to my family lies. Because if they would ask me to do something, if I didn't do it, I would feel guilty about it.

T-3: What sort of things did they ask you to do?

P-4: Well, they felt that it just wasn't right for an unmarried girl to move out. Also, I find it easier to lie than to tell the truth, if the truth is unpleasant. I'm basically afraid of men and afraid to find a good relationship with a man that would lead to marriage. My parents have never approved of anyone I have gone out with.

T-4: Do you go with anyone now?

P-5: Yes, two people.

T-5: And are you serious about either one?

P-6: I really don't know. One is sort of serious about me, but he thinks there's something the matter with me that I have to straighten out. I have also at various times been rather promiscuous, and I don't want to be that way.

T-6: Have you enjoyed sex?

P-7: Not particularly. I think—in trying to analyze myself and find out why I was promiscuous, I think I was afraid not to be.

T-7: Afraid they wouldn't like you?

P-8: Yes. This one fellow that I've been going with—in fact, both of them—said I don't have a good opinion of myself.

T-8: Do you do all right with your work?

P-9: I worked very hard. My family always emphasized that I couldn't do well in school, so I have to work hard. Whenever I set my mind to do anything, I really worked at it. And I was always unsure of myself with people. Consequently, I've almost always gone out with more than one person at the same time, maybe because of a fear of rejection by one. Also, something that bothers me more than anything is that I think that I have the ability to write fiction. But I don't seem to be able to discipline myself. Instead of spending my time wisely, as far as writing is concerned, I'll let it go, let it go, and then go out several nights a week—which I know doesn't help me. When I ask myself why I do it, I don't know.

T-9:   Are you afraid the writing wouldn't be good enough?

P-10: I have the basic fear.

T-10: That's right: it is a basic fear.

P-11: The basic problem is that I'm worried about my family.

T-11: Why are you worried about your family? Let's go into that first of all. What's to be concerned about? They have certain demands which you don't want to adhere to.

P-12: I was brought up to think that I mustn't be selfish. I think that is one of my basic problems.

T-12: That's right. You were brought up to be Florence Nightingale.

P-13   Yes, I was brought up in a family of sort of would-be Florence Nightingale, now that I analyze the whole pattern of my family history . . . My father became really alcoholic sometime when I was away in college. My mother developed a breast cancer last year, and she had one breast removed. Nobody is healthy. My mother feels that I shouldn't have left home—that my place is with them. There are nagging doubts about what I should—

T-13: Why are there doubts? Why should you?

P-14: I think it's a feeling I was brought up with that you always have to give of yourself. If you think of yourself, you're wrong.

What might be the patient's patterns:

1. _____

2. _____

3. _____

4. _____

Reprinted with the permission from Ellis, A. (1974). *Growth through reason* (pp. 223-225). Hollywood: Wilshire Books.

2. The excerpt from a transcript of Dr. Rockland

The patient is a 42-year-old married woman. She is an upper-middle-class mother of one child and a part-time social worker. She has severe marital difficulties and is in marital treatment with another therapist. She describes chronic feelings of unworthiness, of emptiness, and of marked dissatisfaction with most aspects of her life.

P-1:   I'm furious at David again. He always acts so superior. He is cold and self-centered. I don't really know how much he really cares of me. He thinks he is the world's greatest husband. But where it really counts, emotional support, he is just not there. All he cares about is his work and how he looks, and getting new clothes for himself. I want him to look nice too and I bought him an eighty-dollar tie the other day, but I don't think he really appreciated it. And the terrible thing is that he can't see any of this in himself. He thinks he is perfect and I am the sick one in the family. He likes to see himself as cool and me as not only impossible to satisfy but an unreasonable, demanding, impossible person. Sometimes I wonder why I even stay with him. Sometimes I think I really do care about him, but so much of the time I am so angry, that I don't know what I feel toward him. He constantly criticizes me and describes how difficult I am to live with. If I try to fight back, he says I am losing control and he refuses to talk.

T-1:   I believe you when you talk about your husband having problems too. That's one of the reasons that you are in marital therapy, and that is the place to talk about these conflicts between you. But I am also struck by the fact that thus far you have talked only about his difficulties. Furthermore it seems to me that some of the problems that you ascribe to David are very similar to things you have said about yourself in the past. It's always easier to focus on the other person's problems rather than your own. What are your contributions to the difficulties between you?

P-2:   That's not what I am concerned about in myself. What I am concerned about is why does everything have to be so perfect for me? And why do I swing from feeling powerful and good to totally worthless with relatively minor stimuli?

T-2:   I think those are good questions. Tell me some more.

P-3:   If David is good to me I feel good and strong and when he is not I feel worthless, angry, and I feel as though my life has no meaning. I know why. Mother used to always dress me up and always asked me if people liked me and were pleased with me. She gave me the feeling that I would get my feelings of worth from other people's reaction to my face and clothes. But she always said also that everything I did was wrong. She made me feel that I was worthless, but I could be a golden girl when other people thought I was pretty and smart. What are your thoughts about that?

T-3:   You are doing fine.

P-4:   What? Are you kidding? That enrages me. I pay you a lot of money to come here. I want answers when I ask for them. I am entitled to answers to my questions. I've been doing all the talking so far.

T-4:   I don't think you actually asked a specific question. I am also struck by the fact that when you asked me what my thoughts were about that, it seemed like you were turning the tables on me in here.

P-5:   I am furious at you! Why don't you answer my question? I want the answer! This is important!

T-5:   I think you were doing fine. What did you want from me?

P-6:   You have to agree with what I say or it feels to me like it isn't worth anything. You have to endorse it.

T-6:   Why is it worthless unless I endorse it?

P-7:   You are playing games with me. I talked a lot, now you talk.

T-7:   Remember that at the beginning of this treatment, I said that I would talk when I had something useful to say. At that point I didn't. But I am curious as to why you would feel worthless without out my endorsing your thoughts.

P-8:   Oh, I always feel that way. I need feedback, I need feedback or I feel that I am doing badly, and I feel terrible.

T-8:   You are telling me that you are entitled to answers when you want them. And at the same time that what you say is worthless if it doesn't receive endorsement from the other person. It sounds like there is a powerful, demanding, and entitled aspect of you that exists side by side with the feeling that you are utterly worthless.

P-9:   You are just like my husband. You want to control everything.

Describe her basic patterns with herself, her husband and the therapist.

1. _____

2._____

3. _____

4. _____

Developing Psychotherapy Competence—A Guided Inquiry
(Post-module 3)

Name (optional)_____   Date_____

1. What was the most important thing that happened in training during past several weeks?

2. What changes are making in your thinking/feeling about psychotherapy issues as a result of this module?

3. What in this module is *helping you* achieve your desired changes?

4. What aspects/influences *outside* of this module are *helping you* achieve your desired change?

5. What in this module is *keeping you* from making your desired changes?

6. What aspects/influences *outside* of this module are *keeping you* from making your desired changes?

7. Did you find yourself thinking about topics related to this module between training sessions during past several weeks? If so, what *thoughts have you had?*

8. Are you deriving any *benefits* from this module that you did not expect to happen? If so, what are these benefits?

9. Please state the *most immediate concerns* you are having about your psychotherapy competence.

Reprinted with permission from Heppner, P. P. & O'Brien, K. M. (1994). Multicultural counselor training: Students' perceptions of helpful and hindering events. *Counselor Education and Supervision, 34,* 4–18.

As you answer the following questions, please try to think about how you will behave as a therapist now (after module 3)

Counseling Self-Estimate Inventory
(Post-module 3)

Name (optional)_____   Date_____

This is not a test. There are no right and wrong answers. Rather, it is an inventory that attempts to measure how you feel you will behave as a therapist in a therapy situation. Please respond to the items as honestly as you can so as to most accurately portray how you think you will behave as a therapist. Do not respond with how you wish you could perform each item, rather answer in a way that reflects your actual estimate of how you will perform as a therapist at the present time.

	Strong Disagree	Some Disagree	Little Disagree	Little Agree	Some Agree	Strong Agree
1. When using responses like reflection of feeling, active listening, clarifying, and probing, I am confident I will be concise and to the point.	1	2	3	4	5	6
2. I am likely to impose my values on the patient during the interview.	1	2	3	4	5	6
3. When I initiate the end of a session, I am positive it will be in a manner that is not abrupt or brusque and that I will end the session on time.	1	2	3	4	5	6
4. I am confident that I will respond appropriately to the patient in view of what the patient will express (e.g., my questions will be meaningful and not concerned with trivia and minutiae).	1	2	3	4	5	6
5. I am certain that my interpretation and confrontation responses will be concise and to the point.	1	2	3	4	5	6
6. I am worried that the wording of my responses like reflection of feeling, clarification, and probing may be confusing and hard to understand.	1	2	3	4	5	6
7. I feel that I will not be able to respond to the patient in a non-judgmental way with respect to the patient's values, beliefs, etc.	1	2	3	4	5	6
8. I feel I will respond to the patient in an appropriate length of time (neither interrupting the patient or waiting too long to respond).	1	2	3	4	5	6
9. I am worried that the type of responses I use at a particular time, i.e., reflection of feeling, interpretation, etc., may not be the appropriate response.	1	2	3	4	5	6

	Strong Disagree	Some Disagree	Little Disagree	Little Agree	Some Agree	Strong Agree
	1	2	3	4	5	6
10. I am sure that the content of my responses, i.e., reflection of feeling, clarifying, and probing, will be consistent with and not discrepant from what the patient is saying.	1	2	3	4	5	6
11. I feel confident that I will appear confident and earn the respect of my patient.	1	2	3	4	5	6
12. I am confident that my interpretation and confrontation responses will be effective in that they will be validated by the patient's immediate response.	1	2	3	4	5	6
13. I feel confident that I have resolved conflicts in my personal life so that they will not interfere with my therapy abilities.	1	2	3	4	5	6
14. I feel that the content of my interpretation and confrontation responses will be consistent with and not discrepant from what the patient is saying.	1	2	3	4	5	6
15. I feel that I have enough fundamental knowledge to do effective psychotherapy.	1	2	3	4	5	6
16. I may not be able to maintain the intensity and energy level needed to produce patient confidence and active participation.	1	2	3	4	5	6
17. I am confident that the wording of my interpretation and confrontation responses will be clear and easy to understand.	1	2	3	4	5	6
18. I am not sure that in a therapeutic relationship I will express myself in a way that is natural without deliberating over every response or action.	1	2	3	4	5	6
19. I am afraid that I may not understand and properly determine probable meanings of the patient's nonverbal behaviors.	1	2	3	4	5	6
20. I am confident that I will know when to use open or close ended probes, and that these probes will reflect the concerns of the patient and not be trivial.	1	2	3	4	5	6
21. My assessment of patient problems may not be as accurate as I would like it to be.	1	2	3	4	5	6

	Strong Disagree	Some Disagree	Little Disagree	Little Agree	Some Agree	Strong Agree
22. I am uncertain as to whether I will be able to appropriately confront and challenge my patient in therapy.	1	2	3	4	5	6
23. When giving responses, i.e., reflection of feeling, active listening, clarifying, and probing, I am afraid that they may not be effective in that they won't be validated by the patient's immediate response.	1	2	3	4	5	6
24. I don't feel I possess a large enough repertoire of techniques to deal with the different problems my patient may present.	1	2	3	4	5	6
25. I feel competent regarding my abilities to deal with crisis situations which may arise during the therapy sessions—e.g., suicide, alcoholism, abuse, etc.	1	2	3	4	5	6
26. I am uncomfortable about dealing with patients who appear unmotivated to work toward mutually determined goals.	1	2	3	4	5	6
27. I may have difficulty dealing with patients who don't verbalize their thoughts during the therapy session.	1	2	3	4	5	6
28. I am unsure as to how to deal with patients who appear noncommittal and indecisive.	1	2	3	4	5	6
29. When working with ethnic minority patients, I am confident that I will be able to bridge cultural differences in the therapy process.	1	2	3	4	5	6
30. I will be an effective therapist with patients of a different social class.	1	2	3	4	5	6
31. I am worried that my interpretation and confrontation responses may not over time assist the patient to be more specific in defining and clarifying the problem.	1	2	3	4	5	6
32. I am confident that I will be able to conceptualize my patient's problems.	1	2	3	4	5	6
33. I am unsure as to how I will lead my patient toward the development and selection of concrete goals to work toward.	1	2	3	4	5	6
34. I am confident that I can assess my patient's readiness and commitment to change.	1	2	3	4	5	6

	Strong Disagree	Some Disagree	Little Disagree	Little Agree	Some Agree	Strong Agree
35. I feel I may give advice.	1	2	3	4	5	6
36. In working with culturally different patients I may have a difficult time viewing situations from their perspective.	1	2	3	4	5	6
37. I am afraid that I may not be able to effectively relate to someone of lower socioeconomic status than me.	1	2	3	4	5	6

Strategies for Change

As therapists and patients define "well-formed" dysfunctional patterns that need to be changed, psychotherapy enters the next stage—change. In this module, we focus on the strategies of change.

A primary goal of psychotherapy is to help patients to change rather than to cure them (Kleinke, 1993, p. 28). "Cure" implies that the problem will never recur—a questionable claim for any helping professional. Therapists help patients to be aware that change is possible, encourage them to take responsibility for change, and facilitate new thinking and/or behavior. In module 3 we emphasized inferring dysfunctional patterns; however, not all psychotherapeutic relationships focus directly on *pattern* change. Some crisis intervention requires the suppression of negative affect without necessarily changing the patterns that led to the difficulty. Some therapeutic relationships strive primarily to prevent the recurrence of symptoms, in this way providing support to prevent sliding backward. And some patients change major dysfunctional patterns without clearly explicating them simply by deciding what needs to be done in the context of the therapist's willingness to listen.

ELEMENTS OF CHANGE

What Produces Change in Psychotherapy?

Although we focus on the strategies of change in this module, other factors influence the process of change (Garfield, 1995).

- *Therapeutic relationship* (see Module 2)
- *Patient variables* (readiness to change, types of social support, degree of disturbance, ego strength, patient expectations, placebo response, the fit between patient and type of therapy)
- *Therapist variables* (personal qualities, personal therapy, personality, experience, degree of development of observing self)

While further exploration is needed to determine how much each factor contributes to outcomes, it is clear that psychotherapeutic change results from many factors. To some degree, emphasis upon strategies and techniques may simply meet therapists' need to feel effective. Yet, therapists may need to pay more attention to "What is the likely impact of this strategy or technique on the patient?" or "How is the patient hearing what I am saying?" Therapists attempt to influence patients to use what they say. It may be difficult for therapists to know which part of what they say is useful for a specific patient. Some patients will pick up what the therapist intended. Some will hear something quite different. Consider an analogy to listening to music. Different listeners will be touched by different parts of the music— melody, lyrics, and rhythm. Sometimes, when a therapist expects a patient to change in response to an intervention, the patient does not respond at all, and when the therapist expects little change, the patient changes greatly.

Although we don't know the degree to which strategies and techniques contribute to the outcome of therapy, we do know that the wider the range of strategies and techniques therapists have, the more flexible they can be in molding them to the needs of a specific patient with a specific problem. However, it is also quite likely that certain combinations of techniques may be less effective than one clearly defined strategy (Lazarus, 1996). For example, in the treatment of panic disorder, Barlow (1990) found that adding relaxation training to behavioral-cognitive therapy (BCT) reduced positive outcomes compared to BCT alone. In other words, more is not necessarily always better.

What Do We Mean by Change?

Change for a car mechanic means fixing the broken part or replacing it. Change for a surgeon means excising diseased tissue or facilitating the repair of the damaged tissue. For an internist who is treating infectious disease, change means eliminating the effects of noxious bacteria. But for a psychotherapist, change means collaboration with the patient to help the patient do what is in his or her best interest. In psychotherapy, the patient plays the primary active role in the change. In most cases, change comes about more directly as a result of what the patient does than what the therapist does. In fact, while therapists' techniques provide a means to change, patients sometimes change before therapists have the opportunity to try some of their prized methods.

Like so many key elements, change has many meanings: "modifying," "stopping," "increasing," "reducing," "eliminating," and "maintaining." Pattern change refers to modifying the dysfunctional (maladaptive) patterns by reducing their intensity and frequency and/or initiating functional (adaptive) patterns by increasing their intensity and frequency.

Pattern change has three substages: (1) *relinquish the dysfunctional patterns* (e.g., less frequent drug consumption, fewer passive responses, less avoidance of phobic stimuli, decreasing the number of times washing hands, less self-referential thinking, and less blaming others for problems), (2) *initiate (develop) functional patterns and increase their duration, intensity, and/or frequency* (for example, becoming more relaxed when facing fears, increased confidence in frequency of saying "no" to people, more frequent challenging of self-depreciating thoughts, and increased willingness to attempt to trust other people), and (3) *maintain the new functional patterns.* New patterns do not develop suddenly and endure; instead, they often develop in fits and starts—the patient progresses and then slips back, but not quite so far as before. (Picture a man climbing a cliff. He moves two feet upward but slips back one foot with each upward surge.)

Pattern change is one form of change that occurs during psychotherapy. Two others may also take place. The first type (order) may be considered more superficial, less enduring, and more likely to be initiated during crisis intervention. The third type (order) offers a yet more extensive means to change and represents the desired outcome of long-term therapy as well as personal growth:

First order: The therapist helps the patient do something different in the very near future in a single instance. For example, a battered woman might decide to enter a shelter, an alcoholic might go to an AA meeting, a social phobic might fill out a job application, a distraught husband may seek a lawyer. No new patterns are necessarily initiated. The system does not change. The battered woman might return to her husband; the social phobic might decide not to go to the job interview.

Second order: The therapist helps patients to alter a pattern in a way that generalizes to new situations and/or is maintained in a situation where the dysfunctional pattern was more likely to occur. In systems thinking a change in the system leads to new rules for behavior. For example, the alcoholic in AA might reach out for help or examine more closely his emotional reactions before reaching for a drink, the distraught husband may learn to be more assertive in asking to have his needs met and his wife might then accept his new behavior by changing her own.

Third order: The patient learns how to change patterns without the help of the therapist, a psychological equivalent of "learning how to learn." For example, a patient who learned how to disengage from his anxious thoughts about his body's health may also learn how to disengage himself from his employer's irritability.

Strategies For Change

Some strategies and techniques for change are common to most psychotherapy approaches. Some are limited to a specific approach. For example, clarification and confrontation might be used by therapists who hold a variety of psychotherapy orientations, while the "empty chair" is more likely to be utilized by gestalt therapists. In order to help trainees organize the various strategies for change, we list *general* or common and *school specific* strategies separately.

General Strategies

In Figure 4–1 we list general strategies based on our estimates of the frequency with which these strategies are associated with different substages. The substages have heuristic value in helping to conceptualize the progression of change from defining a pattern to maintaining it. In clinical reality, the simple recognition of a modest dysfunctional pattern or a modest change in one area can initiate a cascade of events leading to new patterns and their maintenance. This cascade of events can occur without a clear demarcation between relinquishing and initiating a new pattern or between initiating and maintaining a new pattern. Some of the strategies and techniques listed in Figure 4–1 are directly associated with a substage, but others appear to take transitional roles. For example, "deciding what to change," "generating alternatives," and "taking responsibility" bridge relinquishing and initiating. "Corrective experiences" may be useful in both initiating and maintaining change. "Self-disclosure," on the other hand, may be equally useful in all three substages. See Appendix II of this module for definitions of the terms used in Figure 4–1.

A word of caution regarding the distinction between "strategy" and "technique." Psychotherapists have tended to blur the meanings of these terms. The problem arises because some strategies imply specific technical behaviors, while some techniques incorporate a general plan of approach. For example, the strategy "face fears" implies a direct, behavioral confrontation of a feared stimulus, while the technique (listed in Table 4–1) "changing self talk" can imply a search for the cognitive schemas generating maladaptive self-talk. For the purposes of these discus-

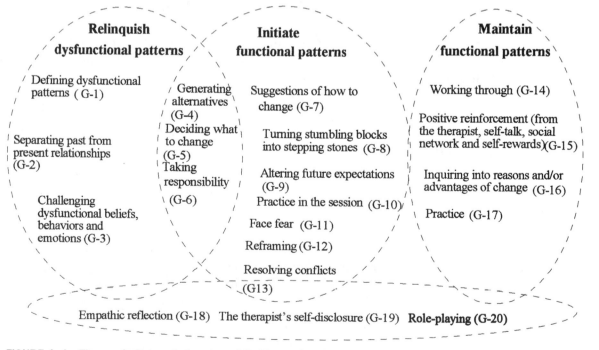

FIGURE 4–1 Three substages of change and their associated generic strategies and techniques (see Appendix II for definitions)

sions a *strategy* is defined as a plan, expectation, or guideline for accomplishing a goal, while a *technique* is defined as a specific behavior or set of behaviors used to carry out a strategy.

Another word of caution, this time regarding the relationship between any specific technique and a specific substage of change: We have listed only our probable estimates of this relationship. Some techniques may be equally useful in different substages. Moreover, the purpose of any technique may be molded by the therapist's intentions of the moment.

ECBIS (Emotion, Cognition, Behavior, Interpersonal, and System)

Different schools not only have different strategies for change but also emphasize different parts of the psychological field: Cognitive therapy emphasizes changing cognitive distortions; behavior therapy focuses on modifying dysfunctional behaviors; emotion-focused therapy emphasizes emotional awareness; interpersonal therapy focuses on change of maladaptive interpersonal schemes; and systems therapies examine ways to alter multiple interacting elements. Change strategies, in fact, are often organized by their targets: emotion, cognition, behavior, interpersonal relationships, and systemic interactions. However, emotion, cognition, behavior, interpersonal relationships, and social systems strongly interact with one another. Although we verbally separate them in real life, they are mutually influential. If one element changes, the other elements usually follow suit.

Since principles of system theory apply to this interaction, we regard the psychotherapy patient from five interacting perspectives: emotion, cognition, behavior, interpersonal, and social system (ECBIS). ECBIS categories represent the general areas toward which change can be directed; they are five conceptual handles by which to grasp patient patterns. Different therapists, or the same therapist for different patients, might start with different handles. Cognitive therapists prefer to go for patient thoughts, while behavior therapists prefer to focus on patient behaviors (as well as stimuli and/or reinforcers). Since the interpersonal component is built upon a combination of the first three targets, some therapists find interpersonal conceptualizing to be an easy way to organize the three more elementary parts. Others think more easily in terms of family and social systems. All psychotherapists attempt to comprehend individuals' functioning in their social fields. Where to begin the process (thoughts, feelings, behaviors, interpersonal, or system) is often a matter of personal preference.

Furthermore, it may be useful to note that the therapist is also part of the patient's system, and the therapist's behavior can reverberate in the patient's system, for good or ill. For example, a new insight, a useful coping strategy, an invitation to bring in the spouse, or an effective psychoactive medication can spur positive changes in the system, while exploitation of the patient, excessive criticism, failure to properly support, or extending relationship too long can have a lasting negative impact. Figure 4–2 demonstrates how E, C, B, I and S interact.

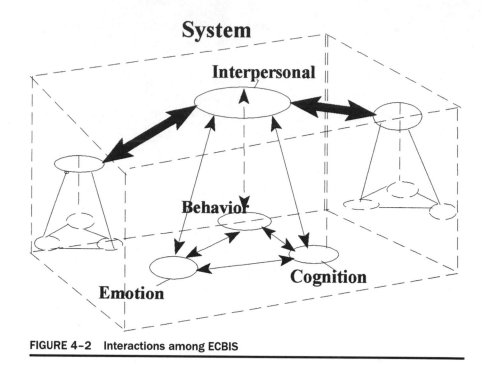

FIGURE 4–2   **Interactions among ECBIS**

Table 4–1 lists in the first column the general change strategies associated with each content area following the sequence of the substages of change. The second column contains the major specific strategies associated with each content area. The third column lists many of the techniques closely associated with the change strategies.

Strategies overlap. The same strategy could be done through different techniques. For example, questioning the evidence and reality-testing can both be used to identify and challenge distorted beliefs; the two strategies are clearly related. And one technique can be used to carry out various strategies. For instance, assertion training can be used to change behavior, restructure emotion, and modify dysfunctional interactive patterns.

The Patient's Observing Self and Change

Most psychotherapeutic techniques rely on the ability of the patient to "step back" from the unwanted pattern in order to recognize what needs to be changed. The triple column technique establishes psychological distance by putting the patterns on paper; the double chair technique puts the patterns in the two chairs; transference development places the patterns between the therapist and the patient. But what then? How does change proceed from this awareness, this clarification of the problematic patterns? As they define the problematic patterns, patients must usually consciously decide that they wish to make the transition and to define an alternative pattern or patterns.

What role, then, does the observing self play in the process of change? The observing self clarifies the pattern(s) to be changed, evaluates the unwanted ele-

TABLE 4–1 Specific Strategies for Addressing Emotion, Cognition, Behavior, Interpersonal, and Systems (ECBIS) (see Appendix III for definitions)

ECBIS	Strategies	Techniques
Emotion: Attend to and intensify emotional experience in order to evoke the conceptsin which they are embedded so that these concepts about emotions can be made more adaptive.	Evoking emotion in the session E-I)	Catharsis (E-I-1) Enactment of conflict splits—two chairs (E-I-2) Exploring "unfinished business"—empty chair (E-I-3) Evoking problematic reactions (E-I-4)
	Restructuring emotional schemas (E-II)	Helping patient to access new information through emotional awareness (E-II-1) Confronting feared emotions (E-II-2)
	Maintaining the reorganized emotion schemas (E-III)	
Cognitive: Capture automatic thoughts that mediate unwanted responses and are embedded in dysfunctional cognitive schemas in order to identify the elements of dysfunction and then to edit for elements of constructive change.	Identifying and challenging the dysfunctional and distorted beliefs (C-I)	Understanding idiosyncratic meaning (C-I-1) Reality testing, questioning the evidence (C-I-2) Guided association/discovery (C-I-3) Triple-column technique (C-I-4)
	Creating (establishing) adaptive and reasonable beliefs. This aim is accomplished by allowing new information discrepant with previous beliefs to enter the information processing (C-II)	Developing alternatives (C-II-1) Fantasizing consequences (C-II-2) Listing positives and negatives of change (C-II-3) Reattribution (C-II-4) Turning adversity to advantage (C-II-5) Editing self-talk (C-II-6) New self-instruction (C-II-7) Thought stopping (C-II-8) Disputing irrational beliefs (C-II-9) Four-column technique (C-II-10)
	Repeating or practicing the modified beliefs in a variety of situations (C-III)	Positive reinforcement (C-III-1)
Behavioral: Define maladaptive behavior in order to (1) desensitize phobic avoidance, (2) reinforce more adaptive behaviors, (3) reduce the impact of stimulus control.	Defining the maladaptive behaviors (B-I)	Description of presenting problems and maintaining variables (B-I-1) Behavioral observation by the therapist and significant others (B-I-2) Self-report and self-monitoring (B-I-3)
	Changing behavior directly (B-II)	Changing reinforcers to change behavior (B-II-1) Self-reinforcement (B-II-2) Relaxation training (B-II-3) Biofeedback (B-II-4) Systematic desensitization (B-II-5) Assertion training (B-II-6) Modeling (B-II-7) Behavioral rehearsal (B-II-8)
	Practicing the modified behaviors in various situations (B-III)	Positive reinforcement (B-III-1)

Continued

TABLE 4–1   **Specific Strategies for Addressing Emotion, Cognition, Behavior, Interpersonal, and Systems (ECBIS) (see Appendix III for definitions)** *Continued*

ECBIS	Strategies	Techniques
Interpersonal-psychodynamic: Use discrepancies between effective and ineffective interpersonal responses to identify the interpersonal schemas of which these maladaptive elements are a part in order to define and incorporatemore adaptive thoughts, feelings, and/or behaviors to create improved interpersonal schemas.	Identifying maladaptive interpersonal schemas (I-I)	Interpretation (I-I-1) Enacting and identifying the patient's interpersonal patterns within the therapeutic relationship (I-I-2) Therapist's examining interpersonal "pulls" from the patient by being both a participant and observer (I-I-3) Cyclical psychodynamics (I-I-4) Analyzing interpersonal transactions (I-I-5) Analysis of faulty communication (I-I-6) Monitoring examples of faulty interpersonal transactions through diaries (I-I-7)
	Modifying role relationship models and altering interpersonal scripts (I-II)	Corrective emotional experience (I-II-1) Helping the patient to rewrite, modify, and correct the assumptions underlying his or her interpersonal scripts (I-II-2) Guiding toward more effective communication (I-II-3)
	Practicing modified roles (I-III)	Therapist's maintaining consistent and reliable behavior to disconfirm the patient's false assumptions about his/her interpersonal reality (I-III-1) Reinforcement from new interpersonal success (I-III-2)
Systems: Identify factors maintaining undesired homeostatic patterns, determine the most available and potentially most effective entry points for change, then induce a change most likely to cascade the system into a more desired homeostasis	Identifying the dysfunctional dynamic interactions among family members (S-I)	Circular questioning (S-I-1) Enactments (S-I-2) Analysis of the sequence of communication (S-I-3) Genogram (S-I-4) Narrative (S-I-5)
	Changing the interaction patterns (S-II)	Paradox (S-II-1) Changing rigid or enmeshed boundaries (S-II-2) Task-setting within the family (S-II-3) Communication skill training (S-II-4) Ritual prescription (S-II-5) Reinforcement and practice (S-III-1)
	Maintaining the new and functional interaction patterns (S-III)	

ments, and directs the development one or more new patterns. The therapist can observe the patient's observing self in operation and provide feedback to reinforce the observing self to continue in the desired direction.

Where Is Change Initiated?

Change may be initiated in two general locations: in the therapist's office or in the patient's real world. Generally therapists have drawn lines between these two arenas, some claiming that change must be initiated in the office through transference interpretation (e.g., Strupp & Binder, 1984) or through deep emotional exploration (e.g., Greenberg, Rice, & Elliott, 1993) and others stressing the patient's real world. This false dichotomy resolves by recognizing that both arenas provide the opportunity for change. Keep in mind, however, that change in the office provides no benefit unless it generalizes to the patient's real world interactions.

Strategy Selection

The most straightforward way to select a strategy is to determine which goal is most likely to be achieved by a strategy likely to be acceptable to the patient. At this moment, the therapist considers the most efficient path leading to the most comprehensive change for this given patient. Information influencing this decision includes: patient readiness to change, the strength of the therapeutic relationship, the patient's goals, and the nature of the dysfunctional patterns. Therapists attempt to predict and therefore control the future through the strategies they select.

Ideally, psychotherapy researchers would have provided practitioners with answers to the following set of questions: What technique, for what person, with what problem, at what time? Some empirically validated studies have been undertaken; unfortunately, many of these studies have been performed with highly selected patients who were diagnostically homogeneous, willing to follow research protocols, and recruited through advertising. The degree to which these studies generalize to clinical populations remains a vexing question. Nevertheless, the results of these studies deserve careful consideration in strategy selection. Therapists need to choose well-documented, well-established strategies and methods for a particular disorder, such as exposure for phobias, cognitive and interpersonal therapy for depression, and assertiveness training for passivity. If these well-documented methods do not work or fit for a particular problem with a given patient, therapists should consider other strategies and techniques.

Other researchers have paid less attention to diagnosis and more to patient variables. Their conclusions offer useful guidelines for strategy selection. Some encouraging results have emerged from attempts to match three client variables (motivational stress, external coping style, and resistance to interpersonal influence) with three different strategies (group cognitive therapy, emotionally focused expressive therapy, and nondirective self-awareness procedures) (Beutler, Mohr, Grawe, Engle, & MacDonald, 1991). For example, clients who are highly reactant (rebellious against directives) were more successfully treated with nondirective self-awareness procedures. They reacted against the directive qualities of cognitive and emotionally focused approaches. There is even some evidence that excessive direction in highly reactant people can foster deterioration. Externalizers (clients who looked outward rather than inward for problems and solutions by avoidance and blaming others) responded more positively to the directive, symptom-focused approach of cognitive therapy.

Many psychotherapy dilemmas have escaped research scrutiny, leaving therapists without clinically developed guidelines for strategy selection. Simple problems, for example, should respond to simple techniques, but some do not and so a second and possibly third strategy may be required. Complex problems may require multiple, simultaneous strategies.

Finally, despite all the clever research or clinical innovations, individual therapists find their own personal predispositions influencing treatment selection. Therapists who have personally benefited from facing fears, changing cognitions, clarifying past present relationships, etc., are likely to use their favorite strategy when caught at an ambiguous choice point. Training programs also influence practitioner strategy choice, as does the latest psychotherapy book read or the latest seminar attended. In addition, patient preference must always play a role in strategy selection. Just as some patients do not want to take psychoactive drugs but prefer psychotherapy, some patients, based on their own experiences, are predisposed to one strategy or another.

SESSIONS

The goals of module 4 are (1) to understand the substages of change, (2) to understand the various strategies for change, and (3) to begin to understand principles for strategy selection.

The tools of module 4 are:

1. Transcripts for change strategies (Form 18–1 and Form 18–2)
2. Case vignettes for change strategies (Form 19–1 and Form 19–2)
3. Appendix II (Generic Strategies and Techniques) and Appendix III (ECBIS Glossary)
4. Psychotherapy videotape vignettes (Greenberg, Mirris, Persons, Beitman, and Kaslow)

Session 1

1. The seminar leader goes through the module 4 introduction.

2. Homework: Trainees are asked to read the text of this module, Appendix II, and Appendix III.

Session 2

1. Continue to discuss the text.

2. Homework: The seminar leader assigns the Transcripts for Change Strategies (Form 18–1). In Form 18–1, there are multiple choices after each transcript; trainees are asked to circle the answer that fits best for that question.

Session 3

1. The group discusses Form 18–1.

2. Homework: The seminar leader assigns the Case Vignettes for Change Strategies (Form 19–1). After each case vignette, trainees are asked to consider which strategies or techniques the therapist might to use.

Session 4

The group discusses Form 19–1.

Session 5

Trainees watch the videotape vignettes that focus on E, C, B, I, and S strategies, respectively. Then the group discusses these strategies.

E: View Dr. Greenberg's tape:

Todd is a 34-year-old married engineer. He has taken 15 days of "sick leave" from his job, usually because of exhaustion, an inability to concentrate, and a sense that he "just could not face it." This videotape of the fourth session shows us some strategies and techniques that focus on emotion such as *increasing emotional awareness, emotional catharsis, here-and-now emotion, double chair,* and *empty chair.*

C. View Dr. Mirris's tape:

Tom has problems with his new boss. It seems to him that he can't do anything right. The therapist helps Tom *identify his self-talk (automatic thoughts)* in an attempt to help him become responsible for his reactions. They attempt *"cognitive restructuring":* changing the way he thinks of himself in relationship to his boss.

B. View Dr. Persons' tape:

Lisa is a 29-year-old single woman who suffers from social phobia with a panic component. The videotape is the fourth session which shows us the discussion of a *homework assignment.* The patient was asked to chat informally with colleagues before each regular business meeting during the previous week. She had rated chatting with a colleague as "20" on her scale of 100 points on her hierarchy of feared speaking situations. This exercise demonstrates *exposure-desensitization* and *positive reinforcement* by the therapist, as well as therapeutic change taking place between therapy sessions.

I. View Dr. Beitman's tape:

MC is a 56-year-old married woman who entered psychotherapy because of her generalized anxiety (she was seen in module 3 as well). This videotape of the fifth session demonstrates the *defining of an ineffective interpersonal pattern* (I can't say "no" when I need to). A new, more assertive response is initiated during the session through *role-playing,* during which the patient plays both herself and the other person. She comes to understand how the other person is reacting to her.

S. View Dr. Kaslow's tape:

Alan is a 54-year-old married CEO of an accounting firm with 30 employees. His internist recommended that he see Dr. Kaslow because of his "stress headaches," including dizziness, visual impairment, and an ashen pallor.

Joyce—his wife,

Julie—his daughter (she entered into the family business four years earlier after getting her MBA from Harvard)

Chris—Julie's fiancé

This third session tape shows us how the therapist *views the patient in a family system* and *how to change the family system by changing the person who sees the therapist*. Please pay attention to the triggers to his headache, his concern about Chris's "inordinate interest in the family business," and his thinking about "handing over the firm to his daughter."

Session 6

1. Continue to watch and discuss videotapes.

2. Homework: The seminar leader assigns the Transcripts for Change Strategies (Form 18–2) to be completed before the next session.

Session 7

1. The group discusses Form 18–2.

2. Homework: The seminar leader assigns the Case Vignettes for Change Strategies (Form 19–2) to be completed before the next session.

Session 8

1. Trainees need to complete COSE (Post-module 4) and Guided Inquiry (GI, Post-module 4) during the session.

2. The group discusses Form 19–2.

3. Homework: The seminar leader assigns module 5 introduction for review before the next session.

Generic Strategies and Techniques

G–1. Defining dysfunctional patterns: By confrontation and clarification, the patient defines a well-formed pattern—i.e., the newly defined pattern implies what needs to be done to bring about change. By defining the pattern and seeing what needs to be changed, the patient begins the process of relinquishing it.

G–2. Separating past from present relationships: Individuals often react to present circumstances with past response patterns. When the old response does not fit current circumstances, the past pattern can be distinguished from the current response repertoire.

G–3. Challenging dysfunctional beliefs, behaviors, and emotions: Dysfunctional patterns are usually composed of dysfunctional beliefs, behaviors, and/or emotions. Defining these patterns often requires highlighting one or several of these elements for the patient to consider.

G–4. Generating alternatives: Patient and therapist develop a list of possible responses (thoughts, behaviors, feeling awareness) that could lead to a desired change.

G–5. Deciding what to change: As change alternatives are generated, one is selected for action.

G–6. Taking responsibility: As an alternative is selected, the patient comes to accept that carrying out this alternative is up to him and no one else. Patients do not necessarily have to assume responsibility for the creation of the dysfunctional pattern, since fixing blame can be problematic and elusive. Rather, they take responsibility for maintaining the old pattern when alternatives are available and doable.

G–7. Suggestions of how to change: The therapist offers an alternative response and encourages the patient to try it.

G–8. Turning stumbling blocks into stepping stones: This involves converting obstacles, problems, difficulties into opportunities, or looking for opportunities when the situation looks bleak. For example, a job loss could be an opportunity, or the symptoms of a panic attack could be a clue to examine a situation more carefully rather than something to be stamped out.

G–9. **Altering future expectations:**   With the therapist's help, the patient comes to realize that a new and better future is more likely than the one the patient has in mind. If the patient changes his expectations of others, then a better future is likely.

G–10. **Practice in the session:**   Rather than risking a new response in the "real world," the patient practices in the office with the therapist.

G-11. **Face fear:**   A high percentage of psychotherapy problems are related to excessive fears, which cause patients to avoid the fearful stimulus. These fears are not only external (e.g., interpersonal performance, shopping malls, closed places) but also cognitive (being abandoned, hurting someone), emotional (anger, love, dependency), behavioral (assertiveness, asking for what one wants), and related to memories (posttraumatic, grief).

G–12. **Reframing:**   Taking an alternative, more constructive view of current circumstances.

G–13. **Resolving conflicts:**   Defining two polarities by clarifying the perspectives of each side and beginning the work of mediating their differences and similarities.

G–14. **Working through:**   Once a maladaptive pattern is defined and better alternatives generated, the patient must repetitively unlearn and relearn the better patterns, until they are ingrained. One major insight rarely brings lasting change; instead, patients enter situation after situation in which to apply their new responses, sometimes falling into the old pattern and then attempting to instate the new one. For example, a couple's fights usually escalate into battles where each retreats to safe isolation. Working through begins when they decrease the time between the fight and their making-up with each other. Working through continues as they cut their arguments short and start looking for a better way to discuss the issue. Working through reaches an end when they both recognize the signs that indicate a fight is likely to start and then find a better interaction pattern before the conflict escalates. Various circular processes are set in motion, involving insight, memory, cognitions, behavior change, and interpersonal relationships.

G-15. **Positive reinforcement:**   If a behavioral response is followed by a generally rewarding event, the behavior tends to be strengthened and to occur more frequently. Praise, interpersonal gratification, and various forms of success can each act in this way. Many different forces can act as reinforcers, including the therapist (praise, encouragement), self-talk, self-rewards, and social network responses.

G–16. **Inquiring into the reasons for and/or advantages of change:** Helping a patient to notice how change has been or will be beneficial.

G–17. **Practice:**   Repetitively doing what has been decided to do.

G–18. **Empathic reflection:**   Usually considered an essential technique for establishing the therapeutic alliance, empathic reflection can also increase patient awareness of inner states and inner motivations, as the therapist acts as an external observer of the patient's inner processes. New awareness can then lead to change.

G–19. **Therapist's self-disclosure:**   The therapist reveals some element of his/her history or current responses to help the patient along the process of change. As with all therapeutic interventions, the patient's need—not the therapist's desire to talk about him/herself—is the primary reason to self-reveal.

G–20. **Role-playing:**   Two kinds of role-play are commonly used: (1) The patient interacts with an empty chair or the therapist in practicing new behaviors, or (2) the patient interacts with an empty chair talking with a part of him/herself or an important other to resolve intrapsychic conflicts.

ECBIS* Glossary

EMOTION

E-I Evoking Emotion in the Session

In evoking emotion in the session the therapist helps the patient access and reexperience emotion in order to define and restructure dysfunctional emotional schemas.

E-I-1: *Catharsis*

This term originated from Freud's use of hypnosis in treating hysterics. He noticed that after patients discharged their strangulated emotions during hypnosis, their symptoms were reduced. Then Freud found therapeutic results could be obtained without hypnosis by permitting the patient to talk freely, to experience whatever ideas came to mind (free association). Catharsis is not necessarily associated with hypnosis and free association. A patient's verbal expression of traumatic experiences, suppressed feelings such as guilt, fear, anger, or suffering, with or without the help of the therapist, can be called catharsis.

E-I-2: *Enactment of Conflict Splits—Two Chairs*

Two-chair dialogue is generally used to explore two aspects of the self that are in opposition. Two chairs represent the two conflicted parts or the "split." Any conflict is based on cognitive-emotional schemas representing two polarities. One is derived from deeply felt emotions, desires, and needs; the other is derived from externally derived standards that oppose the emotions, desires, and needs. The first one can be called "experiencing self," the second "the critical self." Failure to recognize needs and wants generally leaves the person unclear and confused, whereas failure to meet the standards and values produces negative self-evaluation and loss of self-worth. The two-chair technique is used to evoke these two aspects simultaneously in the session. The therapist helps the patient role-play and explore the

*ECBIS: emotion, cognition, behavior, interpersonal, and system.

"critical" aspect of the self, identifying its harsh, negative evaluations of the "experiencing" aspect of the self. At same time, the therapist also helps the patient to express the experiencing part's affective reactions to the harsh criticism. In this process, the critic part moves from general statements to more concrete and specific criticism of the person and situation, while the experiencing part begins to react in a more differentiated way that is expressed to the critic as a want or a need. Two-chair dialogue can lead to a negotiation or an integration between the two parts.
Sources: Greenberg (1995a), Greenberg, Rice, & Elliott (1993)

E-I-3: Exploring Unfinished Business—Empty Chair

Unfinished business is defined here as those emotional experiences that are so overwhelming, painful, or frustrating that they are held back from conscious experience. The expression of the feelings and the needs from which the feelings emerge are blocked. Those unmet needs do not, however, fully disappear. Rather, they and the situation become encoded in memory and remain as "unfinished business." The empty chair can then represent the significant others with whom the patient has "unfinished" feelings. The patient addresses the empty chair as if the significant other is sitting in it. It is used to evoke this unfinished business in the session in order to help the patient reprocess and reconstruct the blocked emotional schemas.
Sources: Greenberg (1995a), Greenberg, Rice, & Elliott (1993)

E-I-4: Evoking Problematic Reactions

Interactions with other people and difficult situations may trigger "markers" for problematic reactions. Markers for these events consist of three identifiable features: (a) a stimulus situation, such as, "When I saw her walking down the hall"; (b) an emotional or behavioral reaction on the part of the patient, like "I wanted to run"; (c) and an indication that the patient views the reaction as puzzling, inappropriate, or in some way problematic. The therapist helps the patient vividly evoke the incident and then reprocess it more slowly and completely. The patient discovers that his problematic reaction was a direct consequence of his views of the eliciting stimulus. This, in turn, can stimulate further exploration, which may lead to recognition that the particular problematic reaction was an example of a broader pattern that is interfering with meeting the patient's goals and needs.
Sources: Greenberg (1995a), Greenberg, Rice, & Elliott (1993)

E-II Restructuring Emotional Schemas

One basic assumption of emotion oriented therapy is that the barriers to current healthy functioning result from dysfunctional, emotion-laden cognitive schemas. In other words, key cognitions are usually "hot"; that is, they are laden with emotion.

E-II-1: Helping Patients to Access New Information Through Emotional Awareness

Some dysfunctional emotional schemas are beyond the patient's conscious awareness. Helping patients to become aware of and experience these emotions is a prerequisite to the emotion-cognition reconstruction process. As patients directly experience their warded-off emotions, the therapist helps them access new information which had been beyond their awareness.

E-II-2: *Confronting Feared Emotions*

Patients generally try to avoid experiencing feared emotions. Patients' dysfunctional patterns result from this avoidance. In confronting feared emotions, the therapist helps patients access emotions in a safe, supportive therapeutic environment, and then to change their responses to them.

E-III Maintain the Reorganized Emotional Schemas

The patient's new and more functional emotional schemas can be maintained by repeated reexperiencing and reconstructuring until they become part of the patient's response system.

COGNITION

C-I Identifying and Challenging Dysfunctional and Distorted Beliefs

The primary foci of cognitive therapy are distorted beliefs. Therapists help patients identify, challenge, and change these distorted beliefs.

C-I-1: *Understanding Idiosyncratic Meaning*

The therapist should not assume he or she completely understands the terms used by the patient without asking for clarification. Therefore, it is essential to question the patient directly on the meaning of verbalizations. By doing this, the therapist can make sure that he or she is on the right track. Patients often overgeneralize, understate, or exaggerate their problems. They may leave some information unstated. Therapists do not necessarily take every self-criticism or every negative statement about others as true; instead, they help patients define more explicitly what they mean. If, for example, a patient claims that she is a "loser," the therapist should explore what she means rather than simply accepting the idea that nothing she does ever "wins."
Source: Freeman & White (1989)

C-I-2: *Reality Testing, Questioning the Evidence*

Patients often use certain evidence to maintain and support their distorted thoughts and beliefs. One effective way to challenge these dysfunctional thoughts is to examine the extent to which it is supported by the available evidence and whether other explanations fit the evidence better. It is essential for the therapist to show the patient how to identify and then question the evidence he or she uses to maintain or strengthen a belief in order to find ways to let go of it.
Source: Freeman & White (1989)

C-I-3: *Guided Association/Discovery*

Guided association differs from free association in psychoanalysis. In guided association/discovery the therapist helps the patient explore and expand the per-

sonal understanding of specific experiences as the patient lets ideas come to mind under the therapist's guided questions. These questions may focus on the patient's distorted ideas, thoughts, and images and take the form, "Then what?" "What would happen then?" "What if . . . ?" etc.
Source: Freeman & White (1989)

C-I-4: Triple-Column Technique

This technique is used to identify the dysfunctional thoughts. The first column is the situation and context in which the symptom or dysphoric event is taking place. The second describes the type and intensity of the emotion associated with each event. In the third column the patient records the "automatic thoughts" that link the situation to the consequence. The three-column technique can help both the patient and the therapist to identify a connection between when and where the symptoms occur and what thoughts and feelings the patient has at that time.
Source: Beck, Rush, Shaw, & Emery (1979)

C-II Creating Adaptive and Reasonable Beliefs

This aim is accomplished by allowing new information discrepant with previous beliefs to enter information-processing. After the dysfunctional thoughts are identified, the therapist helps the patient create functional thoughts and beliefs by providing the patient with new information, a broader perspective, and a new way to think. The patient uses this new information to develop more adaptive responses.

C-II-1: Developing Alternatives

Some dysfunctional thoughts result from patients' limited options for interpreting situations. They simply have only one way to understand what they see. For example, "I think people do not like me because one day when I started to talk with one of my coworkers, he hurriedly left." The therapist helps the patient to generate additional options, and when the patient can see other options, he or she begins to replace dysfunctional thoughts with more adaptive ones. For this patient, the therapist might help generate such options as, "He may have had an appointment with somebody at that time," "He may have difficulty in his marriage," or "He did not like the topic you brought up rather than he did not like you."
Source: Freeman & White (1989)

C-II-2: Fantasizing Consequences (Related to C-I-3—see Appendix II)

The patient is asked to imagine a situation and fantasize the consequences. For example, a patient is afraid that if she becomes assertive with her abusive husband, he will leave her. The patient is asked to fantasize the consequences of his no longer being in her life. By imagining and verbalizing her fears, the patient can see their irrationality as well as the real concerns. This technique allows the patient to bring into the consulting room imagined events, situations, or interactions that he or she

believes will happen in the future. When the patient clarifies the imagined consequences, concerns and fears become more rational and realistic.
Source: Freeman & White (1989)

C-II-3: *Listing Positives and Negatives of Change*
(Related to G-16—see Appendix II)

This technique helps the patient move away from an all-or-nothing position to one that explores the possibility of new experiences, feelings, thoughts, or behaviors that have both negative and positive qualities. When the patient examines both advantages and disadvantages, a broader perspective can be achieved. This approach is most often used in helping the patient to resolve conflicts about change, about relinquishing dysfunctional thoughts and behavior with clearer ideas about possible benefits.
Source: Freeman & White (1989)

C-II-4: *Reattribution*

There are two common dysfunctional patterns about responsibility. Some patients take responsibility for events and situations that are only minimally attributable to them; some patients always blame others and take no responsibility. Reattribution means the therapist helps the patient distribute responsibility reasonably among the relevant parties. The therapist should not take a position of total support (such as, "It wasn't your fault at all, you're better without her") or total blame (such as, "It is all your fault"); rather, he/she takes a middle ground.
Source: Freeman & White (1989)

C-II-5: *Turning Adversity to Advantage*
(Related to G-8—see Appendix II)

There are times when a seeming disaster can be used to one's advantage. For example, divorce may be the entry point to start a new life, or pressure from the boss can be used as a motivator. Turning adversity to advantage requires the patient to look for the positive aspects in a negative situation, which initially is difficult. Patients will sometimes respond to the therapist's effort to point out positive aspects with greater negativity and opposition. The therapist can point out that the view being offered is no less realistic than the patient's negative view.
Source: Freeman & White (1989)

C-II-6: *Editing Self-Talk*

People talk to themselves. They comment, criticize, and direct their own thinking and emotions. Cognitive therapy contends that the imprecise language with which patients talk to themselves is one of the causes of distorted thinking processes. Changing self-talk means that the therapist pays attention to the patient's imprecise (e.g., exaggerated, minimizing) language patterns, like too many "shoulds," "musts," and "oughts." Therapists help patients to employ new self-statements to substitute for the old language. For example, instead of saying, "It must be awful

if . . . ," they can learn to say "It would be inconvenient if. . . ." Through the process of changing their language patterns and making new self-statements, patients come to think and behave more rationally.
Source: Corey (1996)

C-II-7: New Self-Instruction

We give ourselves orders, directions, instructions, or information necessary to solve problems. Therapists can help patients control some dysfunctional thoughts by introducing orders or directions. The therapist teaches the patient to start with direct verbalization of self-instruction aloud; then, with practice, the patient learns to say the instructions silently; and then the instruction becomes more automatically. New instructions also can be introduced by patients themselves.
Source: Freeman & White (1989)

C-II-8: Thought-Stopping

Patients' dysfunctional thoughts often have a snowball effect. Once they start, they are hard to stop. Thought-stopping is used to inhibit their progression. The patient can be taught to picture a stop sign, "hear" a bell, or think the word "stop." Any of these procedures can help stop the progression of the thought. Finding a way that the patient accepts and practicing in the session are important in this technique. The memory of that intervention can then be used by the patient to assist his or her thought-stopping between sessions.
Source: Freeman & White (1989)

C-II-9: Disputing Irrational Beliefs

The therapist actively disputes patients' irrational beliefs and teaches them how to challenge their own thinking. These challenges take two general forms: (1) the logical debate and (2) testing by comparing the beliefs with external evidence. The logical debate may take the form: "What does it matter if life is not exactly as you want it to be?" The testing approach has the therapist quickly challenge irrational beliefs by asking questions like, "Where is the evidence of your beliefs?" Through a series of logical and empirical refutations, therapists help patients develop more rational and adaptive beliefs. This technique may be used when it is clear to the therapist that there is strong working alliance between the therapist and the patient.
Sources: Corey (1996) and Freeman & White (1989)

C-II-10: Four-Column Technique (Related to C-I-4)

This technique is built on the three-column technique. Three-column technique is used to detect the dysfunctional patterns. In order to correct these dysfunctional patterns, the fourth column is introduced. This is a rational response that is a more appropriate interpretation of the stimulus situation that had contributed to the maladaptive automatic thought and emotion. In this way the patient learns to respond to and adjust dysfunctional thinking patterns.
Source: Beck, Rush, Shaw, & Emery (1979)

C-III Repeating or Practicing the Modified Beliefs in a Variety of Situations

In order to maintain the patient's more adaptive thoughts and/or beliefs, therapists need to help patients practice these new thoughts and beliefs in different situations. One major task in this process for the therapist is to provide positive reinforcement and teach patients how to positively reinforce the change on their own.

C-III-1: Positive Reinforcement (see Appendix II, G-15)

BEHAVIOR

B-I Defining the Maladaptive Behaviors

Behavior therapy focuses on patients' maladaptive behaviors. In order to change these behaviors, therapists need to identify them.

B-I-1: Description of Presenting Problems and Maintaining Variables

Describe behaviors targeted for change and the stimuli and/or reinforcers that are maintaining them.

B-I-2: Behavioral Observation by the Therapist and Significant Others

Direct observation of maladaptive behavior generally is clinically useful during assessment. These observations may be made by the therapist and/or by significant others. The patient's interaction with the therapist during the session may provide a sample of his problem behaviors. The observations by significant others in the patient's life, including the patient's parents, spouse, and best friends, can be very informative because they have more opportunities to observe the patient's behaviors in various situations and can provide valuable descriptive information connecting stimuli and/or reinforcers to behaviors targeted for change.
Source: Goldfried & Davison (1976)

B-I-3: Self-report and Self-monitoring

Self-report and self-monitoring also provide a window into the real-world correlates of symptomatic behavior. The patient is asked to observe his own targeted behaviors in particular situations and to record them. For example, if the patient wishes to reduce excess food intake, monitoring and recording foods could be a target for self-reporting.

B-II Changing Behavior Directly

B-II-1: Changing Reinforcers to Change Behavior (Related to G-15)

The use of reinforcement to change behavior is the cornerstone of modern behavior therapy. Changing reinforcers to control behavior comes from the theory of operant conditioning, which proposes that behavior can be changed by manipulat-

ing its consequences. Reinforcers can be regarded as events that increase the probability of the behavior they follows. Reinforcers can be positive or negative. A positive reinforcer is an event which, when presented to the individual, increases the behavior. A negative reinforcer means an event which, when removed from the target behavior, increases the behavior. For example, the therapist's approval (positive reinforcer) may increase the patient's new behavior. A parent's refusal to continue financial support (negative reinforcer) of a grown child may increase the the likelihood that the child will find ways to support himself.
Sources: Goldfried & Davison (1976) and Corey (1996)

B-II-2: *Self-reinforcement*

Self-reinforcement can include participating in pleasant activities, buying something for oneself, or positive or negative self-appraisal. Self-reinforcement, ideally, leads to the automatic implementation of the desired behavior.

B-II-3: *Relaxation Training*

There are many relaxation training methods, including graded muscle relaxation, breath control, visualization of pleasant scenes, and meditation. An effective and simple method requires gentle focus of attention on the mechanics of breathing. For example, patients can be instructed to focus their attention on the rise and fall of their abdomen with each breath. As their attention inevitably drifts to other thoughts, they are instructed to gently return their attention to their breathing.
Source: Kabat-Zinn (1990)

B-II-4: *Biofeedback*

Individuals can learn to control activities of their autonomic nervous system. Biofeedback machines help them to be aware of their own biological functions. These biological functions include skin temperature, heart rate, muscle tension, blood pressure, and brain wave activity. The patient is taught to regulate one or more of these biological states through feedback from the machine monitoring these functions in order to reduce symptoms and reach a desired physiological state. For example, the ability to raise the temperature of one's hand may be used to reduce the frequency of migraine headache through learning how to alter regional blood flow.

B-II-5: *Systematic Desensitization*

The basic assumption underlying systematic desensitization is that an anxiety response is learned, or conditioned, and can be inhibited by substituting an activity that is antagonistic to it. It includes three steps: (1) The therapist helps the patient analyze stimuli that evoke anxiety in order to construct a hierarchy of situations which they then arrange in order of increasing aversiveness; (2) the therapist teaches the patient relaxation techniques; and (3) the patient pairs relaxation with imagined scenes from the hierarchy, beginning with the least fear-provoking item. Anxiety-producing stimuli are repeatedly paired with relaxation until the connection between those stimuli and the response of anxiety is eliminated. Systematic desensitization can be conducted in the session, where the patient imagines each situation under conditions of deep relaxation, so that he is able to tolerate greater and greater levels of anxiety. Or it can be conducted between the sessions, where the patient can use the learned relaxation to reduce his or her anxiety while directly confronting stimuli in the real world.

Sources: Goldfried & Davison (1976) and Corey (1996)

B-II-6: *Assertion Training*

Assertion training is one form of social-skill training. The basic assumption underlying assertion training is that people have the right to express their wants and needs directly to others. There are many assertion training methods, most of which focus on the patient's negative self-statements, self-defeating beliefs, and faulty thinking. Assertion training includes two parts: One challenges patients' beliefs that inhibit self-assertion; the second provides people with skills and techniques for dealing with situations in which they are better served if they state their beliefs and/or desires. Assertion training can be useful for (1) those who cannot express anger or irritation, (2) those who have difficulty saying no, (3) those who are overly polite and who allow others to take advantage of them, and (4) those who find it difficult to express affection and other positive responses.

Source: Corey (1996)

B-II-7: *Modeling*

The terms *modeling, observational learning, imitation,* and *social learning* are used interchangeably to refer to the process by which the observer learns to perform the model's desired thoughts, attitudes, and behaviors. Several types of models are used in therapeutic situations. A live model can teach patients appropriate behavior, influence attitudes and values, and teach social skills. Sometimes therapists can serve as live models for their patients. Behavior therapists also use symbolic models. A model's behaviors can be shown on film or videotapes. Multiple models are especially relevant in group therapy. The observer can change attitudes and learn new skills through observation of successful peers in the group. People seem to learn better from models who are imperfectly successful than from ones who perform tasks perfectly.

Source: Corey (1996)

B-II-8: *Behavioral Rehearsal (Related G-20—see Appendix II)*

Behavioral rehearsal is used primarily to help the patient learn new ways of responding to specific life situations by selecting a target situation, simulating the situation in the session, initiating new behavioral patterns, and carrying out of this new role with its specific new behaviors in real-life situations. Sometimes this term is used interchangeably with "role-playing"; however, behavioral rehearsal is more specifically focused on training new response patterns.

Source: Corey (1996)

B-III Practice the Modified Behaviors in Various Situations

In order to maintain the new behavioral patterns, the therapist needs to encourage patients to practice these new behaviors in real-life situations until they can carry them out on their own.

B-III-1: Positive Reinforcement (See Appendix II, G-15)

INTERPERSONAL/PSYCHODYNAMIC

I-I Identifying Maladaptive Interpersonal Schemes

Interpersonal-psychodynamic therapy regards the patient's problems as a function of disturbed interpersonal relationships. In the interpersonal approach, the patient's intrapsychic conflicts, dysfunctional thoughts, emotions, and behaviors are seen to both reflect and impinge on relationships with significant persons in the patient's life. Therefore, identifying maladaptive interpersonal patterns (role relationship models, the way patients view their intimate and important relationships) involving thoughts, emotions, and behaviors is crucial. Those who think of themselves as "interpersonal" tend to focus more on current relationships outside the office, while those who consider themselves "psychodynamic" tend to focus more on the here-and-now relationship with the therapist. In fact, both transference and current relationship patterns, coupled with patterns developed in the family of origin, can flesh out patterns to be changed.

I-I-1: Interpretation

This term was used by Freud to describe attempts to translate the potential hidden meanings of dreams into the language of ordinary consciousness. This idea was then applied to the psychoanalytic relationship, in which the analyst "translated" the hidden meanings in the patient's words with reference to transference reactions. Translation gradually took on a causal quality, as interpretation came to suggest how early childhood events influenced or "caused" the pattern in the present, especially with the analyst. Interpretation also became associated with understanding resistance, as the therapist and patient looked for reasons (e.g., fear) behind reluctance to continue the therapeutic process. Interpretation then came to mean a variety of things, including probing for the history, cause, purpose, or meaning of a repeated dysfunctional pattern.

The interpretation of a resistance or transference reaction usually contains three elements: an empathic summary (or confrontation), a clarification of the pattern, and a suggestion or guess about its origins. For example, a patient becomes silent. An interpretation might be: It seems very difficult for you to talk about your feelings (empathic reflection); you have had similar problems with your wife as well as your boss (pattern repetition); (and) perhaps you are afraid that people will take advantage of you if they know how you are feeling (avoidance because of a fear).

I-I-2: *Enacting and Identifying the Patient's Interpersonal Patterns within the Therapeutic Relationship*

The patient repeats with the therapist patterns from current and past relationships in a safe environment. These patterns are usually repeated to some extent no matter what the therapist does. However, the longer the therapeutic relationship and the less active the therapist, the more likely that details of the patient's adaptive and maladaptive interpersonal schemas with intimate others will be enacted with the therapist. There are times when discussion of this enactment is irrelevant to the patient's purpose in seeking help. At other times, the repetition illustrates clearly the problems which the patient must overcome. Therapists can welcome these real-life imitations or divert attention away from them, depending upon their relevance to the therapeutic aim. For begining therapists and for psychotherapeutically unsophisticated patients, bringing the therapeutic focus into the office and into the relationship between the participants can be anxiety-provoking. Beginners must learn to be effective users of their observing selves, so that they can "step back" from the interaction to observe their own as well as the patient's responses. With a well-activated observing self, the therapist can help the patient step back to observe the interactional patterns and explain how the therapist's office can be a laboratory in which to study and learn to alter the maladaptive patterns. The patient might then be able to observe and describe the patterns in ways that suggest possible change.

I-I-3: *The Therapist's Examining Interpersonal "Pulls" from the Patient by Being both a Participant and Observer*

This technique for identifying patterns is related to the previous one. Patients (like everyone else) usually attempt to elicit responses from others that fit their consciously or unconsciously desired role relationship models. The observing self of the therapist asks: What does the patient expect me to do? What am I expected to be? What response is the patient trying to "pull" from me? What reciprocal role does the patient wish to assign to me? (See module 6, on patient-originated countertransference.)
Source: Strupp & Binder (1984)

I-I-4: *Cyclical Psychodynamics*

From a cyclical psychodynamic perspective, the psychodynamic process is not located in the past reemerging in the present. Instead, the maladaptive process is understood as a vicious cycle generated both by the patient and by reactions of others. Like the problem of which came first, the chicken or the egg, therapist and patient may have difficulty deciding what starts the vicious cycle. The key, however, is not in identifying a single initiating source but in helping patients identify points in their interaction patterns at which they can intervene. Patients treat themselves in the same way that they see others treating them. For example, a patient who is highly self-critical often feels as if others are critical of him and/or induces others to be critical of him. Similarly, a patient whose identity seems to be determined by the expectations of others is usually unable to define and respond to her own wishes and needs. Patients unconsciously shape their relationships with others to confirm their

intrapsychic views of themselves. This concept can be useful in identifying a dysfunctional pattern, since the same pattern is being played out in three different arenas: intrapsychic, interpersonal, and transference.
Sources: Strupp & Binder (1984) and Wachtel & Wachtel (1986)

I-I-5: *Analyzing Interpersonal Transactions*

Analyzing interpersonal transactions involves focusing on the contributions of the patient's thoughts and feelings to relationships with others and the behaviors that result from those thoughts and feelings. This analysis takes into account the expressed or imagined actions (thoughts, wishes, fears, motives), as they form the individual's role relationship models. For example, "That is a pretty painting" does not describe an interpersonal event, but this sentence does: "When he saw that I was drunk again, he got angry, and slammed the door, and I imagined that I would never see him again." The action of drinking is understood as evoking the action of the other person's anger, as demonstrated by slamming the door, which in turn evokes imagining the final separation.
Source: Strupp & Binder (1984)

I-I-6: *Analysis of Faulty Communication*

Faulty communication may be responsible for failure in interpersonal relationships. Communication analysis is used to examine and identify these communication failures, which often result from one partner's mistaken assumptions about the other's thoughts, feelings, or intentions. Some common communication failures include: expecting the other person to "read my mind," ambiguous statements or nonverbal communication that contradicts verbal communication, incorrectly assuming that one has communicated clearly, and abrupt silence that closes off communication.
Source: Klerman, Weissman, Rounsaville, & Chevron (1984)

I-I-7: *Monitoring Examples of Faulty Interpersonal Transactions through Diaries*

Repetitively studying the situations in which the patient responds in ways that are ineffective and self-defeating can foster relinquishing these responses. Asking the patient to keep a diary facilitates this analysis.

I-II Modifying Role Relationship Models and Altering Interpersonal Scripts

After identifying the dysfunctional interpersonal schemas and their associated behaviors, the therapist needs to help the patient reconstruct, modify, and change these schemas by incorporating more reasonable and adaptive thoughts, feelings, and/or behaviors.

I-II-1: *Corrective Emotional Experience*

Some therapists believe that what the patient understands intellectually is far less important than what the patient experiences emotionally in the context of the psychotherapeutic interaction. The term "corrective emotional experience" was used by Alexander and French (1946) to refer to the positive effects of the difference between how the therapist responds to the patient and the patient's expectations of the therapist's responses. (These expectations are usually developed from previous experiences with parents and other caregivers.)

The term now has a more general meaning. It refers to any aspect of the therapeutic encounter that enables the patient to experience an unexpected form of interaction that leads to a change in dysfunctional patterns.

Psychotherapy is a specialized subset of human relationships. The therapist's basic attitudes toward the patient, such as caring, empathy, interest, and positive regard, can be corrective in themselves. The therapist may be able to bring about a corrective emotional experience through active understanding of the patient's interpersonal expectations. For example, if the patient expects to be dominated by a punitive authority figure, the therapist may take a warm and permissive manner. *Sources:* Alexander & French (1946), Strupp & Binder (1984), and Beitman (1987)

I-II-2: *Helping the Patient to Rewrite, Modify, and Correct the Assumptions Underlying His or Her Interpersonal Scripts*

Any intense relationship can provide an opportunity to begin modifying a patient's role relationship models and scripts. Role relationship models refer to the concepts or schemas the patient has about specific interpersonal roles. They start usually with one person being dominant and the other submissive. Then the roles carry with them implied descriptions of how the roles are to be played out (scripts). Some interpersonal approaches use the "here-and-now" therapy relationship, especially when the patient reacts to the therapist with characteristic maladaptive scripts. This interaction in the therapist's office provides a model for the patient's study of interactions with others; it also provides direct access for both participants to the unrealistic concerns, distorted views of others, faulty assumptions, and unrealistic scripts and expectations. The enactment of more adaptive responses in the office provides a template for similar responses in the patient's interpersonal environment. Similar changes can be initiated outside the therapeutic relationship. For example, the patient can ask friends, "Am I exaggerating or does that person really dislike me?" The answer can lead to new set of response patterns.

I-II-3: *Guiding Toward More Effective Communication*

Sometimes patients' problems result from their faulty communication. Therapists guide them to initiate effective communication, to practice these communication skills within the session, and then to try them out in various interpersonal situations.

I-III Practice Modified Roles and Patterns

New interpersonal patterns need to be practiced or worked through in different contexts in order to maintain them. While they can be reinforced within the therapeutic relationship, the degree of generalization to other relationships varies. The factors that promote generalization from the therapeutic relationship (e.g., from therapist to husband) or from any other relationship (e.g., from wife to mother) remain to be studied.

I-III-1: The Therapist's Maintaining Consistent and Reliable Behavior to Disconfirm the Patient's False Assumptions about the Interpersonal Reality

Interpersonal-dynamic therapists believe that patients change through experiencing a new interpersonal relationship. In the context of that experience, patients come to understand the meaning of their faulty learning, which they have carried forward from the past. In order to maintain patient change, the therapist must maintain consistent and reliable behaviors (by not being drawn into the patient's attempts to recreate old roles). The new human experience helps the patient repetitively understand (work through) the differences between beliefs, feelings, and behavior patterns generated from the past and the beliefs, feelings, and behavioral patterns currently being established.

Source: Strupp & Binder (1984)

I-III-2: Reinforcement from New Interpersonal Success (Related to G-15—See Appendix II)

New interpersonal behavior is often rewarded in patients' lives and leads to increases in the desired direction. And, as often happens with successful adaptation, success breeds success.

(However, it must also be recognized that some interpersonal change can lead to negative responses in others. Perhaps married patients in individual psychotherapy should be told that "psychotherapy can be dangerous to your marriage," since, in a minority of cases, the changes in one spouse can disrupt a comfortable equilibrium for the other spouse, who then attempts to dampen the patient's change. Therapists may need to be vigilant for negative reinforcement of change. In addition, the spouse may find him/herself experiencing anxiety or depression with the new equilibrium, requiring the therapist to be vigilant for the emergence of problems in the spouse that lay hidden because of the apparently bigger problems of the patient. There are other situations where family members commonly resist disturbances of their system—when, for example, a passive, compliant son or daughter starts to become assertive.)

SYSTEM

S-I Identifying the Dysfunctional Dynamic Interaction among Family Members

S-I-1: Circular Questioning

Circular questions are systemic questions that link one member of the family to another. It is a technique for interviewing families. One person is questioned about the relationships among others. The responses are then utilized by the therapist to introduce new formulations. Circularity is based on the idea that family members are connected to each other in particular patterns through time and that the problem in the family system often results from these interacting patterns. In order to perceive the architecture of the system, therapists use circular questioning to define and clarify the interacting patterns and specific connections, as well as to introduce information back to the family in the form of new questions. Circular questioning is also regarded as a change strategy, since it allows families to get a comprehensive systemic view of their situation in the context of history and environment. This enables the family to open up new patterns and new levels of meaning in the system. In the following example of circular questioning, the therapist asks the son in the family:

Q: Who is the most upset by the problem? **A:** mother.

Q: What does mother do about it? **A:** She tries to motivate John to go to school.

Q: Who agrees with mother? **A:** The school psychologist.

Q: Who disagrees? **A:** Father.

Q: Why do you think he disagrees? **A:** He thinks they are pushing John too hard.

Q: Who feels the same with father? **A:** Grandmother.

Sources: Boscolo, Cecchin, Hoffman, & Penn (1987) and Small (1984)

S-I-2: Enactments

The conflict situations and problems in the family are reproduced in the session. In order to identify interactional patterns in the family, family therapists often try to initiate the interaction between the family members, rather than listening to their report. Therapists may have spouses talk to each other, have the mother negotiate with the child, or have the family enact interacting patterns associated with the presenting problems. The therapist becomes an observer and director for in-session interaction. These in-session interactions usually reproduce out-of-session patterns. Family therapists may emphasize different content areas, for example, boundary patterns, transgenerational patterns, ineffective coummunication patterns, or distorted beliefs, ideas, and attitudes in the family culture.
Source: Griffin (1993)

S-I-3: Analysis of the Sequence of Communication

Ineffective communication between family members creates problems in the family system. Common ineffective communication patterns include withholding information, expecting the other to read one's mind rather than informing directly, sending vague and double messages, as well as attacking and defending. This analysis also includes defining complementary relationships and symmetrical relations. Complementary relationships are defined by the taking of reciprocal roles, the simplest example being one person is dominant and the other submissive. Symmetrical relationships are characterized by similarity of response, the simplest example being the escalation of an argument in which each one retaliates with something similar to the last statement of the other. Punctuation refers to an aspect of communication

concerning when one person stops talking and the other begins. Sometimes, for example, a family member begins to speak and another one regularly interrupts.
Source: Sherman, Oresky, & Rountrees (1991)

S-I-4: *Genogram*

A structural diagram of a family's three or four generational relational system. Through the creation of the genogram therapists can see patterns that cross the generations.

S-I-5: *Narrative*

A story told by an individual about his/her perspective on selective experiences within the family that reflects the patterns of this person living in this family. The narrative can, like many stories, contain multi-level meanings of the family as a unit in society as well as its internal modes of operation.

S-II Changing Interactional Patterns

S-II-1: *Paradox*

A paradoxical intervention is one that, if followed, will accomplish the opposite of what it is seemingly intended to accomplish. This technique, also called prescribing the symptom, is based on the following assumption: Symptoms or problems in the family act as a mechanism for regulating the dysfunctional parts of the system and maintaining family homeostasis. The pull toward homeostasis explains why families are very resistant to change, even when they are seeking psychotherapeutic help. Paradoxical techniques can be used to handle this homeostatic resistance and initiate change in the system. The three major techniques used in designing and applying systemic paradoxes are: redefining, prescribing, and restraining. The purpose of redefining is to change the perception of the problem. Behavior that maintains the symptom is defined as positively motivated to preserve family stability; for example, anger is defined as caring and distancing as a way of reinforcing closeness. Then the symptom-producing interaction is prescribed to the family. The key in doing this is to ask the family not only to continue to believe what they are doing is right, but to also dramatically exaggerate or increase the behavior. The third step is, whenever the family shows signs of changing, to insist that the change be restrained. If the paradoxical prescription is successful, the family will rebel against the therapist and decrease the behavior. Paradox is neither always necessary nor always desirable. One important criterion for its use is based on the evaluation of the degree of resistance to change. Generally, paradoxical intervention is used for those covert, longstanding, repetitive patterns of interaction that do not respond to direct interventions such as logical explanation or rational suggestions.
Sources: Minuchin & Fishman (1981), Sherman, Oresky, & Rountrees (1991), and Boscolo, Cecchin, Hoffman, & Penn (1987)

S-II-2: *Changing Rigid or Enmeshed Boundaries*

This strategy comes from structural family therapy, which assumes that dysfunctional behavior reflects an inadequate structure in the family system. Family structure is maintained by appropriate boundaries between subsystems. Therapists help to establish clear and effective boundaries that individuals can cross to an optimal degree. Rigid boundaries are loosened and overly flexible or enmeshed boundaries are defined and strengthened. The therapist helps the family to change inappropriate boundaries by restructuring relationships and setting tasks within the family that force new interactions between and among subsystems, leading to a realignment of the subsystems.

Sources: Minuchin & Fishman (1981), and Griffin (1993)

S-II-3: Task-setting Within the Family

In order to alter the structure of the family, the therapist increases the likelihood of new transactions by making specific suggestions about how to behave differently.

S-II-4: Communication Skill Training

Changing communication patterns between the family members can change the structure of the family. Ineffective communication can be changed through many techniques, such as having the members be aware of their ineffective communication patterns, direct instruction and coaching, blocking specific types of communication, task-setting, avoiding counterattacking and defensive talk, and having members keep a diary of their communication patterns.

Sources: Kramer (1985), and Sherman, Oresky, & Rountrees (1991)

S-II-5: Ritual Prescriptions

Rituals are ceremonial acts that mark life activities of a family and that are used to provide meaning and an atmosphere of security. Ritual prescriptions are intended to begin the establishment of such acts in order to give the family the opportunity for increased meaning and security.

S-III Maintain the New and Functional Interaction Patterns to Create Virtuous Cycle

S-III-1: Reinforcement and Practice

The family is instructed to practice new behaviors in the office as well as at home. If effective, the new patterns will reinforce themselves. The spiral of change ideally creates more benefit until better functioning equilibrium is reached.

FORM 18-1

Transcripts for Change Strategies

Name (optional)_____   Date_____

The following pages are transcripts. Some transcripts are followed by the following three questions: (1) Through which stage(s) of change does the dialogue move? (2) Which generic strategies and techniques were used in the transcript? (3) Which ECBIS strategies and techniques were used? Some transcripts are followed only by the last two questions. There are four answers (a, b, c, and d) for each of these questions, but *only one* is the best. Please circle the answer you think best fits that question. As you answer these questions, please review Figure 4-1 and Table 4-1 for reference. Try to get a general sense for the sub-stages and general and specific strategies for your responses.

I.

The Hanson family consists of father and mother; Alan, age 19; Kathy, 17, who is close to Alan; Peg, 21, the parental child; and Pete, 12. The therapist is Salvador Minuchin.

Alan 1:   Would you give me a hand, Peg?

Peg 1:   Tell Daddy that you want to make decisions by yourself. If you really want to do it.

Alan 2:   Yeah, I would like to be more independent, but I guess it's a habit of letting people do things for me, and I've gotten into it.

Peg 2:   And I guess it's going to be very hard for Daddy to stop. It will be hard for all of us, but especially Daddy, because he and Mommy tend more to be protective. And it's going to take a long time, and it's going to take a lot on your part, too, to make decisions and say, "Well, look, I don't want Peg to help." You can't be afraid to say it.

Alan 3:   Yeah.

Minuchin 1: Peg, do you find yourself frequently in the job of being the helper?

Peg 3:   Yes.

Minuchin 2: Who else is asking you for help?

Peg 4:   Uh—my mother.

Minuchin 3: Pete, exchange seats with your mom, because I want your mother to talk with Peg. (*Pete unhooks his microphone to change chairs, and Peg starts to help him.*) No, let him do it. (*to Pete*) Very good. You did it on your own. Nobody helped you. Maybe you will still be safe, Pete, since nobody will help you. Mom, talk with Peg because I think Peg gets herself saddled with helping a lot in the family.

Mother 1:   She does. Peg wants—

Minuchin 4: Talk with *her* about how you saddle her.

Mother 2:   About how I saddle her with the problems?

Minuchin 5: Yeah.

Peg 5:   Right. Well, I never realized it. It just happened that grandmother—

Mother 3:   My mother used to live with us, and she was around all the time when Peg was growing up, and then when she wasn't there, I just automatically used to ask Peg—I didn't realize that I was putting pressure on Peg. I thought it was more or less conversation. Right, Peg?

Peg 6:   Maybe you didn't realize it, but I knew that you wanted me to help you decide things.

Mother 4:	I always considered it more like we would talk over things together and then I would make my own decision, but I think maybe you felt that it was left on your shoulders to make the decision.
Peg 7:	A lot of times you did. You would say, "What do you think I should do?" or, "What do you think about this?" And I made a lot of decisions.
Minuchin 6:	You did ask Peg to make decisions?
Mother 5:	Not about important things, like about if you're going to buy a house or something like that, but about—
Peg 8:	About family things.
Mother 6:	Yeah.
Minuchin 7:	Family things. She would ask you?
Mother 7:	Yes—I would ask her to help.
Minuchin 8:	Father, where were you? You that are so helpful. You that are helping Alan. Where were you? Why didn't your wife ask you?
Father 1:	I wasn't around too much then.
Minuchin 9:	Oh, that's why. Are you saying that you were alone and that you used Peg because Nels was not around?
Mother 8:	Nels was working two jobs for a long time. He's always working two jobs, but now he has more of an interest in the house. I feel Nels has time if it's something he's interested in, and if it's something he doesn't want to think about, he's just not there to hear it.
Minuchin 10:	Peg, come here and move out from that center. Mom, you sit near your husband. You know, Peg, I think that it's a pity for you to be sitting here between them. I bet that you are too available. I bet you like that job.
Mother 9:	How do you think we can go about correcting this mess?
Father 2:	Well, I think I should start being home nights for one thing. I'll leave the other job—
Minuchin 11:	Can you stop shaking your head, Peg? It's not your function.
Father 3:	Much as I feel I have to change an awful lot, I think you have to change.
Mother 10:	In what way?
Father 4:	Or, general mannerisms, your attitude toward me personally. I feel very deeply hurt many times.
Mother 11:	How do I act that makes you feel I look down on you?
Father 5:	Sometimes you don't have to act, you can just look.
Mother 12:	But I don't understand what—like what do I do that gives you that impression? How do I— obviously I—
Father 6:	I'm trying to look for an answer here.
. . . . . .	
Father 7:	You are not respectful of me.
Mother 13:	I don't think I'm not respectful with you. I don't mean to be not respectful of you.
Minuchin 12:	You said that she doesn't treat you as a full man. You make Nels feel that you are not on his side.
Mother 14:	And I guess I have feelings that he doesn't understand me, either.
Father 8:	I think we've been throwing this back at each other for a long, long time, and it's—

Minuchin 13:   You have not been helpful. You, Peg, have not been helpful.

Peg 9:   What do you mean? Now? Or in the past?

Minuchin 14:   Whenever Mom chose to talk with you instead of talking with Dad. Will you resign from that job or are you stuck with it?

Peg 10:   I don't know. Let me think for a minute. I don't think that my mother is going to stop—

Minuchin 15:   Using you?

Peg 11:   Yes, you're right.

Minuchin 15:   It's a job that you like for life? Do you want that job for life?

Peg 12:   No, because I'm not her mother. I'm only 21 years old. If I wanted to be the mother, I'd get married.

Minuchin 16:   She's not using you as a mother really. She uses you when she feels she does not know how to talk with your father. (*to parents*) So Peg is in between both of you. Who is on the other side?

Father 9:   Oh, Peg is there with her mother and the mother is with Peg.

Minuchin 17:   What about the other ones?

Father 10:   Pete is fairly independent. He'll speak his piece. And Kathy is—I'd say she'll look at both sides. Alan will form an opinion, I feel, but he will keep it inside him rather than take sides.

Minuchin 17:   Do you think he is taking sides but he is keeping it silent?

Father 11:   I feel so.

Minuchin 18:   And with whom is he siding?

Father 12:   I think Alan feels about his mother like I do. I honestly, sincerely feel that. I don't think he wants to take sides, but I feel Alan feels a lot of times I may be right, but he'll never say it.

1. Generic strategies and techniques used in this transcript include:
   a. Taking responsibility
   b. The therapists's self-disclosure
   c. Turning stumbling blocks into stepping stones
   d. Inquiring into reasons and/or advantages of change

2. ECBIS strategies and techniques used in this transcript include:
   a. Catharsis
   b. Reality testing
   c. Assertion training
   d. Changing interaction patterns by changing enmeshed boundary

Reprinted with permission from Minuchin, S. & Fishman, H. C. (1981). *Family therapy techniques* (pp. 155–159). Cambridge, MA: Harvard University Press.

II.

C1:   One of the things that drives me sort of crazy is the kids fooling around when they're eating. My kids and their friends. Particularly when Betty invites a friend for dinner. And they get up and look out the window and come back and eat, and slowly, like an hour to eat. And I get so furious and so controlling and they have to only eat and no silliness and you know very demanding. And really overreacting to little kids against ordinary manners.

T1:   Let's make sure that I understand. When the kids are eating and they dawdle and take their time— That just seems to drive you around the bend. And you feel that you're overreacting.

C2:   Right.

T2:   OK. I wonder if we could go back to the situation, the way you visualize it in your mind. So I could get the flavor of that. You say that the kids are all sitting around the table, and there's Betty on one side and Larry on the other, and—James is it—across?

C3:   Mhm.

T3:   So you're watching, maybe standing by the sink in the kitchen?

C4:   And I'm watching. Betty is leaning over to Larry, and the place mats are getting moved slightly. And Larry is leaning over there. And then there's some noise outside and he gets up and looks out the window and he comes back and sits down and says, "I don't like tomatoes."

T4:   And there's something about the way they play and they joke—that really seems to bug you—just something . . .

C5:   The way they are dawdling. They don't care. There's absolutely no caring on their faces. And yet I know that the whole eating thing is a lot more than just eating. It's a whole social occasion. And there I am denying it to my kids.

T5:   So you're telling them, "Cut all the fun and games. Get down to that task!" Do you have any awareness of what's going on inside you? I imagine you clenching your teeth—

C6:   I'm anxious for it to be over. I'm angry. I'm impatient. And then what I mentioned about evaluating myself as a mother.

T6:   So then you're not just getting mad at them.

C7:   I'm getting mad at myself for being the kind of person I am, the kind of mother.

T7:   It's not just the problem of getting upset with them, but you're kind of adding insult to injury by questioning yourself and asking yourself "Maybe there's something wrong with the kind of mother I am." And yet I think what really interests me is what it is about their silliness that seems to upset you so much.

C8:   There's a look or a small action that happens. And then they start looking at each other through the corners of their eyes and giggling. And half the meal seems to be made up of giggles.

C9:   I feel almost as if they're pulling something on me because they know my needs and despite it all, they're doing this.

T9:   At the moment it does feel as if they were doing it to spite you.

C10:   I almost don't allow it to feel any way, because at the moment I'm saying "Jeez I'm bitchy." So I don't allow my immediate reaction to come. I'm too busy putting a trip on myself for what I've already done.

T10:   And—yet my hunch is that there's something going on that is making you very angry, and that's what we're trying to understand.

C11:   Yeah, I think—I don't understand why I get like that. Because sometimes it would be a specific things that I have to do, and I understand why I'm impatient. But sometimes there isn't anything else I'm supposed to be doing.

T11:   Do you have a sense of what that impatience feels like?

C12:   (long silence) Hmm—It has something to do with feeling the responsibility.

T12:   Hmm.

C13:   And it's at that time I'm feeling that my job, my responsibility, is to be there with the kids, and prepare lunch.

T13:   Hmm.

C14:   And I separate—I tend to—It's almost like I separate my whole life, or a day or whatever into—little sections. And I can't go on to any section or do anything until one is over. (*pause*) And I can see that in other things too. I used to draw and paint, and I couldn't start a picture because there were going to be other things that interfered with it, so that meant that I couldn't start it at all.

T14:   Oh. So by kind of making these little slots for yourself—in a way it—you kind of stop yourself from—

C15:   I stop myself from doing anything else. And them being silly and taking a long time—they're stopping my life.

T15:   Oh, I see. If they cooperated, then you could be over and finished with that particular section, and you could feel like you did your job well, and then get on to something else.

C16:   That's right—(*pause*) And I think the only times I've really enjoyed having lunch with them, is when I've been—when I've been more involved with it and made it . . . part of my life . . . almost . . . as if they were people, rather than seeing it as a job in that slot.

T16:   The times you've enjoyed have not been when you've been in the role of the good mother, but when you've just been able to view them as human beings whom you're eating with, just as if they were adults.

C17:   That's right. That's when they get into that slot, you know, without that work section. And there's just a tremendous difference!

T17:   Hmm.

C18:   And then I realize that there I am demanding them not to be silly. And I love being silly (*laughs*). And I joke with them and we just get right off on it.

T18:   Ah—like during those times you're one of them.

C19:   Yeah. And there's a tremendous—you know—the whole core is just so different. So much closer and feels so much better.

T19:   You don't feel like that nagging mother.

C20:   Oh no, no. And the thing is that nagging mother wants so much to be in control of them, for them to hurry up. But when I'm—when I'm part of the whole scene, I feel myself being in control.

T20:   When you imagine yourself being silly with them and having that good rapport with them, feeling kind of like a real sense of control—It's a whole different feeling—

C21:   It's just a happier sense, a sense of well-being, of feeling the qualities I like about myself.

T21:   I'm guessing that your life must be quite full, that you've got to structure and organize it this way.

C22:   That's right. I've got my studying to do. And the home responsibilities—

T22:   And those damn kids are just completely wrecking—

C23:   My computer.

T23:   And you'd like to say "For heaven's sakes would you just—"

C24:   Yeah—"Don't you realize the stress I'm under?" I guess I'm feeling it—but I guess I'm also saying "I have no right to ask them to feel the stress in my life when it's chosen for myself, apart from them." I guess I feel guilty about spending so much time away from them and spending so much time being at the university and writing papers that I didn't want to say "These are my particular needs."

T24:   But what comes before that? "Don't these kids know how much stress I have in my life?"

C25:   Don't they know how hard I work? Can't they see that they have to cooperate so I can continue doing it?

T25:   Mhm.

C26:   Can't they see how important it is for me?

T26: Our time is almost up. And I want to ask you where this leaves you.

C27: Well I feel better about it actually. I feel that I can go and say—that it is OK for me to say "You know these are all the things I'm doing. This is why I need you to hurry up and not fool around." Because I can see that this is something we can work out together, rather than continuing to feel worse by the minute. Because that's when there's this build-up, you know.

1. Generic strategies and techniques used in this transcript include:
   a. Separating past from present relationship
   b. Empathic reflection
   c. Positive reinforcement
   d. Inquiring into reasons and advantages of change

2. ECBIS strategies and techniques used in this transcript include:
   a. Disputing irrational beliefs
   b. Assertion training
   c. Restructuring emotional schemes by helping patient to access new information through emotional awareness
   d. Practice modified roles by reinforcement from new interpersonal success

Reprinted with permission from Rice, L. A., & Greenberg, L. S. (1984). *Patterns of change* (pp. 47–51). New York: Guilford.

III.

The patient is a 35-five-year old foreman for a construction company. He was referred from the general medical clinic because no physical basis could be found for the gastrointestinal symptoms that were troubling him. Shirley is his wife.

P1: (*Sits down, looks cheerful and animated*) I want to tell you, Doctor, I don't know when I've felt this good. Everything is so much better now that me and my wife are really communicating. She really is interested in me if I give her a chance.

T1: In other words, you have learned something very important about relationships. Once you sort out the present from the past things go much better.

P2: Shirley is certainly a lot more understanding than my mother ever was. I can't believe I treated her so mean when all she wants is for us to get along.

T2: Of course your wife doesn't have an alcoholic husband, a houseful of kids to raise, and no money.

P3: That's true. She had her hands full. I think I knew that for as long as I can remember. That's why I tried to be a good boy. I did an awful lot for her—watched the kids, did the dishes, went grocery shopping.

T3: Was your mother appreciative of your efforts?

P4: Oh yes, in her own way. She'd sometimes say she wouldn't know what to do without me; called me the man of the house the way I looked after her and showed her I care. But you know, when you're a kid you don't understand everything the way you do later. When she was crabby, like she usually was, no matter what you did she'd get mad. You should have done it sooner, or different: nothing satisfied her then. I used to think she didn't like me. (*Tears well up*) Look at me, I can still feel it hurt now just thinking about it.

T4: Yes, exactly. That's what I meant. Old feelings and the attitudes they create are still very much in evidence in all of us.

P5: When will I get over that, Doc?

T5: In a way we never really get over our childhood experiences. They are the building blocks of everyone's personality, it's what makes you you, and me me. But as you found out when we learn to understand the reason for our behavior we get a new control over our feelings and can stop ourselves from being self-destructive. You, for instance, based on certain early experiences, have come to expect disinterest where your emotional needs are concerned. That attitude hasn't disappeared, but knowing about it makes it possible to prevent its spoiling your relationship with your wife.

P6: Not only with her, Doc. I've been noticing what I do in other places too. I used to think no one ever appreciated what I was trying to do at work, I only heard them complaining. Now I can hear it when they say "thank you," or when the boss tells me the job went good. It's funny how you can have your mind made up to something and never know it, even when it gets you into trouble.

T6: It's a revelation when you first see it, isn't it?

1. The stage(s) of change the dialogue move through:
   a. Relinquish dysfunctional patterns
   b. Relinquish dysfunctional patterns and initiate new patterns
   c. Initiate functional patterns
   d. Maintain functional patterns

2. Generic strategies and techniques used in this transcript include:
   a. Suggestions of how to change
   b. Resolve conflict
   c. Separating past from present relationship
   d. Role-playing

3. ECBIS strategies and techniques used in this transcript include:
   a. Confronting feared emotion
   b. Challenging the distorted beliefs by questioning the evidence
   c. Modifying role relationship models
   d. Modeling

Reprinted with permission from Basch, M. F. (1980). *Doing psychotherapy* (pp. 32–33). New York: Basic Books.

IV.

Bob entered counseling for the purpose of solving "career problems." As counseling progressed, the problem became more clearly defined as an interpersonal conflict between Bob and his boss.

Bob: I don't know what this exercise is going to prove. Every time we discuss my problem, I end up at the same conclusion. My boss is insensitive and completely unconcerned about my situation. He'll never change, and I'm not going to change, so the only solution is for me to look for another job.

Counselor: Before we reach that conclusion, let's try the role reversal exercise we discussed last week. It may not change anything, but at least we can say we looked at the problem every way we could imagine. Are you still game?

Bob: Well, I can't imagine what you have in mind, but I'll go along with whatever it is.

Counselor: Good. I'd like you to play devil's advocate with your problem for a few minutes. I'd like you to imagine that you are your boss, and I'll be you. Try to be as accurate in this role as you can. That way, I'll have a much better idea what your boss is like. And I will try to be as accurate as possible in my role as Bob. If I tend to respond inaccurately, stop the role reversal and give me some coaching on how I should respond. Are you ready?

Bob: I suppose so. I know I can imitate him. I know him like the back of my hand. But I don't see how it can do any good.

Counselor:	Maybe you're right. Let's give it a try and see what you think. You begin as your boss.
Bob (as Boss):	Bob, I see you have missed another deadline for the production report. What the hell's going on?
Counselor (as Bob):	I couldn't get the information I needed, and I didn't want to bother you yesterday.
Bob (as Boss):	What do you mean "You didn't want to bother me?" If you have to bother me to get the report done, then bother me. But don't miss the deadline.
Counselor (as Bob):	I wish you wouldn't get upset with me. I was just trying to take care of you.
Bob (as Boss):	Look, Bob, you can't have it both ways. If you don't ask for help when you need it and that leads to missing deadlines, then you have to expect some consequence. And if anger is the consequence, then you've got to understand that it is due to your avoiding me. You've got to stop avoiding me.

(End of role reversal)

Counselor:	Well, Bob, what do you think of that scenario?
Bob:	I guess it took an unexpected turn. His anger does upset me, but I haven't been thinking about bringing it on myself. Maybe I could learn to handle him better.

1. Generic strategies and techniques used in this transcript include:
   a. Challenging dysfunctional beliefs, behaviors and emotions
   b. Self-disclosure
   c. Positive reinforcement
   d. Inquiring into reasons and advantages of change

2. ECBIS strategies and techniques used in this transcript include:
   a. Catharsis
   b. Creating adaptive beliefs by fantasizing consequences
   c. Circular questioning
   d. Relaxation training

Reprinted with permission from Cormier, L. S., & Hackney, H. (1987). *The professional counselor* (pp. 126–127). New Jersey: Prentice Hall.

V.

Wife 1:	I mean that maybe I'm making an excuse for us, but in this particular occasion, and maybe there are others, I feel we are both turning around when one of us slips off and does the parent and child thing (to each other) and then we come back (on track again).
Therapist 1:	O.K., then, if you want to make that part of the relationship, do you have a "contract" for that as to how that's going to work so the other person doesn't get bent out of shape so much?
Husband 1:	No, we don't, and sometimes it comes as a surprise to me.
Therapist 2:	Yes?
Husband 2:	You know, that's when it's the worst. When it comes as a surprise (to me/to us).
Therapist 3:	You still have to have a "contract" for that, you see.
Husband 3:	Yeah????
Wife 2:	What do you mean? A contract that we're going to do it, but we don't know when or where?
Therapist 4:	Yes. An open-ended contract on that line that would make something work for you as an interlude or a change of pace of deviation from what your normal discourse is, you see. (*Pause*) And then you can assign yourself roles. You will know much more about what to expect from one another. Know that it may be time limited. It's not going to go on for weeks and

weeks, and then, even though it may be a surprise in terms of the exact moment it starts, it's not a surprise as to what you both can expect from that point on, you see. I'm hearing there is a genuine surprise and then one or both of you aren't quite sure how the scenario is going to come out.

Wife 3: (*to husband*) I think for the most part you're expecting me to act like the adult that I normally do. So, when I start my pouting, you're kind of like, oh, boy, there she goes again . . .

Husband 4: Yeah.

Wife 4: And I think you click into adult; I mean, I think you click into parent.

Husband 5: Well, I don't know. Parent is part nurturing, so I try to try that angle and sometimes that doesn't work, and then sometimes I get "Well, you should" and that doesn't work either. So, if we get a contract, I can say, "This is going on and this is what is happening and here's what my role should be and then let it take its course." You know, real surprises are the school times and sometimes when I come home from work or whatever and you're banging away at homework and say, "I'm almost done" or "It stinks" or "Life's horrible" . . .

Therapist 5: It seems to me the two of you can do something in terms of contracting here. I'd like to see you give that some real attention and let me know what to come up with. I think you can discuss, for example, Mrs. Jones, whether you need to pout for awhile and what kind of role you need Mr. Jones to be in? Do you need him in a nurturing, parent role, or do you need him in an adult role, or do you need him to be silent? What are the expectations? What is most helpful and facilitative to you as well as to the relationship?

Wife 5: At that time? You mean I have to tell him at that time which one of those roles?

Husband 6: Yes, in advance.

Therapist 6: Contract in advance so he knows whether he should click into the parent, as he was saying a minute ago, or whether he should click into something else or just click off.

Wife 6: Well, I wouldn't know until I was doing it which of those I would want. Is that what you mean? I would never say every time I pout I want you to act like this.

Husband 7: Oh, then, how will I know?

Therapist 7: You mean there's a differentiation then for outcomes for pouting?

Wife 7: I think there are differentiations in terms of what's going on in terms of what I need from him.

Therapist 8: O.K., but, does the differentiation fall into several predictable categories?

Wife 8: I don't think it's predictable.

Husband 8: Well, I do.

Wife 9: I mean, I think there are several categories.

(The couple continued on and agreed upon some contract categories with which they were satisfied).

1. The stage(s) of change the dialogue move through:
   a. Relinquish dysfunctional patterns
   b. Relinquish dysfunctional patterns and initiate functional patterns
   c. Imitate and maintain functional patterns
   d. Maintain functional patterns

2. Generic strategies and techniques used in this transcript include:
   a. Generating alternatives
   b. Turning stumbling blocks into stepping stones
   c. Separating past from present
   d. Self-disclosure

3. ECBIS strategies and techniques used in this transcript include:
   a. Modifying role relationship by guiding toward effective behaviors
   b. Confronting feared emotions
   c. Disputing irrational beliefs
   d. Positive reinforcement

Reprinted with permission from Turner, N. (1994). Nuclear family vs. family of origin: A paradox. In G. Weeks, & L. Hof, (Eds.). *The marital relationship therapy casebook* (pp. 113–115). New York: Brunner/Mazel.

VI.

T1: I'd like you to close your eyes now and imagine yourself in the following situation: You are sitting on stage in the auditorium together with the other school board members. It's a few minutes before you have to get up and give your report to the people in the audience. Between 0 and 100 percent tension, tell me how nervous you feel.

C1: About 50

T2: (*Now to get into his head*) So I'm feeling fairly tense. Let me think. What might I be telling myself that's making me upset?

C2: I'm nervous about reading my report in front of all these people.

T3: But why does that bother me?

C3: Well, I don't know if I'm going to come across all right . . .

T4: (*He seems to be having trouble. More prompting on my part may be needed than I originally anticipated.*) But why should that upset me? That upsets me because . . .

C4: . . . because I want to make a good impression.

T5: And if I don't . . .

C5: . . . well, I don't know. I don't want people to think that I'm incompetent. I guess I'm afraid that I'll lose the respect of the people who thought I knew what I was doing.

T6: (*He seems to be getting closer.*) But why should that make me so upset?

C6: I don't know. I guess it shouldn't. Maybe I'm being *overly* concerned about other people's reactions to me.

T7: How might I be overly concerned?

C7: I think this may be one of those situations where I have to please everybody, and there are an awful lot of people in the audience. Chances are I'm not going to get everybody's approval, and maybe that's upsetting me. I want everyone to think I'm doing a good job.

T8: Now let me think for a moment to see how rational that is.

C8: To begin with, I don't think it really is likely that I'm going to completely blow it. After all, I have prepared in advance, and have thought through what I want to say fairly clearly. I think I may be reacting as if I already have failed, even though it's very unlikely that I will.

T9: And even if I did mess up, how bad would that be?

C9: Well, I guess that really wouldn't be so terrible after all.

T10: (*I don't believe him for one moment. There is a definite hollow ring to his voice. He arrived at that conclusion much too quickly and presents it without much conviction.*) I say I don't think it'll upset me, but I don't really believe that.

C10: That's true. I would be upset if I failed. But actually, I really shouldn't be looking at this situation as being a failure.

T11: What would be a better way for me to look at the situation?

C11: Well, it's certainly not a do-or-die kind of thing. It's only a ridiculous committee report. A lot of the people in the audience know who I am and what I'm capable of doing. And even if I don't give a sterling performance, I don't think they're going to change their opinion of me on the basis of a five-minute presentation.

T12: But what if some of them do?

C12: Even if some of them do think differently of me, that doesn't mean that I *would* be different. I would still be me no matter what they thought. It's ridiculous of me to base my self-worth on what other people think.

T13: (*I think he's come around as much as he can. We can terminate this scene now.*) With this new attitude toward the situation, how do you feel in percentage of anxiety?

C13: Oh, about 25 percent.

T14: OK, let's talk a little about some of the thoughts you had during that situation before trying it again.

1. The stage(s) of change the dialogue move through:
   a. Relinquish dysfunctional patterns
   b. Initiate functional patterns
   c. Initiate and maintain functional patterns
   d. Maintain functional patterns

2. Generic strategies and techniques used in this transcript include:
   a. Turning stumbling blocks into stepping stones
   b. Positive reinforcement
   c. Inquiring into reasons and advantages of change
   d. Challenging dysfunctional beliefs

3. ECBIS strategies and techniques used in this transcript include:
   a. Restructuring emotional schemes by increasing the patient's emotional awareness
   b. Creating adaptive and reasonable beliefs by disputing irrational beliefs
   c. Desensitization
   d. Therapist's examining interpersonal pulls from the patient by being both a participant and observer

Reprinted with permission from Goldfried, M. R. (1995). *From cognitive-behavior therapy to psychotherapy integration* (pp. 91–93). New York: Springer.

VII.

The client, an attractive 23-year-old woman, came for help because she claimed she was self-punishing, compulsive, afraid of males, had no goals in life, and was guilty about her relationship with her parents.

T1: How are things?

C2: Things are okay. I went to visit my parents on Monday night. And every time I was tempted to fall prey to their emotional blackmail, I remembered what you said, and I was able to fight it.

T3: Fine!

C4: My mother is having a rough time yet, because of having her breast removed. She hardly says anything. She's really in a world of fog. She gets confused, and she uses the confusion to give her a hold on the family. She was putting on a martyr act the other night; and usually I would have given in to her, but I said, "Quit being a martyr! Go to bed." She just looked at me as though I was a strange creature!

T5:   And you didn't get upset by it?

C6:   No, I didn't get upset by it. I had the feeling that I was doing the right thing. And that was, I think, the major accomplishment in the past few days.

T-7:   Yes, well that was quite a good accomplishment.

C8:   Now if there are any bigger crises that will come, I don't know how I'll face them; but it looks like I can.

T9:   Yes; and if you keep facing these smaller crises as they arise—and they tend to be continual—there's no reason why you shouldn't be able to face the bigger ones as well. Why not?

C-10:   I guess it's a case of getting into a good habit.

T-11:   Yes, that's right: getting really to believe that no matter what your parents do, no matter how hurt they get, that's not your basic problem. You're not deliberately doing them in; you're just standing up for yourself.

1. Generic strategies and techniques used in this transcript include:
    a. Turning stumbling blocks into stepping stones
    b. Defining dysfunctional patterns
    c. Role playing
    d. Positive reinforcement
2. ECBIS strategies and techniques used in this transcript include:
    a. Evoking problematic emotions
    b. Fantasizing consequences
    c. Identifying maladaptive interpersonal schemes
    d. Assertion training

Reprinted with permission from Ellis, A. (1974). *Growth through reason* (pp. 223–286). Hollywood: Wilshire Books.

VIII.

T1:   Hello, Susan, what is your goal in coming in?

C1:   My marriage is not going well. I think Bill has fallen out of love with me and he won't talk about it. Whenever I try to talk about our problem or bring it up, he just puts me off with, "Not that again," and then he walks away. If I pursue him, we fight. He says there is nothing wrong, but I don't believe him. If he would just talk to me or show me that he loves me, I wouldn't be so upset. I tried to get him to come to therapy with me, but he said there was no way he was going to listen to more of my complaints in front of a stranger.

T2:   I am sorry about all this. Can you tell me what the two of you will be doing differently when this is not a problem anymore?

C2:   Well, if this changes, he will be talking with me. If he is unhappy with me, he will tell me instead of this silence. He will be more communicative and I think we'll be spending more time together.

T3:   So he will be more communicative. What will you be doing differently?

C3:   I guess I won't be so worried.

T4:   That sounds better for you. When you are not so worried, what will you be doing differently or at least different in his eyes?

C4:   I guess he would say I would be more relaxed and secure, and I think I would.

T5:   What will he see or hear you doing differently that will tell him that you are a little more relaxed?

C5:   I will be getting more into my own things, my own friends, my own chores and hobbies. He thinks I am too dependent on him right now.

T6: So you think he thinks you are too dependent on him and that he does not like that. When he thinks that way, what would he say he does?

C6: He probably says that I disgust him and he wants to get away. Maybe he thinks he has to make me more independent.

T7: So you don't want him to pull away or make judgments about you. And when he thinks you are more relaxed or secure, what would he say he would do differently?

C7: He would probably say that he likes that more and . . . I don't know what he would do.

T8: If he were here, what would you guess he would say he would do?

C8: I suppose he might say that he would feel like spending time with me or that he just likes to see me happy.

T9: Are there times now when you think you appear a little more relaxed to him, maybe when you are a little more into your own things or friends?

C9: Sometimes. Sometimes, I just give up on him and just do my own thing. Then he comes around. He probably thinks I am more independent then.

T10: You think he likes you acting independently. How do you do that?

C10: Oh, sometimes I just feel like it, or sometimes I just tell myself I can't look at him all the time.

T11: Is that different for you to tell yourself that?

C11: Yes, I have been thinking that way more lately, more independently.

T12: So, how are you getting yourself to think and act more that way lately?

C12: My friend has been suggesting it and I think she's right.

T13: Well, as you continue to think and act in this different way, what do you think the chances are of his thinking of you more favorably and you getting more of what you want?

C13: Yes, I really need to be looking to myself first.

T14: So, how will you continue to do this?

1. Generic strategies and techniques used in this transcript include:
   a. Practice in the session
   b. Altering future expectations
   c. Resolving conflicts
   d. Role playing

2. ECBIS strategies and techniques used in this transcript include:
   a. Modifying and alter interpersonal script
   b. Catharsis
   c. Reality testing
   d. Modeling

Reprinted with permission from Walter, J. L., & Peller, J. E. (1992). *Becoming solution-focused in brief therapy* (pp. 193–195). New York: Brunner/Mazel.

IX.

The patient had been unable to give up the grieving process because of excessive guilt associated with her anger toward her husband before and after his death. She had responded to his illness with self-denial but secret resentment. As he became progressively more debilitated she was at once horrified at the deterioration of a man on whom she had depended and angry at him for becoming such a burden on her. Her desire for him to die was conscious and even acted upon during a fit of anger. Moreover, she saw her decision to hospitalize him as signing his death warrant. After he died she felt continued resentment at being deprived of his company and his help in handling affairs, including the bills for his illness. Given her anger and her guilt in reaction to it, the patient could not allow herself to pleasurably pursue a life alone. Although she had many personal and social resources, she could not bring herself to take advantage of them.

T1:   You know, last week we had discussed, we had talked about the fact that you know, it seems like . . . getting back to what we talked about a little earlier . . . that really, this is one of the first times in your life that you've been really *been* as free as you are.

P1:   Yeah, in all my life, I think it's my . . .

T2:   Mm-hm.

P2:   This is the freest I've ever been. And I really sometimes get very annoyed with myself, that I don't put my time to better use.

T3:   Like . . . ?

P3:   Well, like doing something for somebody else, you know, I still have . . . perhaps doing some, doing some volunteer work somewhere . . .

T4:   Hm.

P4:   I've been talking to a couple people that I know who are doing some, one of the women working in the convalescent home . . . goes in a couple of times a week and she loves it.

T5:   Hm.

P5:   And it gives her a feeling of, you know, usefulness.

T6:   Mm-hm. That seems like a big step to take?

P6:   Yes . . . it's a big step for me to take to call up. I'm . . . not a telephone person. I hate telephones, I've got to be . . . really desperate to pick up a telephone and call somebody . . . or something.

T7:   Mm-hm. What about dropping by?

P7:   I never thought of that (*chuckles*). That to me would be easier than telephoning.

T8:   Mm-hm, mm-hm. Well, I mean, I . . . I suppose most places where you would volunteer, there must be someone there, you could . . . just go by and see. Or maybe you could go with a friend, or something like that.

P8:   Yeah . . . mm-hm . . . Well, I-I-I'm still busy trying to get myself . . . in order, that, I'll . . . sort of let that rest a little while.

T9:   Mm-hm. Well, I guess the thing about, though, having a lot of freedom is that it really, always brings up . . . issues like—you know, what are the things that are satisfying to you? You know, what is it that you want out of life?

P9:   Well, see, I always wanted to go, I'd always . . . I grew up thinking that I never was able to go to college.

T10:   Hm.

P10:   So . . . now I've got this freedom, and my son said, "Why don't you take a course? That'll keep you interested and occupied . . ."

T11:   Mm-hm.

P11:   So (*sighs*) he said, "Why don't you go down to . . ." you know . . . the one down on . . . Anyway, I took South Central, because I thought it was easier for me to get there than it was to go to Southern.

T12:   Mm-hm, mm-hm. I think South Central also generally does have more . . . community people.

P12:   Yeah . . .

T13:   Instead of, you know, Southern tends to be more eighteen-year-olds.

P13:   Yeah . . .

T14:   That kind of thing. Mm-hm.

P14:   Of course, as a senior citizen, there are a lot of things that are open to you, like I don't have to pay for the courses that I take.

T15:   Hm.

P15:   I pay for my books, but I don't have to pay . . .

T16:   Mm-hm, mm-hm. Well, have you thought of taking more than one course? Or are you really trying to get a degree?

P16:   Well, I have, I have . . . well, I thought I would like to get an associate degree. I don't know in what, but I always like that, because South Central . . . South Central . . . is a two-year course anyway. So I have to talk to, I have to go down, to get to talk to a counselor there, see what's open for me.

T17:   Mm-hm, mm-hm.

P17:   Well, this course that I'm taking now, English course, is . . . a lot of writing, I . . . think, my goodness, if I took two courses I'd go crazy.

T18:   Mm-hm. Well, I guess that's the thing about freedom, is that you have to—decide on what you're . . .

P18:   Yeah.

T19:   What it is that you want?

P19:   Because I still want some freedom. For myself.

T20:   Mm-hm.

P20:   To do . . . other things that I like to do.

T21:   Well, so, so one of the things then, that you want to have in your—as part of your life—picture—the way that you would be organizing your life—would be . . . at least a minimum amount of time at home, or, you know, taking care of the house and I guess being *in* the house that you like.

P21:   Yeah . . .

T22:   And . . . you know, just having a sense that it's yours, and relaxation, that sort of thing. And, you know, another aspect of it I guess would be that you'd want to make sure that you *had* time to . . . you know, do some socializing.

P22:   Mm-hm.

T23:   To, maybe . . . After all, one of the advantages of being retired is that you can . . . spend time doing recreation.

P23:   That's right.

T24:   That kind of thing.

P24:   As long as you're healthy enough to do that.

T25:   Mm-hm. But . . . on the other hand, it seems like . . . there are other things . . . that you want to be able to have a sense of building, or of accomplishment.

P25:   Yeah, I've got to, I've got to really sort of pinpoint what I really want to do because my mind whirls around . . . doing this, this, this, this, and . . . uh . . .

T26:   Well, what . . . ?

P26:   And I don't think that you can . . .

T27:   Mm-hm.

P27:   You can (*sighs*) do a good job at everything that you want to do, you know.

T28:   Mm-hm, mm-hm. Well, what are the things that you've been considering?

P28:   Nothing specific, it's just that my mind is just whirling around . . .

T29: Well, where does it whirl?

P29: Well, first the volunteer stuff, that, that part . . .

T30: Mm-hm. Any particular kind of volunteer?

P30: No, I hadn't really thought about any kind of volunteer work, and I've been sort of . . . I don't know, I don't know whether I want to work with the elderly or the children . . .

T31: Mm-hm.

P31: Sometimes I think I'd like to work with the elderly, and, you know, then I think maybe I'd rather work with children, so I have to make up my own mind about that.

T32: Mm-hm.

P32: And I think that . . . I haven't really . . . gone into it, I think the senior citizens do have a program . . . for volunteer work too, so that . . .

T33: Hm.

P33: I might be into something there.

T34: Mm-hm.

P34: As I get better acquainted.

T35: Mm-hm. So one possibility would be to do some . . . volunteer work, which I guess would be satisfying in the sense that . . .

P35: Yeah, if it's just one day a week, I think it would sort of satisfy me . . .

T36: Mm-hm, mm-hm.

P36: I think this woman I was talking about, I think she started with one day and decided she had to go two days, because she enjoyed it, and they . . . really looked forward to having her come.

T37: Mm-hm.

P37: So it sort of gives her a sense of being needed, and accomplishing something too

T38: Mm-hm. Then another whole idea, though is the area of—I guess learning more: I'm going to still be curious about things, and . . .

P38: Yeah.

T39: Want to . . . ?

P39: Yeah, I certainly don't want to just sit in a chair and watch television. I don't . . . watch that much television anyway. Nothing much on, you know?

1. Generic strategies and techniques used in this transcript include:
   a. Suggestions of how to change
   b. Self-disclosure
   c. Role-playing
   d. Positive reinforcement

2. ECBIS strategies and techniques used in this transcript include:
   a. Reconstructing emotional schemes
   b. Identifying and challenging distorted beliefs
   c. Modifying and alter interpersonal scripts
   d. No ECBIS strategies and techniques

Reprinted with permission from Klerman, G. L., Weissman, M. M., Rounsaville, B. J., & Chevron, E. S. (1984). *Interpersonal psychotherapy of depression* (pp. 178–182). New York: Basic Books.

X.

The patient was a career woman in her late thirties, who sought psychotherapy for feelings of anxiety and depression that has persisted for several years.

T1:   What comes to mind about why you would respond automatically that way as opposed to some other way?

P1:   Because I think that's the way I was treated.

T2:   By whom?

P2:   Primarily by my mother.

T3:   Your mother would yell at you and criticize you.

P3:   She was a very criticizing person, very critical, and I am aware of that and I'm aware of how critical I am a lot of times in the relationship to my husband and my children and everybody, and that bothers me and I've tried to work on it. I've made some progress slowly and I don't want my children to grow up being criticized all the time. I have to work very hard to praise them for things they do that are worthy of praise.

T4:   You feel you didn't get much praise from your mother?

P4:   Yeah.

T5:   How was your father different?

P5:   He wasn't a very critical person and he didn't have a lot to do with disciplining us on a day-to-day basis. He would get involved periodically. I can remember being spanked by him one time and that was because I told a lie. He asked me if I washed my hands and I hadn't and I told him I had. And he would say things like "don't talk back to your mother," if I said something wrong, snippy. He would always support her and not allow us to act that way toward her. But mother is the one who would pick the switch off the bush and switch us if we did something that annoyed her. I don't remember getting a lot of spankings. It was a lot more verbal: "Why did you do that? You shouldn't have done that."

T6:   So on a day-to-day basis you felt that you were constantly under the gun of mother's criticism and didn't get much support, much praise, and it sounds like you might have liked father to be on your side and balance it but he wouldn't. He was kind of in the background or he took mother's side.

P6:   Supporting her, yeah.

T7:   You felt kind of ganged up on.

P7:   The way I think of him is he set the standards for what—I think this is right, this is my perception but I may be wrong—for how things were. But mother was the enforcer.

T8:   But what happened if you tried to stand up to mother? Talk back?

P8:   Well, I was told I couldn't talk like that or mother would hang up the phone on me, wouldn't allow me to continue, or the conversation would be cut off. She would leave the room.

T9:   What about father?

P9:   I never got into any confrontations with dad that I can remember.

T10: Why not?

P10: I don't know why not. It seems like it always came from mother. The decisions were made and partly because probably he wasn't there some of the time and he never seemed to be that much involved in the arguments, about what was going on, and I don't know why.

T11: So your experience was that if you tried to stand up for yourself, talk back when you were getting criticized, or there was an argument, that if you did you'd be—mother would turn away from you, and you'd just be left there.

P11:   Or she'd just say, "I don't want to hear any more. That's the end of it. I don't want to talk about it anymore. I said no." Period.

T12:   Do you think that influences your fear of speaking out to your husband? That he'd do the same thing except maybe even worse?

P12:   Well, I think it probably is my preconditioned pattern of response and there've been times when we have gotten into confrontations and he really overpowers me and I back off. I get really upset with that kind of force.

T13:   I would say, "you ought to get out of that relationship," and you would say, "I'm not so sure," and I would get angry and what do you imagine would happen? How would that hurt you?

P13:   I don't know how it would hurt me except the anger. I guess I just have this thing about anger. Just from our last meeting when I said, "When did you want to get started," and you said, "Right away," I felt really pushed. I wanted to say, "No I've got to wait a couple of weeks," but I didn't say that. But you said, "I'd like to get started right away." And that made me nervous for some reason. I don't know why. Maybe because I was still feeling a little unsure about the whole thing. Part of it too is because I know my schedule is like unreal this week and next week. But I felt when you said, "I want to get started right away," I felt pressured. And I think I probably thought, "Okay what other kinds of pressures are you going to lay out on me that I'm not going to be able to say, Stop, wait a minute I can't deal with that or that's not for me."

T14:   Well it sounds like, looking back over and kind of pulling together what you've talked about today, our earlier interchange about getting started right away stirred up in you a feeling that once again you were going to be caught in a situation that is very familiar for you, where you were feeling like either the wife being dragged along with things that she didn't want to do but had to for fear of something even worse happening, or like a child—"this is the way it's going to be and I don't want to hear anything from you." Like you experienced when you were a kid. And once again this would happen again here with me. And the only way you would have, the most comfortable way at this point that you would have in dealing with that, is to try to kind of pull back, not speak up about it, but protect yourself and draw back.

P14:   That's my pattern.

T15:   Which maybe is what's behind your concerns about can you afford it, can you fit it in your schedule. All of these things that are very reasonable, and behind that is really, "Are you going to hurt me, are you going to get angry at me if I don't want to do what you want me to do?"

P15:   Well, I think I have a fear of being boxed in.

T16:   That really seems like an important area to explore, why it is that—I think we looked today at some of the things that make you feel boxed in. You're being pressured or that you feel like you're being told this is the way it's going to be by someone who's important to you, whether it's your husband, your parents when you were a kid, and you feel pressured. But it doesn't explain why you feel so overwhelmed by it. That you're boxed in, you can't do anything about it, you can't stand up for yourself. That might be an important area to explore. When we talked before about one of the characteristics of this kind of therapy is to try to find a circumscribed area of primary importance emotionally and look at that carefully and this certainly seems like that kind of an area. It's what brought you in, or an important part of what brought you in, and we also saw it emerge immediately in our relationship.

P16:   Yeah, I thought about—well I couldn't really talk when you called me at home the other night because everything was just in a mess, but I thought about calling you at home and I thought, no I don't want to do that because he might not like it. (laugh)

T17: Yell at you?

P17: Well, I don't know what I thought. I don't think I thought you'd yell at me. I don't have that perception yet of you. (*laugh*) I just—and then I'd wake up at night and stew around.

T18: Call me to tell me what?

P18: To tell you I was feeling really uneasy about this whole thing. I had some questions that I didn't feel like I'd settled and couldn't we wait. Put it off a couple of weeks. (*laughs*)

T19: How do you feel now?

P19: Well, I feel a little better except I still don't have some of my questions answered.

1. Generic strategies and techniques used in this transcript include:

   a. Turning stumbling blocks into stepping stones
   b. Positive reinforcement
   c. Role playing
   d. Defining dysfunctional patterns

2. ECBIS strategies and techniques used in this transcript include:

   a. Maintaining the reorganized emotion schemes
   b. Disputing irrational beliefs
   c. Changing reinforcers to change behavior
   d. Identifying the patient's interpersonal patterns within the therapeutic relationship

Reprinted with permission from Strupp, H., & Binder, J. L. (1984). *Psychotherapy in a new key* (pp. 200–205). New York: Basic Books.

FORM 19–1

Case Vignettes for Change Strategies

Name (optional)_____   Date_____

The following are case vignettes. Please read and think about which generic and ECBIS strategies and techniques should be used for this given patient. As you answer the questions, you may need to review Appendices II and III. Here is an example:

- -

A 33-year-old pharmacist reported that she did not want to return to work because she did not trust her supervisors. She was afraid they would deny her request for pharmacy technicians if she needed the technicians. She had not asked yet, so the did not know whether her request for the technicians would be denied. She recognized her fear as unfounded, yet she could not help feeling intensely anxious. She wanted a new job somewhere else.

Her mother had been diagnosed with schizophrenia when the patient was six years old. Her father became dependent upon her to take care of her younger siblings. She felt an intense loss of adequate parenting. She felt her needs as a child had been ignored.

The feelings about her supervisors had begun when she returned home for Christmas. Six weeks later, when she saw the therapist, she had not been able to shake the intense anxiety about her supervisors.

The generic strategies and techniques that might be used for this patient are:

Relinquish the dysfunctional patterns:

1. Defining well-formed patterns with the patient and confirming that the patterns are dysfunctional. For this patient, her dysfunctional pattern is that she thinks people in authority over her will ignore her needs; she fears being rejected by them. With a good working alliance, therapist and patient could arrive at this well-formed pattern by questioning.
2. Separating past from present relationship. The patient's fear obviously originated from her early relationship with her parents. Although she is an adult, her fear of being ignored has remained. The therapist could help the patient be aware that she is responding with a past feeling to a present reality.
3. Challenging dysfunctional emotion. This can be done by examining her irrational fear.

Initiate a functional pattern:

1. Suggesting how to change. The therapist may give very specific suggestions for the patient in order to help her initiate change. The therapist can encourage the patient to ask her the supervisors if she can have a technician. If this is too hard for the patient, the therapist can help her think about other less fearful situations in which to practice asking authority figures for help.
2. Face fear. This strategy is related to the previous one. The suggestion should focus on facing fear of being ignored or rejected.

Maintain the functional patterns:

1. Working through. If the patient completes the practice in one situation, the therapist can encourage her to practice the new behavior and thinking in other situations.
2. Positive reinforcement: The patient generally will report her new experiences after she has changed. The therapist can then use the patient's positive response to the new experience to reinforce the patient's change, compliment her, or help her to generate new and encouraging self-talk.

There are still other generic strategies and techniques we can use between the substages of change. These include: taking responsibility (once the patient is aware that her fear originated from her parents' behaviors, she might think she can't change or else blame her parents, so encouraging the patient to take responsibility is the prerequisite to initiating change), corrective experience (the patient might regard the therapist as an authority and anticipate the therapist refusing and ignoring her; the therapist's unexpected supportive reactions to her needs will facilitate change), or role play new behaviors with herself in the two roles of supervisor and self.

The ECBIS strategies and techniques might be:

Emotion:

Evoking the emotion in the session in order to understand her fear:

1. Exploring "unfinished business"—empty chair. This technique allows the patient to reexperience the unresolved feelings in a safe environment in order to access the next step, "reconstructing emotional schemes." For this patient, she can put her father into the empty chair, and the therapist can help her reexperience and express her fear, hurt, and anger at being ignored.
2. Or the enactment of conflict splits (two chairs) in order to reexperience her inner conflict in asking for a technician from her supervisors.

Reconstructuring emotional schemes:

The therapist can help the patient to access new information through emotional awareness, reconceptualizing her internal experience and confronting feared emotions in a safe situation.

Cognition:

Identifying and challenging the dysfunctional belief:

1. Questioning the evidence. The patient thinks that the people in authority over her will ignore her needs and reject her. The therapist can challenge this belief by questioning the evidence with the patient.
2. Reality-testing. The patient thinks her supervisors will refuse her need for a technician, although she has not asked them. The therapist can help the patient to test this belief by encouraging her to bring up her need to her supervisors. (If refused by her supervisors, she can then examine which reasons are most likely realistic.)

Creating adaptive reasonable beliefs by allowing new information that is discrepant with previous beliefs to enter (one's) processing:

1. Developing alternatives. Help the patient understand other possible reasons for being rejected by her supervisors, such as, they might think it is not the right time to hire a technician, they don't have enough money to hire somebody else, they have not found the appropriate candidate, or they believe in her competence to do the work.
2. Fantasizing the consequence. Help the patient to imagine and verbalize what will happen if she tells her supervisors she wants a technician and they refuse. In doing this, the patient can see the irrational fears and thoughts and the therapist can work with the patient to access the realistic reaction.

Repeating or practicing the modified belief:

Help the patient practice her new beliefs and her new self-talk in various situations.

Behavior:

Defining the maladaptive behaviors: her fear responses and avoidance behavior.

Changing reinforcement to control behavior:

Help the patient overcome avoidance behavior (avoiding asking for her needs) by desensitization, relaxation training, and assertion training.

Practice new behavior (she can express her need when she wants) *in various situations.*

Interpersonal/psychodynamic

Identifying the maladaptive interpersonal schema:

Since the patient may repeat her interpersonal pattern with the therapist, the therapist can use the here-and-now relationship to clarify the patient's maladaptive interpersonal schema. (She didn't trust people who are in authority over her, and she is afraid of bringing up her needs to these people because she fears being ignored.) She can discover how these responses originated in childhood.

Modifying and altering an interpersonal script:

1. The therapist can use the here-and-now relationship to provide the patient with new and constructive interpersonal experiences.
2. The therapist can use the here-and-now relationship to help the patient rewrite and correct the assumption underlying her scenarios: Any people in authority over me will ignore my needs.

Practice the modified role:

1. The therapist needs to maintain consistent and reliable behavior (keep caring about her needs in the therapeutic relationship) to disconfirm her false assumptions about interpersonal reality.
2. Generalizing the experience with the therapist to other interpersonal relationships, especially relationships with those she regards as authorities.
3. Reinforcement from new interpersonal success.

System:

Because this case vignette does not provide enough information about her family, possible system strategies are limited.

From this exercise, we can see that the therapist can use different strategies and techniques to help the same patient. As we stated in the module 4 text, the therapist can approach the patient from different orientations. We can't tell which approach is best, and success depends on many factors. In psychotherapy reality, one strategy or technique sometimes initiating change, and so using several strategies and techniques isn't always better than using just one. This exercise can help us to think about how different strategies can help the same patient and how ECBIS strategies overlap.

1. A 23-year-old student entered therapy for depression. She reported having had four different roommates, but each of them had left her. She worries now that her fifth roommate will also leave her. She complained that none of them cared about her. She reported that, "one day I felt a little stomach pain and lay in bed. My roommate should have thought that I was hungry and needed something to eat. But she didn't ask me." As therapy progressed, she continued to ask the therapist to allow her to call and come to see him whenever she needed because she had so much pain and couldn't bear it. When the therapist asked: "What if I am seeing another patient or I am doing other things when you come without an appointment?" The patient replied: "I don't think other patients are in greater pain than I am. Helping me is more important than your 'other things'." What will you do?

_____

_____

_____

_____

_____

_____

_____

_____

_____

2. A high school teacher was criticized by one of her colleagues in front of other teachers. Since then she has had trouble sleeping and concentrating at work. She has become depressed. Two years earlier she had been in a car accident that had injured her brain sufficiently to require that she enter a brain injury treatment program lasting three months. She was able to return to work as a teacher; however, she noticed she required more time to prepare the same lessons for her class. She also noticed that, since the accident criticisms of her work by students, parents and other teachers bothered her much more than they had before the accident. How might you help her?

_____

_____

_____

_____

_____

_____

Form 18-2

Transcripts for Change Strategies

Name (optional) _____   Date _____

The following pages are transcripts. Each transcript is followed by the following questions: (1) Which generic strategies and techniques were used in that transcript? (2) Which ECBIS strategies/techniques were used in the transcript? There are four answers (a,b,c, and d) for each of these questions, but *only one* is the best. Please circle the answer you think best fits that question. As you answer these questions, please review Figure 4–1 and Table 4–1 for reference. Try to get a general sense for the substages and general and specific strategies for your responses.

I.

C1:   I've been looking forward to coming, much more than I did the other times, I've had a crummy week. My job is really bad, and I'm tired of my house, and everything seems flat like I'm just watching, I'm not in it. And I know it's me.

T1:   So everything seems flat and you're not involved in it, just watching. But you know it isn't the job and so on, it's you.

C2:   Well, the job really is bad, what they're doing in that place isn't right, but other times I'd be able to do something with it, I know.

T2:   So, it's true what you feel about them, but also, the way you're being inside you is not OK.

C3:   Yes.

T3:   So we have to go see where your good energy went to. (*long silence*)

C4:   I have lots of energy there, but it's tied up.

T4:   You can feel your energy right there, but it's tied up.

C5:   Yes.

T5:   Can you sense what's tying up? (*long silence*)

C6:   It's like a heavy wall in front of it. It's behind that.

T6:   You can feel a heavy wall. (*long silence*)

C7:   It's whole part of me that I keep in. Yes, a whole part of me, like when I say it's OK when it's not. The way I hold everything in. (*long silence*) There's a part of me that's dead, and a part that isn't.

T7:   Two parts, one is dead, and one . . . ah

C8:   Survived. (*silence*) It wants to scream, to live.

T8:   The dead part wants to scream and be let out.

C9:   And there's also something vague, I can't get what that is.

T9:   Make a space for that vague thing, you don't know what it is yet. There's something vague there, but it isn't clear what it is.

C10: I feel a lot of tension.

T10: OK, take a break. Just step back a little bit. There's the vague thing, and then also, there's the tension.

Let's talk a little. You've come a lot of steps. (*C relaxes, shifts in the chair.*) Yes, that's right. Let the body get whole again, when we come a long way there have to be little breaks.

C11: It's hard to take a breaks.

T11: That's why I'm talking, I'm just saying anything so you can have a break.

C12: Yes, I'm getting a break because I'm listening to what you're saying. (*shifts again*) Now I'm going back.

T12: There was a vague thing, and tension.

C13: It's like I want to run.

T13: Step back just a little step, and be next to the wanting to run. (*long silence*)

C14: Someone will get mad at me if I let that part live, and that's very uncomfortable.

T14: If you let that live, someone will be mad at you, and that's hard to stand.

C15: Yes. (*long silence*) I want to run and never go back, and just be free.

T15: You want to run, just not look back, go free. (*silence*)

C16: Then that's sad.

T16: Somehow it feels sad, if you run and don't look back.

C17: Yes. Running from the vague thing is sad. Some of me wants to find out what the vague thing is. (*long silence*) Some of me doesn't.

T17: You can feel a part of you that doesn't want to find out, and a part that does. (*C looks angry.*) Be friendly to this place, just step back a little bit, like, OK this could take a while, it's OK if it takes a week to find out, slowly. Make room for a part that doesn't want to find out, a part that does.

C18: I don't feel friendly. I want to jump on it.

T18: Yes, that's what I thought. Well, make a space for the anger too. The anger gets to be here too. Just don't let it get on this thing. Let the anger flow through.

C19: I'm very angry.

T19: Lots of anger. (*long silence*)

C20: It's a big loss, something missing. That's what the vague thing was.

T20: A big loss. Something big missing. (*long silence*)

C21: And my energy is right there too.

T21: So that's also where your energy is. It is there with the vague thing that turned out to be a big loss of something big, missing.

C22: Yes, I feel lighter!

T22: It feels better.

C23: Yes, I don't know what that is yet, that's missing, but even though I don't know what it is, I feel lighter. I feel all right inside myself again.

1. Generic strategies and techniques used in this transcript include:
   a. Challenging dysfunctional beliefs, behaviors, and emotions and suggestion of how to change
   b. Inquiring into reasons for and/or advantages of change
   c. Separating past from present
   d. Reframing

2. ECBIS strategies and techniques used in this transcript include:
   a. Evoking emotion in the session and restructuring emotional schemes
   b. Fantasizing consequences

   c. Assertion training

   d. Identifying the patient's interpersonal patterns within the therapeutic relationship

Reprinted with permission from Rice, L. N., & Greenberg, L. S. (1984). *Patterns of change* (pp. 235–237). New York: Guilford.

II.

In the Reynolds family, the parents, Vera and George, have two married children and a younger daughter, Martha, a 17-year-old anorectic who alternates starvation and food binges. The parents see themselves as concerned people, who have been successful with the older children and are trying their best with the identified patient. Martha spends a large part of her life monitoring the parents' nontalking and trying to meet the mother's and father's needs for companionship. Minuchin is the therapist.

Minuchin 1:	(*to mother*): What do you do?
Mother 1:	I work for the city.
Minuchin 2:	That means it's a nine-to-five job?
Mother 2:	Yes.
Minuchin 3:	Do you have any help?
Mother 3:	No. I never did. Recently my husband has been helping me.
Martha 1:	Mom, that's a lie and you know that. I've always helped you. I've done the dishes and vacuumed or washed the floor when I'm home on my summer vacation, and I put supper in the oven before you come home.
Mother 4:	Martha, don't get all hyper now—
Martha 2:	You said you had no help and that's what I—
Mother 5:	Sometimes I did get help. When I asked for help, I got it, Martha.
Martha 3:	Other times you didn't ask and I helped.
Father 1:	Martha was helping quite a bit.
Mother 6:	Okay, she was. She was making supper sometimes. But don't say it like she did it routinely every night. She did not.
Father 2:	For a while there, it was pretty routine.
Martha 4:	It was.
Mother 7:	It was. Right until she started getting real bad.
Minuchin 4:	Vera, do you find that George and Martha sometimes team up and put you down? Martha, just now, got kind of hepped and kicked you.
Mother 8:	I don't care. She does that a lot.
Minuchin 5:	And then what happened with George
Mother 9:	He came to her rescue.
Father 3:	Did I?
Minuchin 6:	Yes, you did here. Absolutely you did. He does this at home?
Mother 10:	He does that at home now that you mention it. Yes. Because when I used to reprimand her and scold her, he would tell me to be quiet and to stop the noise and leave her alone. He always came to her defense.

Father 4:	That works both ways, too. Sometimes I would also tell Martha not to bother Mother at certain times of the day. I'm just trying to keep a happy medium. I'm sitting in the background. I'm just watching.
Minuchin 7:	Vera says that she experiences you being more in Martha's corner than in hers. (*to Martha*) Are you very frail? I saw you taking Mom out very easily. You were not afraid of taking her on. You didn't need his help.
Martha 5:	No.
Minuchin 8:	No. Does that happen frequently that Dad feels that his weight will help you if you are in an argument with Mother? Will he try to make peace by joining with you?
Martha 6:	No, not really. He'll just tell me, like, "Simmer down and leave her alone," or "Why don't you stop bothering her, let her do what she wants," or whatever, and then I feel guilty because my mother gets hurt in the situation, and I don't want anybody to be hurt.
Father 5:	Don't get the wrong impression there. You've got the impression that I'm always doing this. No. Very seldom do I speak up.
Martha 6:	But when he does, that's how it works.
Father 6:	I don't want to see two people arguing foolishly. It's a foolish argument. If I'm sitting in one room and I hear an argument going on in the kitchen and I feel it's foolish—one will say one thing, another one will say another thing—it's nothing constructive, it's foolish—and they're both getting hot under the collar about it, naturally, I'll step in.
Minuchin 9:	So, you are a referee?
Father 7:	You might call it that.
Minuchin 10 (*to mother*):	Why would he do a thing like that? Do you get hurt easily?
Mother 11:	I used to. I've got a shell on me now.
Father 8:	We have a pillar of fire here (*pointing to wife*) and we have a pillar of fire here (*pointing to daughter*). We have two positives. They are very outspoken, both of them.
Minuchin 11:	George, is it necessary to monitor their fights?
Father 9:	No, it's not necessary, but I feel I should step in before somebody says something they will be sorry for later on.
Minuchin 12:	You don't like a fight in your family?
Father 10:	No, I don't.
Minuchin 13:	What about between you and Vera?
Mother 12:	We don't talk.
Father 11:	If I feel a fight coming on, my wife gets excited or I get excited—but she'll get excited more than me, and then she'll get excited more and more up to a point where I feel I better stop—I just get up and either walk out of the house or walk into another room just to stop it.
Minuchin 4:	And that works?
Father 12:	It works, but then she's mad at me for a couple of days. She won't talk to me.

Mother 13:	We've gone where you don't talk to me for a month and I give you the same treatment.
Minuchin 15 (*to Martha*):	What do you do then?
Martha 7 (*laughing*):	Well, I withdraw into my own world. It's more safe and secure there.
Minuchin 16:	That means then Mom is in her corner, Dad is in his corner, and you go into your corner? Great family! How do you get out of it? Don't you try to talk with Mom or with Dad or try to patch it up?
Martha 8:	Sure, I try to, but it is very uncomfortable. They're not talking with each other, and then I feel I've done something because my mother, without realizing it, accidentally might snap at me for something. I figure what did I do and I just better keep quiet, and I'll go into my own world and not have to worry about getting rejected again by them—by their snapping at me.
Father 13:	Martha, I don't snap at you.
Martha 9:	No, Mom does though. But my father will always talk to me, though. It's like, "Well, if your mother doesn't want to talk, that's fine." He'll just say something like that. But then I feel guilty, because I should be doing something. I'm living in the same house and I should be making them have a more pleasant life. You know, I have to make them talk and enjoy their life.
Minuchin 17:	And are you successful?
Martha 10:	No. So I punish myself for this and go on a binge.
Minuchin 18:	Then is that helpful?
Martha 11:	Well, to me it is. It just temporarily relieves the problems. It's like alcohol or drugs. It doesn't solve anything.
Minuchin 19:	So, I see here two therapists already—Father, who when you are fighting with Mom, tries to put oil on rough waters, and you, who try to monitor and help these people. And you are not a very good therapist. You are not very successful.
Martha 12:	I can't. They won't let me. They say, "Mind your own business."
Mother 14:	It's none of your business what goes on between us.
Martha 13:	That, to me, is a rejection, because I feel I'm part of the family. I should be doing something.
Minuchin 20:	How long have you been trying to cure them?
Martha 14:	I never thought about it. Now that I think about it, it's about the time the anorexia started.
Minuchin 21:	That means for four or five years you have been trying to cure them.
Martha 15:	Yeah.
Minuchin 22:	Oh, my girl, you need better techniques than the ones that you have. In four or five years, you should have changed them. (*to parents*) She tries to heal you. She tries to bring happiness to you, and she's just not good at that. (*to daughter*) Have you ever tried to get some training in how to increase harmony and happiness?
Martha 16:	No. The only thing I would ever do is ask them, "Why aren't you talking?" "It's none of your business." Then I feel they're uncomfortable by my trying to do anything. So I wasn't even much thinking of myself as a therapist before, but now I think I can help this family.

Minuchin 23:	Maybe not a therapist, but a healer. Somebody who tries to bring harmony and happiness in a family. I would like you, Martha, to talk with your parents about the ways in which they frustrate your attempts to help them.
Martha 17 (*to parents*):	How am I going to say this so it makes sense, so you can understand it? It's like I have to go on a guilt trip because you aren't talking. You're my parents and I love you, but if you don't love each other, I feel guilty, and I can't live my life unless I know you're happy. You see, you try to hid it. Like you say it's your own business, but still it isn't your business because I live in the same house and I have to see this. It's not the fighting, it's the not talking that bothers me.
Mother 15:	We don't get into arguments that way.
Martha 18:	Well, see how it's affected me? I see you don't talk to people, so I go to school and I figure, subconsciously, I can't talk to people. I don't know how to, you know. If I heard you having a conflict and resolving it, then I could learn from that, you know.
Mother 16:	But, Martha, it's taken us thirty years to arrive at this attitude that we have—thirty-three years.
Martha 19:	But the thing is I can't be happy unless I know you're happy.
Mother 17:	But I'm happy in my little world and your father's happy in his little world.
Parents:	And you should be happy in your little world.
Martha 20:	Do you think it could be better? I know you don't want it to be better, but could it be?
Minuchin 24:	You see, it's a very interesting thing what Martha is saying. She is saying that you really need her very badly because you, together, cannot hack it.
Martha 21:	I feel that I'm bringing you happiness in some way, you know.
Minuchin 25:	I don't think your parents understand you. I don't think that they understood what you just said.
Martha 22:	Neither do I.
Minuchin 26:	I don't think that they are hearing you. You are saying something very simple. You are saying that unless you can help them, they cannot make it.

The therapist has been egging the identified patient on to continue her job as her parents' healer for over fifteen minutes. In the process, the identified patient addresses herself to the parents as a couple, instead of pursuing her usual negotiation with each of them separately. The parents respond—sometimes annoyed, at times placating—as a holon. The therapeutic construction's exaggeration is intended to produce the parents' rejection of the girl's help and to create distance from her.

Minuchin 27:	Talk with Dad and talk with Mom.
Martha 23:	It's things like—you guys figure that's your life and I should just stay out of it. Is that how you feel? Is that what you're trying to tell me?
Mother 18:	Um-hum.
Martha 24:	I don't understand it. None of it makes any sense.
Minuchin 27:	You see, my feeling is, Martha, that your parents know that they need you. You couldn't have such a strong feeling toward helping them unless they are telling you—

Martha 25:	That they want it.
Minuchin 28:	That they want it. How does your mother tell you that she likes you to help? They must be doing it in some way. I don't know that they know how they do it, but they must be doing it. They must be telling you in some way. How do they do it?
Minuchin 29:	Martha, you are really an exploited little girl. You are pretty, you are seventeen, and you don't have a boy friend. Do you have many girl friends?
Martha 26:	No, I won't be close to anybody. I'm too afraid. I can't do that.
Father 14:	You had a close girl friend once.
Martha 27:	Who? No, I'm not close to her. No.
Father 15:	That's your closest girl friend though.
Mother 19:	She was your closest girl friend.
Father 16:	You went on vacations together—
Minuchin 30 (*to parents*):	Hold it a moment.
Martha 28:	How do they know I'm close to her? How can they say that? How can they say that?
Minuchin 31:	That is one of the ways in which they pull you. Just now, you were telling me something about your life and then—
Martha 29:	They think they know about it.
Minuchin 31:	They entered and they are pulling you. You see, I am concerned that you will never, never leave your home.
Minuchin 32 (to mother):	How old are you?
Mother 20:	Fifty-four.
Minuchin 33:	Fifty-four. So probably you have what—25 more years of life?
Mother 21:	If I'm lucky.
Minuchin 34:	If you are going to 80. And how old are you, George?
Father 17:	Fifty-four.
Minuchin 35:	Okay. So, maybe—how old are you, Martha? Seventeen. They will die around 80, so you have 25 years to remain at home. So, 25 and 17—you will be a very immature, 42-year-old single woman when you are ready to leave home.
Martha 30:	No, I don't want that to happen.
Minuchin 36:	I think that will happen, because they are busy asking you to help them to become happier. And you are spending all of your time looking at your dad and your mom. You look so much at them that you don't have time to look elsewhere. Don't you want to have a boy friend?
Martha 31:	I'm too afraid. I don't want to go out of the house.
Minuchin 37:	Oh, that is—that means—you are saying that you are using them also? They are using you and you are using them?
Martha 32:	Yeah, this one kid keeps calling me, and I tell my father to tell him I'm not home. And he does; he says, "Oh, you just missed her. She just walked out the door."
Minuchin 38:	That means you use them to defend yourself against the world outside.
Martha 33:	These are my weapons.

Minuchin 39:   You are a very interesting family. It's very, very interesting, because clearly she uses you also. I thought that you used her, but she uses you.

1. Generic strategies and techniques used in this transcript include:
   a. Working through
   b. Positive reinforcement
   c. Generating alternatives
   d. Defining dysfunctional patterns and challenge dysfunctional thoughts and behaviors
2. ECBIS strategies and techniques used in this transcript include:
   a. Helping the patient access new information through emotional awareness
   b. Identifying and challenging the distorted beliefs and creating adaptive beliefs
   c. Defining the maladaptive behaviors and changing reinforcers to control behavior
   d. Identifying the dysfunctional dynamic interactions among family members (enactment of situations in the family)

Reprinted with permission from Minuchin, S. & Fishman, H. C. (1981). *Family therapy techniques* (pp. 234–242). Cambridge, MA: Harvard University Press.

III.

The patient, a 35-year-old foreman for a construction company, was referred from the general medical clinic because no physical basis could be found for the gastrointestinal symptoms that were troubling him. The following transcript is excerpted from session 3. Shirley is the patient's wife.

T15:   Well, how are things going since I last saw you?

P1:   Pretty good. I don't have those stomach-aches much anymore.

T2:   But you do have them sometimes?

P2:   I still get some twinges when I first get home, but I tell myself it's nerves and try to relax.

T3:   Relax?

P3:   Instead of going right in the house I stay in the back yard a little bit. Smoke a cigarette and fool around with the flowers. That's sort of my hobby. I've planted most everything we have back there. I got some nice rosebushes, but you really have to watch it with roses. They're like kids—you have to feed them right, when they get sick give them medicine. Next year, though, I'm going to put in some vegetables too—tomatoes, beans. Maybe we can save some money, everything is so high at the store.

T4:   Your sister-in-law and her kids don't upset you so anymore?

P4:   I've got to hand it to Shirley, she's really trying to make things better. Now she gets supper ready on time and, anyway, they leave pretty soon after I get home. Sometimes they're even gone by the time I get there.

T5:   It does sound as if your wife is trying to accommodate your needs. Yet as I mentioned last time, you have indicated that you felt she wasn't that interested in you as a person.

P5:   I thought a little about that too after I left last time. I asked Shirley about it when we were talking about her sister the other night; we're talking more now and it's sort of nice. She was telling me some funny story Grace had told her about the people at her office and I said, "You know all about everybody at her office, but I'll bet you ten dollars you can't even tell me the name of my two bosses at the company." She started to get mad at me then and said there was no talking to me when I always came in with a chip on my shoulder. If she asked anything about my day I'd snarl and tell her she wouldn't understand anyway. So how should she know what I did or who I did it with. Then she clouded up and it looked like we were going to have a fight right then and there, but I told her she was probably right, that I didn't mean to be like that, and I've tried to change things. She cried a little, but not angry-like, and told me she could tell I was trying.

T6:   You've been trying to change your behavior with your wife in some ways?

P6:   I'm really trying to talk to her now. If something bothered me at work I tell her about it. I think she doesn't really understand it all, but it feels better to have talked about it to someone anyway.

T7:   It sounds as if you really are on the right track to a much better relationship with your wife and to a better feeling about yourself. Once you've surmounted a problem it's often easier to look back and get an understanding of how it developed in the first place. I get the impression that your feeling that she didn't care about you was based on lack of communication between the two of you.

P7:   I think you've got it there, Doc. We weren't communicating. I wouldn't tell her what was wrong or what I wanted from her. Maybe I expected her to understand me without saying anything.

T8:   Like the expectations a child has of its mother.

P8:   Not my mother!

T9:   Oh?

P9:   No, I always thought she had too many troubles of her own to pay attention to mine. I remember once I got hurt on my bike and came to her all bloodied up. When she saw me she got mad and yelled at me for making more trouble for her when she already had her hands full with my father.

T10: Do you remember how you felt them?

P10: I can't remember, but I know that after that I never brought my troubles to her again.

T11: How old were you?

P11: Nine. I know that because I got that bike for my ninth birthday. It was a little too big for me still, that's why I got hurt on it.

T12: Perhaps you carried this attitude into your marriage.

P12: What attitude?

T13: The feeling that your wife, like your mother, would be unsympathetic to your difficulties. That there was no point in telling her about your experiences because she was too preoccupied or too busy to care.

P13: She's so different from my mother. I come first with her.

T14: On one level you know that. On another, deeper level there may well be the fear that people—or maybe only women, or maybe only women you're close to—are all the same, and you can't take a chance of being rejected again in your need.

P14: Maybe you're right Doc, but all that was so long ago, and I should be over that by now.

T15: That's not the way the mind works. If a shock or a disappointment is strong enough it can permanently freeze our picture of ourselves and our expectations of the world. The rest of us grows up—that is, we let ourselves learn about life from experience and from what we see, hear, or read of the experiences of others, but that one area where we really got hurt stays unchanged. So what I mean when I say you might be carrying that attitude into your relationship with your wife is that when it comes to your hopes of being understood and catered to when you feel hurt or abused by life, you still feel very much like that nine-year-old boy who was rebuffed in his need and gave up hope that anyone would or could respond to him.

1. Generic strategies and techniques used in this transcript include:
   a. Separating past from present and positive reinforcement
   b. Suggestions of how to change
   c. Defining dysfunctional patterns
   d. Self-disclosure

2. ECBIS strategies and techniques used in this transcript include:
   a. Helping the patient rewrite, modify and correct the assumptions underlying his scenarios and practice modified roles: reinforcement from new interpersonal success
   b. Creating adaptive beliefs by disputing irrational beliefs
   c. Catharsis
   d. Modeling

Reprinted with permission from Basch, M. D. (1980). *Doing psychotherapy* (pp. 27–30). New York: Basic Books.

IV.

Paula was a 17-year-old high school senior who had recently been invited to go on a skiing weekend with several friends. After much thought and family discussion, her parents had finally agreed to let her go on this "first of its kind" excursion. A few days later, both Paula and her parents became aware that the ski trip was to be unchaperoned. Learning this, her parents reversed themselves and told Paula she could not go. Paula felt both embarrassed and relieved. She also thought she felt insulted that her parents did not trust her enough, but she was not really sure about this latter reaction. In the counseling session following this development, Paula wanted to talk about her conflicting feelings. The counselor suggested that Paula begin as the insulted self and talk to the relieved self.

Insulted Paula:	I am so upset by this whole matter. I don't know why my parents would do this to me. Don't they trust me?
Relieved Paula:	Trusting you isn't what they are thinking about. After all, you didn't tell them the trip wouldn't be chaperoned.
Insulted Paula:	I didn't know. They didn't tell me that. And whose side are you on, anyhow?
Relieved Paula:	I'm not on their side, if that's what you mean. But it would be pretty uncomfortable with this bunch of kids at the ski lodge and no adults around in case someone got hurt.
Counselor:	Excuse me just a moment. Why don't you ask the other Paula why she's feeling so good about this decision?
Insulted Paula:	Okay, why aren't you mad, too? Didn't you want to go on this ski trip?
Relieved Paula:	Yes, I wanted to go, but I didn't want it to be so complicated. I don't really think it would be as much fun if I knew Mom and Dad were worrying, or if I had to worry about things.
Counselor:	Okay, now turn the tables. Ask the other Paula what she's so mad about.
Relieved Paula:	What are you mad about?
Insulted Paula:	I don't know if mad is how I feel. It's just so uncomfortable having to face my friends and admit that my parents won't let me go.
Counselor:	Now talk to Paula about her discomfort.
Relieved Paula:	Okay. Sure it's uncomfortable. But remember, it would have been pretty uncomfortable at the ski lodge, too. And being mad isn't going to make you feel more comfortable.

1. Generic strategies and techniques used in this transcript include:
   a. Inquiring into reasons and/or advantages of change
   b. Resolving conflicts
   c. Separating past from present relationship
   d. Turning stumbling blocks into stepping stones
2. ECBIS strategies and techniques used in this transcript include:
   a. Relaxation training
   b. Enactment of conflict splits
   c. Behavioral rehearsal
   d. Paradoxical technique

Reprinted with permission from Cormier, L. S., & Hackney, H. (1987). *The professional counselor* (pp. 130–131). Englewood Cliffs, NJ: Prentice Hall.

V.

T1:   I would like do something with you. I'm going to describe a certain attitude or belief to you, and I'd like you to assume for a moment that I actually hold this belief. What I would like you to do is to offer me as many reasons as you can why it may be irrational or unreasonable for me to hold on to such a belief. OK?

C1:   All right.

T2:   Assume that I believe the following: Everybody must approve of me, and if this doesn't happen, it means that I am really worthless person. What do you think of that?

C2:   I don't think it makes such sense.

T3:   But why doesn't it make much sense?

C3:   You really can't expect that people are going to do that.

T4:   Why not?

C4:   It just seems unreasonable for you to expect that they would.

T5:   I feel that every single person that I run into during the course of the day is going to have to smile and say nice things to me. And if this doesn't happen, I really feel down.

C5:   But the world is simply not set up that way. There may be people who don't react to you positively because of things that are going on with themselves.

T6:   What other reasons could there be? I tend to think that everything is somehow caused by me.

C6:   But that's ridiculous. It's possible that someone you meet may have had a bad night's sleep, or may have had an argument with his wife, and is in no mood to deal with you.

T7:   So you think that some of the day-to-day variations in the way people react to me can be due to things completely apart from my own adequacy?

C7:   Of course.

T8:   OK, that certainly is a possibility. But what about when someone is really disapproving of *me*? For example, a close friend may disagree with something I say. Now in that case, I usually feel that I am wrong, and I must be worthless for him to have disagreed with me.

C8:   But you can't expect him to agree with everything you say.

T9:   Why not?

C9:   If you did, you would really be dishonest.

T10: But I feel that it is more important for me to get everyone to approve of me and like everything I say and do, than it is for me to really express the way I feel. In fact, I sometimes feel like a weather vane, shifting whichever way the wind might be blowing.

C10:   But that's ridiculous! What happens to you as a person?

T11:   That seems to be a big problem with me; I often don't know who I am as a person. I seem to be so concerned about defining my own worth in terms of what everyone else's reactions are toward me. But how else can I think?

C11:   Maybe you should consider how *you yourself* feel about certain things you do. Provided you're not really hurting anybody else, if you feel that what you are doing is right, perhaps you should be satisfied with that and realize that not everyone is going to agree.

T12:   That seems to make some sense. If I can only really accept it.

C12:   You'll have to, because the other way is not at all reasonable.

T13:   OK. You seem to have a very good perspective on the rationality of that belief. Why don't we move on to another notion?

1. Generic strategies and techniques used in this transcript include:
    a. Defining dysfunctional patterns
    b. Taking responsibility and facing fear
    c. Challenging dysfunctional beliefs and role-playing
    d. Resolving conflict and self-disclosure

2. ECBIS strategies and techniques used in this transcript include:
    a. Creating adaptive and reasonable beliefs by disputing irrational beliefs
    b. Assertion training and overcoming avoidance
    c. Corrective emotional experiences
    d. Confronting feared emotions

Reprinted with permission from Goldfried, M. R. (1995). *From cognitive-behavior therapy to psychotherapy integration* (pp. 85–87). New York: Springer.

VI.

(Mother sitting, reading a newspaper, while Andrew, her five-year-old "hyperactive" son, is playing about 20 feet away with some blocks.)

Mother: I really like that building you've made, Andrew.

Andrew: I don't like it at all.

Mother: Well, that's O.K.

Andrew: (*whining*) Well, why did you say you like it?

Mother: (*about to respond when therapist speaks to her via the earphone*)

Therapist: Go back to your newspaper and do not respond.

Andrew: (*whining still more loudly*) Hey! Why don't you answer me.

Mother: (*once again looks up from her paper as if about to respond*)

Therapist: Even though it may be difficult, go back to your newspaper, please, and let's see if this passes.

Andrew: (*turns back to his blocks and plays quietly. After a few minutes*) Mommy, would you help me with this building?

Therapist: Now go and play with him since he's not whining.

Mother: (*walking towards Andrew*) I'd like to very much Andrew, because you asked me so nicely.

Therapist: That was fine.

1. Generic strategies and techniques used in this transcript include:
   a. Altering future expectation
   b. Taking responsibility
   c. Positive reinforcement
   d. Role-playing
2. ECBIS strategies and techniques used in this transcript include:
   a. Changing reinforcers to control behavior
   b. Restructuring emotional schemas
   c. Cyclical psychodynamics
   d. Disputing irrational beliefs

Reprinted with permission from Goldfried, M., & Davison, G. C. (1976). *Clinical behavior therapy* (pp. 219). New York: Holt, Rinehart and Winson.

VII.

The couple, Bob and Janet entered counseling for their marital difficulties.

Janet: Bob, are you going to cut the grass tomorrow?

Bob: You know people don't cut the grass on Sunday.

Janet: Well, I just thought it would be good to cut it before Monday.

Bob: Well, that's just not what one does on Sunday.

Counselor: Bob, when you say, "People don't cut the grass on Sunday," aren't you also saying "I don't cut the grass on Sunday"?

Bob: Right.

Counselor: What would happen if you just said, "I don't want to cut the grass on Sunday?"

Bob: Nothing, I guess. Maybe Janet wouldn't understand why.

Counselor: Could you tell her why if she didn't understand?

Bob: Yeah, I guess so.

Counselor: Why don't you tell Janet why you don't want to cut the grass?

Bob: O.K. I don't what to cut the grass on Sunday because I don't think it looks good to the neighbors.

Counselor: Janet, is it different when Bob says it that way?

Janet: Yes, I like it better when Bob tells me what he is thinking, but I think it is silly to feel that way.

Counselor: Janet, you answered my question, and then you said something to me that Bob needed to hear.

Janet: What do you mean?

Counselor: You told me your opinion of Bob's reason for not cutting grass on Sunday. I think you really wanted Bob to hear your opinion. Is that right?

Janet: Well, yes, I guess so.

Counselor: Then turn to Bob and tell him.

Janet: He already knows now.

Counselor: I know, but this is just for practice.

Janet: I don't think you need to worry about what the neighbors think. They all work on Sunday.

1. Generic strategies and techniques used in this transcript include:
   a. Separating past from present relationship
   b. Challenging dysfunctional behaviors, suggestion of how to change
   c. Self-disclosure
   d. Turning stumbling blocks into stepping stones
2. ECBIS strategies and techniques used in this transcript include:
   a. Restructuring emotional schemas by confronting feared emotions
   b. Modifying interpersonal scripts by guiding toward effective communication
   c. Establishing adaptive and reasonable beliefs by fantasizing consequences
   d. Modeling

Reprinted with permission from Cormier, L. S., & Hackney, H. (1987). *The professional counselor* (pp. 219–220). Englewood Cliffs, NJ: Prentice Hall.

VIII.

The patient, Roger, was a 36-year-old man. His major complaint was agoraphobia, which had grown progressively worse over the past 12 years. Along with the agoraphobia, his intake sheet noted that he drank heavily, was overweight, was dissatisfied with his job (which he had managed to keep only at the expense of considerable anxiety), had multiple specific phobias, and was actively homosexual.

C1: If I threw myself out the window right now, nobody would shed a tear.

T1: Do you think any of them would try and stop you?

C2: No. Why would they? They might get their names in the paper tomorrow. That's why they would stop my . . . .

T2: Supposing somebody grabbed you [before you jumped out]? What would you feel?

C3: Maybe they'd want to go to bed with me, I don't know.

T3: But that's the only reason?

C4: They'd probably push me out after one night.

T4: So it's inconceivable that anybody would really care?

C5: People really don't care about people that much. They put on a good front, but basically—

T5: Are you speaking about people or are you speaking about Roger?

C6: Just in general.

T6: Roger—Do I care?

C7: I'd like to think you care. I'm not sure though.

T7: What makes me the exception?

C8: Financial gain.

T8: I don't get one penny for seeing you.

C9: I know that—I appreciate that. But, you get (money) from these people in here [the class].

T9: I get not one penny from them.

C10: (*surprised*) I apologize. I didn't know that. (*apologizes repeatedly*)

T10: So the best you can do is accuse me of being interested in you as a case study . . .

C11: (*still apologizing sheepishly*)

T11: You've got to find some other reason [than financial gain]—that ain't it. What makes me different? Why might I possibly care for you? Because I'll tell you—You try and go out that window and I'm going to grab you.

C12:   Maybe you don't want the notoriety—bad for business.

T12:   Yeah, you're right. But on the other hand, maybe I want the fame? . . . My name would get in the paper. (*long pause*) Why might I possibly care?

C13:   I was thinking about that—I'm really confused . . . I mentioned it to a friend as a matter of fact—I asked "Why is this man even bothering?"

T13:   That's my question . . .

C14:   Feelings of being a great humanitarian?

T14:   Not really. Not by seeing one patient for free . . .

C15:   Yeah, that's true.

T15:   What's my game?

C16:   Maybe you thought it was an interesting case? . . .

T16:   You know, Roger, after thirty years—

C17:   Nothing is new—

T17:   Yeah . . . (*I've dealt with about everything.*) Why am I bothering?

C18:   (*subdued*) Give me a week to think about it.

T18:   I will. I hope you will.

C19:   I am going to think about it.

T19:   Good, because that's crucial issue . . . it is not only important in terms of your therapy, but it's important for your life. Because if one person can care for you, then you'll have to ask another question, and that is, maybe two can.

C20:   (*somewhat choked up*) It's very difficult for me to believe it.

1. Generic strategies and techniques used in this transcript include:
   a. Challenging dysfunctional beliefs and separating past from present relationship
   b. Inquiring into reasons and/or advantages of change
   c. Role-playing
   d. Practice and working through

2. ECBIS strategies and techniques used in this transcript include:
   a. Changing self-reinforcers to control behaviors
   b. Restructuring emotional schemas
   c. Modeling
   d. Questioning the evidence and reality test

Reprinted with permission from Mosak, H., & Maniacci, M. (1995). The Case of Roger. In D. Wedding & R. Corsini (Eds.), *Case studies in pychotherapy* (pp. 35–37). Itasca, IL: F. E. Peacock.

IX.

T1:   Immediately before you told your boss that you couldn't work late that evening, what thoughts ran through your head?

C1:   I don't know, it all happened so fast. I didn't want to stay late, but I was afraid to say anything about it.

T2:   And some of your fears were . . . ?

C2:   I was afraid my boss was angry with me, that she would think I was not interested in my job. I didn't think that she would fire me or anything like that, but rather that she'd be annoyed with me.

T3: And despite these thoughts, you nonetheless decided to say something. What did you say to yourself that helped you to do that?

C3: That I worked hard all day, and that I really had other things to do.

T4: But these are thoughts you've had in past instances, where you *didn't* assert yourself. What did you think differently this time?

C4: Well, I had a fleeting thought that maybe I was being unrealistic. I also thought that I no longer wanted to always go along with what other people want, especially when it's not good for me.

T5: And what were your feelings right before you said anything?

C5: I was scared and nervous, but I spoke up anyway.

T6: And your response itself?

C6: It was straightforward and very matter-of-fact, even though inside I was shaking in my boots.

T7: And your boss's response?

C7: It wasn't really bad at all. In fact, she was even a little bit apologetic about having asked me. As I mentioned to you earlier, everything worked out okay anyway.

T8: Right. And how did you feel after it was all over?

C8: Well, I was certainly relieved. Nothing terrible happened; in fact, it turned out just fine.

T9: And how did you feel about *yourself*?

C9: Okay, I guess.

T10: You don't sound all that positive about this experience. If you had to evaluate yourself on a one to five scale, with five being most satisfied with yourself and one being least, how would you rate yourself?

C10: (*pause*): About a three.

T11: What would you have needed to do differently to have given yourself a five?

C11: (*pause*) I don't know that I really could have done anything *any* differently. I guess it's just difficult for me to fully accept the fact that I handled it well. It's difficult for me to see myself in that way.

T12: I can understand that. But aren't you being overly harsh on yourself? At least in this situation?

C12: When you put it that way, I guess I am. I guess I did handle that situation fairly well.

T13: I think it's important for you to be real clear about what went on and how you handled it. If we step back and look at what went on, we have the following: You started out by being reluctant to say anything, for fear that something negative would happen. You were nervous, but still were able to talk yourself into speaking up. What you said certainly sounded appropriate, and was well received by your boss. The payoff was good, in that things turned out well.

C13: Right.

T14: There is a second payoff that you need to recognize as well, and that is that you have every right to feel good about yourself in that situation.

C14: I see what you're saying.

T15: Although this is only one small instance, it nonetheless can provide you with a good turning point, or something that you can fall back on in the future. Next time you're in a situation where you're afraid that something negative will happen if you speak up, and you also feel yourself apprehensive about doing so, think back about how these very same feelings occurred in this situation, how you were able to overcome them, and how things worked out well. It will probably take a number of such instances before you start to feel more self-confident about your ability to stand up for your own rights, but if you continue as you have, there's every reason to believe you'll eventually get there.

1. Generic strategies and techniques used in this transcript include:
   a. Role-playing
   b. Deciding what to change and face fear
   c. Positive reinforcement
   d. Turning stumbling blocks into stepping stones
2. ECBIS strategies and techniques used in this transcript include:
   a. Catharsis
   b. Identifying maladaptive interpersonal schemas by analysis of faulty communication
   c. Editing self-talk and increasing self-assertion
   d. Changing the rigid or enmeshed boundary

Reprinted with permission from Goldfried, M. R. (1995). *From cognitive-behavior therapy to psychotherapy integration* (pp. 111–113). New York: Springer.

FORM 19–2
Case Vignettes for Change Strategies

Name (optional)_____   Date_____

The following are two case vignettes. Please read and decide which generic and ECBIS strategies and techniques should be used for each patient. As you answer the questions, you may want to review Appendices II and III.

- -

1. The patient saw the therapist for depression. After the first session, the therapist and the patient scheduled the date and time of the next session and then the patient left. Several minutes later, the patient came back and very timidly asked, "I am afraid I can't come on that day. Would you mind changing the appointment time?" Next session, the therapist asked the patient why he didn't ask for the more convenient time during the last session instead of afterward. The patient said: "I wanted to ask, but I thought you would be angry at me for that." Suppose that the pattern between the patient and therapist was related to the depression symptoms, what would you do?

_____

_____

_____

_____

_____

_____

_____

_____

_____

_____

_____

_____

_____

_____

_____

_____

_____

_____

_____

_____

_____

2. A 63-year-old man reported many continuing fights with his wife of 35 years. Following are two examples of their fights:

   a. They decided to move from another town to their current location because he was offered a new job there. They discussed the move in great detail. She agreed to go. After they had been there a few months, she became dissatisfied. She blamed him entirely for the move. He accepted the blame.

   b. His wife accused him of having a sexual problem. She said he was impotent. The patient, however, stated that he was able to have an erection if he masturbated. However, if he penetrated his wife, and became "a little soft," she got angry at him and his erection went away. She told him it was all his problem and that he should do something about it. He agreed. How do you help this couple?

_____

_____

_____

_____

_____

_____

_____

_____

_____

_____

_____

_____

_____

_____

_____

_____

_____

_____

_____

_____

_____

_____

_____

_____

_____

Developing Psychotherapy Competence—A Guided Inquiry
(Post-module 4)

Name _____   Date _____

1. What was the most important thing that happened in training during past several weeks?

2. What changes are you are making in your thinking/feeling about psychotherapy issues as a result of this module?

3. What in this module is *helping you* achieve your desired changes?

4. What aspects/influences *outside* of this module are *helping you* achieve your desired changes?

5. What in this module is *keeping you* from making your desired changes?

6. What aspects/influences *outside* of this module are *keeping you* from making your desired changes?

7. Did you find yourself thinking about topics related to this module between training sessions during past several weeks? If so, what *thoughts have you had*?

8. Are you deriving any *benefits* from this module that you did not expect to happen? If so, what are these benefits?

9. Please state the *most immediate concerns* you are having about your psychotherapy competence.

Reprinted with the permission from Heppner, P.P., & O'Brien, K. M. (1994). Multicultural counselor training: Students' perceptions of helpful and hindering events. *Counselor Education and Supervision, 34,* 4–18.

As you answer the following questions, please try to think about how you will behave as a therapist now (after module 4)

Counseling Self-Estimate Inventory
(Post-module 4)

Name _____   Date _____

This is not a test. There are no right and wrong answers. Rather, it is an inventory that attempts to measure how you feel you will behave as a therapist in a therapy situation. Please respond to the items as honestly as you can so as to most accurately portray how you think you will behave as a therapist. Do not respond with how you wish you could perform each item, rather answer in a way that reflects your actual estimate of how you will perform as a therapist at the present time.

	Strong Disagree	Some Disagree	Little Disagree	Little Agree	Some Agree	Strong Agree
1. When using responses like reflection of feeling, active listening, clarifying, and probing, I am confident I will be concise and to the point.	1	2	3	4	5	6
2. I am likely to impose my values on the patient during the interview.	1	2	3	4	5	6
3. When I initiate the end of a session, I am positive it will be in a manner that is not abrupt or brusque and that I will end the session on time.	1	2	3	4	5	6
4. I am confident that I will respond appropriately to the patient in view of what the patient will express (e.g., my questions will be meaningful and not concerned with trivia and minutiae).	1	2	3	4	5	6
5. I am certain that my interpretation and confrontation responses will be concise and to the point.	1	2	3	4	5	6
6. I am worried that the wording of my responses like reflection of feeling, clarification, and probing may be confusing and hard to understand.	1	2	3	4	5	6
7. I feel that I will not be able to respond to the patient in a non-judgmental way withrespect to the patient's values, beliefs, etc.	1	2	3	4	5	6
8. I feel I will respond to the patient in an appropriate length of time (neither interrupting the patient or waiting too long to respond).	1	2	3	4	5	6
9. I am worried that the type of responses I use at a particular time, i.e., reflection of feeling, interpretation, etc., may not be the appropriate response.	1	2	3	4	5	6

	Strong Disagree	Some Disagree	Little Disagree	Little Agree	Some Agree	Strong Agree
	1	2	3	4	5	6
10. I am sure that the content of my responses, i.e., reflection of feeling, clarifying, and probing, will be consistent with and not discrepant from what the patient is saying.	1	2	3	4	5	6
11. I feel confident that I will appear confident and earn the respect of my patient.	1	2	3	4	5	6
12. I am confident that my interpretation and confrontation responses will be effective in that they will be validated by the patient's immediate response.	1	2	3	4	5	6
13. I feel confident that I have resolved conflicts in my personal life so that they will not interfere with my therapy abilities.	1	2	3	4	5	6
14. I feel that the content of my interpretation and confrontation responses will be consistent with and not discrepant from what the patient is saying.	1	2	3	4	5	6
15. I feel that I have enough fundamental knowledge to do effective psychotherapy.	1	2	3	4	5	6
16. I may not be able to maintain the intensity and energy level needed to produce patient confidence and active participation.	1	2	3	4	5	6
17. I am confident that the wording of my interpretation and confrontation responses will be clear and easy to	1	2	3	4	5	6
18. I am not sure that in a therapeutic relationship I will express myself in a way that is natural without deliberating over every response or action.	1	2	3	4	5	6
19. I am afraid that I may not understand and properly determine probable meanings of the patient's nonverbal behaviors.	1	2	3	4	5	6
20. I am confident that I will know when to use open or close ended probes, and that these probes will reflect the concerns of the patient and not be trivial.	1	2	3	4	5	6
21. My assessment of patient problems may not be as accurate as I would like it to be.	1	2	3	4	5	6

	Strong Disagree	Some Disagree	Little Disagree	Little Agree	Some Agree	Strong Agree
22. I am uncertain as to whether I will be able to appropriately confront and challenge my patient in therapy.	1	2	3	4	5	6
23. When giving responses, i.e., reflection of feeling, active listening, clarifying, and probing, I am afraid that they may not be effective in that they won't be validated by the patient's immediate response.	1	2	3	4	5	6
24. I don't feel I possess a large enough repertoire of techniques to deal with the different problems my patient may present.	1	2	3	4	5	6
25. I feel competent regarding my abilities to deal with crisis situations which may arise during the therapy sessions—e.g., suicide, alcoholism, abuse, etc.	1	2	3	4	5	6
26. I am uncomfortable about dealing with patients who appear unmotivated to work toward mutually determined goals.	1	2	3	4	5	6
27. I may have difficulty dealing with patients who don't verbalize their thoughts during the therapy session.	1	2	3	4	5	6
28. I am unsure as to how to deal with patients who appear noncommittal and indecisive.	1	2	3	4	5	6
29. When working with ethnic minority patients, I am confident that I will be able to bridge cultural differences in the therapy process.	1	2	3	4	5	6
30. I will be an effective therapist with patients of a different social class.	1	2	3	4	5	6
31. I am worried that my interpretation and confrontation responses may not over time assist the patient to be more specific in defining and clarifying the problem.	1	2	3	4	5	6
32. I am confident that I will be able to conceptualize my patient's problems.	1	2	3	4	5	6
33. I am unsure as to how I will lead my patient toward the development and selection of concrete goals to work toward.	1	2	3	4	5	6
34. I am confident that I can assess my patient's readiness and commitment to change.	1	2	3	4	5	6

	Strong Disagree	Some Disagree	Little Disagree	Little Agree	Some Agree	Strong Agree
35. I feel I may give advice.	1	2	3	4	5	6
36. In working with culturally different patients I may have a difficult time viewing situations from their perspective.	1	2	3	4	5	6
37. I am afraid that I may not be able to effectively relate to someone of lower socioeconomic status than me.	1	2	3	4	5	6

Resistance

Many therapeutic relationships, despite a strong working alliance, run into difficulties in which the patient appears not to be following the expectations of the therapist. In order to recognize these "blocks" or resistances, therapists need to have reasonable expectations of patient behavior. Not uncommonly, therapists recognize a resistance first by sensing an internal response of frustration, anxiety, or discomfort. Of course, both the obvious failure of patient to do the expected and a feeling of frustration may occur simultaneously. After recognizing the appearance of resistance, the normal human response might be anger or irritation. Here psychotherapists have the opportunity to play out their unique role. The key to responding to these blocks is to relax and wonder about their origin, keeping in mind that sometimes resistances represent single examples of maladaptive patterns. Resistance can activate the observing self of the therapist. "What is going on here? Why am I feeling frustrated? What is going on in the patient that is helping to create this response in me?" This last question directs the therapist's attention to the internal workings of the patient. What is lacking in this person? What is motivating this person to respond in this self-defeating way? How can I activate the patient's observing self to examine this reaction? What content should we explore? Does this resistance represent a discrete example of a general problematic pattern? Finally, am I expecting too much of this person at this point? It is this "stepping back" from a resistance that makes the therapist role different from most other social roles.

SOURCES AND FORMS OF RESISTANCE

The term "resistance" originated from psychoanalysis, which regards it as originating from forces within the patient opposed to the recollection of repressed memories. Greenson (1967) broadened the concept of resistance and defined it as "all those forces within the patient which oppose the procedures and processes of analysis" (p. 59). In clinical practice, patients' failure to meet the therapist's expectations may have various sources. For example, the therapist's inappropriate intervention can lead to the patient's failure to carry out the homework; lack of support from the patient's social network can lead to a missed appointment. Although resistance manifests itself as the *patient's* failure to follow the therapist's various expectations, resistance does not necessarily originate from the patient.

Resistance has three sources (see Table 5–1): (1) the patient, (2) the therapist, and (3) the patient's social network. Patient-originated resistance, which is the most common, refers to those forces within the patient that block the process of therapy. Patients' *fear* of the process of change is a major source of resistance during all stages of psychotherapy. The usual response to fear is avoidance. Avoidant behaviors in therapy often cause resistance. For example, if the patient is afraid to talk about a specific content area, he or she can avoid this fear by keeping silent, talking about irrelevant topics, or missing an appointment. Patients' *lack of necessary information* can also cause resistance. For example, if a patient is having trouble expressing emotions like anger, he or she may never have learned how to recognize and label such feelings. In another example, the therapist says to a patient: "John, since you are attracted to Mary, why not ask her for a date?" John may not carry out this "assignment" because he lacks requisite social skills. Patients' *dysfunctional patterns* may interfere with the process of therapy in the same way that they interfere with other relationships. For example, a patient who attempts to please others by never saying "no" and by rarely talking about what she wants or experiences may believe the therapist is being critical whenever she talks about herself. This fear may be related to the fact that her parents and husband criticize her whenever she talks about herself. Resistance often merges with *transference* (see module 6). Generally, transference refers to the distorted reactions to the therapist, while resistance refers to the patient's interference with the process of therapy. Because transference often becomes an obstacle to the process of therapy, it can also be a source of resistance. For example, a woman patient who distrusts men may fail to complete the diary of thoughts and behaviors, fearing the information will be used against her by her male therapist.

Therapist-originated resistance refers to the resistance caused by the therapist's inappropriate expectations, ill-advised interventions, and countertransference. Therapists usually expect the patient to follow direct and/or indirect instruction and advice. Sometimes, however, *therapist expectations* may exceed the patient's ability

TABLE 5–1 General Sources of Resistance

Patient	Therapist	Social Network
Low readiness to change	Inappropriate expectations	Criticism of the patient for being in psychotherapy
Lack of necessary information to carry out the therapist's expectations	Poor techniques	
	Countertransference	Antagonism toward change that might disturb the equilibrium of the social network
Fears associated with each stage of psychotherapy		
Dysfunctional patterns expressing themselves during therapy		
Transference		

to accomplish them. When confronted with resistance, therapists need to examine their own expectations, keeping in mind the patient's motivation, the degree of fear, the strength of working alliance, and the patient's functional level and social network. When a patient is resistant, sometimes it means that he or she is being treated incorrectly. Beginners may use *poor interventions* because of their lack of experience. In addition, they are likely to become frustrated with resistance. For these reasons, beginners are more likely to experience resistance than experienced therapists. For example, a first-year trainee became uncomfortable with his male patient's sensitivity to his comments. The patient seemed to be placing the therapist on a pedestal of wisdom and intelligence. The therapist, thinking that the patient was reacting to him as he had to his father, blurted out "I am not your father." The patient was confused, talked idly about baseball for a few minutes, and never returned. In another example, a 19-year-old woman presented with agoraphobia and panic attacks. The beginning therapist moved quickly to define a behavioral hierarchy that would enable her gradually to face the agoraphobic fears. The patient became uncomfortable and seemed distracted. She did not participate in the hierarchy development. Unbeknownst to the therapist (because he did not ask), she had recently been sexually abused, something she felt ambivalent about discussing. Once again she was being pushed into something to which she had not agreed. Because *countertransference* can create inappropriate expectations for the patient and lead to ineffective interventions, it becomes a source of resistance. A therapist who thought his wife was responsible for their divorce, for example, was seeing a woman patient who was in the process of a divorce. The therapist insisted that the patient describe her responsibility for the marital difficulties as a homework assignment. The patient missed the next appointment. The therapist had not discovered that her husband was alcoholic and had physically abused her.

The resistance may come from the patient's *social network*, including family members and work relationships that oppose the process and/or potential outcome of therapy. For example, an 18-year-old alcoholic spoke only positively about her family, blaming her peer group for her tendency to drink excessively, even though most of her drunken episodes occurred at home. Only after her intense loyalty to her family was confronted did she describe the abusive and alcoholic patterns of both parents. Another example—a depressed husband fails to change in part because his wife (perhaps out of awareness) resists his improvement; if he were to become less symptomatic, then her sexual problems would become more obvious.

In order to recognize resistance immediately, therapists must be (1) clear about what to expect from the patient and (2) familiar with the various forms of resistance. Stages of psychotherapy provide a structure for what the therapist needs to do and should expect (see Table 5–2). For example, during engagement, the goal is to establish a good working alliance; the therapist expects the patient to trust him or her and actively collaborate. If the patient fails to trust or collaborate, that suggests resistance. During pattern search, the therapist expects the patient to participate in observing his/her dysfunctional patterns. If the patient is reluctant to participate, the therapist may be dealing with resistance. In Table 5–3 we present some of the many forms of resistance commonly seen in different stages of psychotherapy.

TABLE 5-2   Therapist Expectations in Different Stages of Psychotherapy

| | Stages | | | |
	Engagement	Pattern Search	Change	Termination
The therapist's expectation	The goal is to establish a good working alliance. The therapist expects the patient to trust him or her, keep contracts, and become an active participant in the collaboration.	The goal in this stage is to define well-formed dysfunctional patterns. The therapist expects the patient to join with him or her to observe the patient's dysfunctional patterns, to report his/her experience, and to do homework.	The goals include: relinquishing old patterns, initiating new ones, and maintaining them. Therapists expect patients to use their guidance in change, assume responsibility, take risks, and practice new patterns.	The goal is to terminate therapy. The therapist expects the patient to leave therapy without difficulty and with maintenance of change.

During engagement, resistance occurs around issues of trust, role definition, contract agreements, and belief in the therapist's competence. Common resistances in this stage concern the therapeutic contract. Failure to appear for an appointment without prior notification, especially because the patient "forgot," often indicates a nonverbal statement about the therapeutic relationship. Requests for reduced fee or time shifts may hide attempts by the patient to test the therapist's "flexibility" and willingness to accommodate. Deeper still, these maneuvers may conceal attempts to probe the therapist's ability to manage and maintain the therapeutic contract.

TABLE 5-3   Forms of Resistance in Different Stages of Psychotherapy

| | Stages | | | |
	Engagement	Pattern Search	Change	Termination
Forms of resistance	Resist the establishment of the working alliance, by, for instance: ■ Having difficulty in trusting the therapist ■ Doubting the effectiveness of psychotherapy collaboration. ■ Failing to appear for an appointment. ■ Requesting reduced fee or appointment time changes ■ Criticizing the therapist's age, sex, inexperience, training, race, and/or religion	Fail to report information relevant to defining the patterns, as seen in: ■ Excessive silence ■ Withholding important information ■ Becoming evasive when asked critical questions ■ Lying ■ Talking about subjects irrelevant to pattern definition ■ Providing excessive detail for pattern definition ■ Refusing to do role-playing and/or homework ■ Attacking the therapist's questions or empathic statements	Fail to generate alternatives: ■ Agree to initiate a new pattern but fail to do so ■ Refuse to comply with the therapist's suggestions ■ Discuss terminating treatment before changing	Fail to terminate therapy, such as: ■ Continue to call the therapist or go to see the therapist without appointment after termination ■ Fear that loss of the therapist means return of symptoms ■ Believe that the therapist must be available for effective decision-making

Pattern search involves the clarification of problematic patterns of thought, feeling, and/or behavior by the use of inductive reasoning. Resistance in this stage often occurs around observing and exploring these patterns. The prerequisite for pattern search is the patient's willingness to report his or her personal experiences to the therapist and to join the therapist in observing his or her dysfunctional patterns. Patients may be afraid of reexperiencing pain, fear the therapist's contempt, or worry that the therapist will break the confidentiality agreement. They may not know what the therapist wants reported or how to report. The patient may remain silent, tell lies, withhold important information, become evasive when asked questions, refuse to do role-playing and homework, or attack the therapist's questions or empathic statements.

Consider failure to do homework. Exploring the potential sources for not doing homework will help the therapist move the process of therapy. A woman patient with panic disorder is asked to record the situation, thoughts, and feelings associated with each attack. At the next appointment the therapist finds that the patient has not completed the task despite having agreed to do so. What are the possible explanations that can lead to a resolution of this impasse?

1. Patient was afraid to think about her panic attacks.
2. The patient did not understand the instructions but was afraid of looking stupid by asking for clarification.
3. The patient thought that she needed to describe every panic attack in full detail, felt overwhelmed by the project, and decided not to start it.
4. The patient felt she did not have enough time to complete the task.
5. The patient was afraid that she would not do it correctly and would be criticized.
6. The patient was afraid that someone else would see her doing the diary and then she would have to explain why she was doing it.
7. The patient used alprazolam (Xanax) sometimes to abort panic attacks. She feared that if the therapist had a clear record of Xanax use, he would criticize her for using too much of it.

Usually direct discussion will reveal and clear up these problems. Some resistances to homework imply unconscious motivations and may illustrate a general dysfunctional pattern:

8. The patient was afraid that if she got over the panic disorder, her marriage would dissolve since so much of her involvement with her husband revolved around her agoraphobia.
9. The patient felt resentment toward the therapist because he had too quickly focused on panic problems while she thought depression was the key issue.
10. The patient felt helpless about the panic attacks and believed that she could do nothing to change them.

Change is often the most challenging stage for patients. From the beginning of therapy, some patients avoid having to change themselves. Even when they ask for help, they just want someone else to take away their symptoms or to make others change. Resistance to change may be identified at many different places along the psychotherapeutic journey. A patient may disagree with the therapist's interventions, refuse to comply with the therapist's suggestions, miss appointments, refuse to take medication, terminate treatment, etc. Change is a boundary experience (Yalom, 1980), an event that defines one's own limitations by clearly defining losses as well as gains. To change is to lose one's identity for a new one, to risk the unknown, and to become transformed. Consequently, change may create a sense of danger, even though new patterns promise a better life . The threat of change triggers intrapsychic conflict about the past and the future, about the tried and untried ways of being. Sometimes the patient fails to change because of forces in his/her environment. A patient may be afraid to become more assertive with her husband because she fears she will lose him. Children may be afraid to leave home or assert themselves because their parents might withdraw their love. Other patients may appear to avoid change but simply have not grasped what they must do in order to accomplish what they wish.

Resistance in the termination stage is less important in brief therapy than in long-term psychotherapy. It frequently occurs around the fear of separation from the therapist and lack of self-confidence to handle situations on one's own. Patients may refuse to terminate therapy and activate new problems or symptoms. Therapists must keep in mind the termination context as a partial explanation for new problem behaviors.

Although resistance may occur at any stage of psychotherapy, research shows that it seems to increase during therapy, becoming relatively more common in the middle sessions of treatment than during either beginning or termination stages (Orlinsky & Howard, 1978). A possible explanation for this findings is that resistance is lowest when interpersonal threats are low (for example, when establishing an initial relationship or reviewing the whole progress of treatment) and highest in the middle sessions when the patient is being challenged to change.

Table 5–4 lists sources of resistance during different stages of psychotherapy. These resistances cross stages. For example, transference resistance and the resistance caused by the patient's patterns can be seen in any stages of therapy. However, knowing the appropriate therapeutic expectations (Table 5–2) and the potential forms of resistance in different stages (Table 5–3) will augment the therapist's ability to predict and recognize resistance.

RESPONDING TO RESISTANCE

Having recognized resistance, the therapist proceeds to manage it. Although resistance is an obstructionist force, quickly trying to "get rid of" it may not be the most effective way to dilute its power. Resistances usually must be understood and respected by both therapist and patient. The handling of resistance requires looking at it objectively and if possible connecting it to the process of change. Perhaps stumbling blocks can be turned into stepping stones. Rather than blaming the patient for an unconscious desire to subvert psychotherapeutic change, therapists will be more successful if they take an optimistic, cooperative tack. First, they should clarify the source of the resistance, including patients' lack of knowledge about what to do and/or unconscious or environmental blocks. Does the patient's resistance originate from inappropriate therapist expectations? Are these expectations a manifestation of countertransference? If the resistance does not originate from inappropriate therapist expectations, discussion of resistance with the patient is necessary. Not all patients, however, are willing to reveal or explore their reluctance to change. In that case, the therapist will need to wait until the patient is ready.

There are five general responses to resistance:

1. Empathically encourage the patient to do or not do what is desirable.
2. Explain/discuss how the resistance interferes with the process of therapy and define specifically what the patient can do to get past it.
3. Interpret the cause, reason, or pattern suggested by the resistance.
4. Paradoxically allow or cooperate with the patient's resistance rather than struggle to make the patient relinquish it.
5. Ignore it or accept it without comments.

In responding to the fear of engaging in psychotherapy, one approach is to calmly and sympathetically verbalize how the patient must feel about entering psychotherapy. Putting patients' feelings into words will help them feel safe, accepted, and understood by the therapist; that is likely to accelerate engagement in therapy. Patients' questioning of the therapist's ability can unnerve some therapists in engagement and other stages. Such apparent doubting often makes therapists feel uncomfortable and may even cause anxiety and anger, especially for beginners. Keep in mind that patients' questions generally reflect their fears of not receiving proper assistance. Therapists do not have to defend themselves. Making empathic reflections to the patient and showing the patient that the therapist has requisite strength to deal with his or her problems can increase confidence and trust in the therapist.

Therapists choose various ways to handle patients' resistance to the contract, depending on the type of patients, the strength of working alliance, the setting, and the therapist's personal orientation. Contract violations provide a clear and easily identified focus for discussion. Four general alternatives are available to therapists when the contract becomes a problem:

1. Empathically encourage patients to do what is expected, such as encouraging them to take medication or to come to sessions on time.
2. Explain/discuss the reason for request. For example, the therapist explains to the patient that coming to sessions on time and paying for the session can help him or her use time more effectively.
3. Interpret the behavior. For example, the patient who comes late may be angry with the therapist and may have expressed anger to others in this way.
4. Paradoxically accept the potential breach and then help the patient keep the contracts in other ways. For example, a therapist did not confront a woman's

TABLE 5–4 Sources of Resistance by Stage of Therapy

	Stages			
	Engagement	*Pattern Search*	*Change*	*Termination*
The potential source of resistance	**Lack of information about the contract and ground rules of psychotherapy** **Fears of seeking help from psychotherapy** (Ex: *Afraid of being controlled, exploited and/or humiliated*) **A dysfunctional pattern like:** *attempting to please others by avoiding "selfish" requests (like full attention to one's feelings)* **Transference** (see module 6) **Therapist's inappropriate expectation** (Ex: *The therapist insists on too rapid development of trust, requests additional payments, keeps contracts rigidly, and is overly reassuring about the effectiveness of psychotherapy.*)	**Lack of knowledge about how to define dysfunctional patterns** (Ex: *The patient does not know how to report and what the therapist needs to know.*) **Fears of pattern search** (Ex: *Afraid of reexperiencing the pain, afraid the therapist will not like him or her, will break confidentiality, or use the information against him or her*) **Dysfunctional patterns demonstrated** (Ex: *The patient blames others rather than looks at his or her own patterns; the patient thinks that, whatever he or she reports, his or her needs or wishes will be neglected.*) **Transference** (see module 6)	**Lack of knowledge about how to change** (Ex: *The patient is not clear about what must be done.*) **Fear of change** (Ex: *Afraid of new situations, afraid of failure, afraid of reactions from others to his or her new behaviors*) **Dysfunctional patterns** (Ex: *The patient refuses to take responsibility; "I am always wrong no matter what I do"*) **Transference** (see module 6) **The therapist makes an ineffective intervention** (Ex: *The therapist's suggestion is not likely to work, too threatening, or the therapist is pushing too hard to change.*)	**Fears of termination** (Ex: *The patient is afraid of separation from the therapist; worries about recurrence of symptom.*) **Dysfunctional patterns** (Ex: *Weak boundaries, overdependency*) **Transference** (see module 6) **Therapist's inappropriate expectation** (Ex: *Therapist expects the patient to have no difficulty saying goodbye when the goals of therapy are reached, thinks the patient should never return with the same problem.*) **Social networks** (Ex: *Lack of the support for the change from the patient's environment after termination*)

| The potential source of resistance | **Forces from the patient's social network** (Ex: *The family thinks psychotherapy is not helpful or denies the patient has problems.*)

Faulty inductive reasoning (Ex: *The patient doubts the effectiveness of psychotherapy because one of his friends did not get any help from psychotherapy.*)

Countertransference (Ex: *An alcoholic patient missed an appointment because the therapist criticized him. The therapist's father was an alcoholic.*) | **Therapist's inappropriate expectation** (Ex: *The therapist insists on complete honesty, asks for excessive amounts of homework, or does not ask about homework that was assigned.*)

Faulty inductive reasoning (Ex: *The patient did not do the homework because when he was in high school his diary was stolen and shown to his classmates.*)

Countertransference (Ex: *A patient did not tell the therapist about her affair because she noticed that the therapist became irritated when she mentioned the subject. The therapist divorced his own wife after he found out about his wife's affair.*) | **Therapist's inappropriate expectation** (Ex: *Therapist expects the patient to follow suggestions without hesitation; thinks change should proceed smoothly ahead with no backsliding.*)

Pessimism about change (*doubt the likelihood of change*)

Forces from the patient's network (Ex: *The patient's change might destroy the marriage or close relationship.*)

Faulty inductive reasoning (Ex: *The patient failed to carry out his homework which was to talk with his colleagues, because he noticed that one time they seemed irritated when a new employee talked with them.*)

Countertransference (Ex: *A patient who had been in therapy for several months seemed stuck. The therapist had become very attached to the patient and knew that change was the beginning of termination.*) | **Faulty inductive reasoning** (Ex: *The patient did not want to terminate therapy because his mother committed suicide after her termination of psychotherapy.*)

Countertransference (Ex: *A patient had a hard time terminating because the therapist was excessively concerned about whether the patient would function well without her help.*) |
| --- | --- | --- | --- | --- |

decision to miss the next appointment in order to see her mother, but instead emphasized her ability to choose in many situations and to take responsibility for the decisions. Eventually, the patient decided to come the next appointment and to see her mother another time.

For resistances that indicate interpersonal patterns, therapists need to help patients step back to observe and be aware that what they are doing is related to the reason why they entered therapy. Such patients are trying to guard a vulnerable area of their emotional life and protect themselves from further pain. Not only patients, but every one of us comes to use various protective means to fend off embarrassment, guilt, fear, and pain. These protective behaviors form the problematic aspects of ineffective patterns. For most patients, these mechanisms will not be readily relinquished. Patients often bring these protective mechanisms into therapy and use them in interacting with the therapist. No matter how inappropriate, nasty, sarcastic, and demanding patients' behaviors can be, therapists should know that self-protection is likely to be the motivation. Therefore, keeping calm should be a component of the intervention. Therapists can use patients' here-and-now resistance behaviors as samples of ineffective patterns in their lives. Once this assumption is confirmed, therapists should help patients activate the observing self by encouraging them to examine the resistance as an example of these maladaptive behavior patterns. Therapists can provide feedback about the behavior and its consequences, provide explanations for the pattern, and/or report their own reactions to the resistance behaviors.

If the patient's failure to carry out a homework assignment is based upon a lack of understanding about what to do, therapists should clarify their expectations. Therapists must also ensure that the patient understands the rationale and goals of each homework assignment. A useful way to assess such understanding is to use a role reversal procedure where the patient, in his or her own words, explains the nature of the homework assignment to the therapist. Other useful questions include: How do you feel about this assignment? Do you see the usefulness of this homework? What might prevent you from doing the homework?

Many patients fear the consequences of change. At the very least, their current social and psychological functioning could be disrupted, ushering in new and unknown experiences. The simple fear of the unknown often affects human decisions to change. Acknowledging the fear and examining the feared consequences (like divorce, having to find a new job, anger from important others) encourage patients to decide whether or not the risk of change exceeds the pain of current functioning.

When choosing strategies for handling resistances, therapists should consider the strength of the working alliance and the patient's reactance levels. A good working alliance will facilitate the resolution of a resistance through interpretation. A poor working alliance is likely to require the therapist to approach the resistance indirectly. Research shows the relative value of paradoxical intervention among those who are prone to extreme resistance and oppositional reactions (high reactance), and conversely, the value of directive, interpretive, and confrontive procedures in the treatment of those with low reactance. These studies suggest that patients who feel they need to be in control of situations do better with a nondirective approach, while patients with low resistance respond well to directive and structure-enhancing techniques (Beutler & Consoli, 1992).

SESSIONS

The goal of module 5 is to understand the sources, forms, and management of resistance. The tools are:

1. Resistance Case Vignettes (Form 20)
2. Resistance Case Vignettes (Form 21)

Session 1

1. The seminar leader goes through the text of this module. The discussion focuses on the concept of resistance, its sources, forms, and management.

2. Homework: Trainees are asked to compete Form 20 (Resistance Case Vignettes).

Session 2

1. The group discusses Form 20.

2. Homework: Trainees complete Form 21 (Resistance Case Vignettes).

Session 3

1. Trainees complete COSE (Post-module 5) and Guided Inquiry (GI, Post-module 5) during the session.

2. The group discusses Form 21.

3. Homework: Trainees are asked to preview the text of module 6 before the next session.

FORM 20

Resistance Case Vignettes

The case vignettes show patient resistance. Each case vignette is followed by two questions: (1) What is the source(s) of the resistance? and (2) How do you handle this resistance? There are four possible answers (a, b, c, and d) for each of these questions, but only one is the best. Please circle the answer you think best fits that question. As you answer these questions, please review Table 5–4.

I. The patient entered therapy because of difficulties in the relationship with his boss. The patient remains silent and is not able to tell the therapist any details. The therapist feels frustrated. The therapist discovers from the patient's wife that he has troubles telling anyone what he thinks.

1. The source of this resistance is:
   a. Lack of information about the contract and ground rules of psychotherapy
   b. Pessimism about change
   c. The therapist's ineffective interventions
   d. A dysfunctional pattern

2. How do you handle this resistance?
   a. Empathically encourage the patient to talk
   b. Explain the reason for the need for the patient to talk
   c. Interpret the patient's silence
   d. Remain silent and wait patiently

II. After three sessions of therapy about her marital problems, the patient reluctantly "confessed" she was frigid and felt disgusted by any sexual activity. During her initial history and early phase of therapy she maintained that she fully enjoyed and actively participated in sex with her husband. She had deliberately lied about her sexuality out of her fear that the therapist would immediately focus on her sexual difficulties.

1. The source of this resistance is:
   a. Fears of discussing painful subject
   b. Lack of information about how to define dysfunctional patterns
   c. The therapist's ineffective techniques
   d. Forces from the patient's network

2. How do you handle this resistance?
   a. Encourage the patient not to lie again
   b. Explain the reasons for being truthful to therapists
   c. Interpret her fear of talking about sex
   d. Paradoxically tell her to keep hiding her sexuality

III. A female agoraphobic came for help in learning to control panic attacks. A major consequence of these panic attacks was that the patient stayed as close as possible to her husband. An important contributing factor to this patient's difficulties involved the husband's reinforcement of her dependence. In fact, the marriage depended on this type of relationship. It became apparent that if the patient learned to control her panic attacks and became more independent, the husband would probably leave the marriage.

1. The source of this resistance is:
   a. Dysfunctional patterns brought to therapy
   b. Pessimism about change
   c. Forces from the patient's network
   d. Lack of knowledge about how to change

2. How do you handle this resistance?
   a. Empathically encourage the patient to do what is expected
   b. Discuss the advantages and disadvantages of change
   c. Interpret her avoidance of changing her agoraphobia as a desire to punish her husband
   d. Remain silent and wait patiently

IV. A woman came to psychotherapy because her husband wanted her to discuss their interpersonal problems, but she found herself unable to do so. She became frustrated with not being able to comply with this reasonable request and began taking some of her husband's clonazepam, which had been prescribed for his panic disorder. She told neither the therapist nor her husband about taking the pills. Her husband called the therapist to discuss her lack of progress and mentioned that he believed she was taking the pills, although she had denied it.

1. The source of this resistance is:
   a. Forces from the patient's social network
   b. Pessimism about change
   c. A dysfunctional pattern demonstrated
   d. The therapist's ineffective interventions

2. How do you handle this resistance?
   a. Empathically encourage the patient to do what is expected
   b. Explain the reasons for telling the truth
   c. Interpret the reasons for avoiding the truth
   d. Remain silent and wait patiently

V. An anxious, unassertive, and somewhat depressed woman was married and had two children. She was unable to make any effective change, although she came for sessions regularly and punctually. After several sessions she revealed that she was extremely reluctant to become assertive for fear of destroying her marriage and thereby damaging her children. She knew her husband seemed to enjoy the role of her comforter and protector. She felt that she probably could manage without him. Developing her potential and abandoning her dependent role would probably destabilize her marital relationship to the point of rupture.

1. The source of this resistance is:
   a. Lack of knowledge about how to change
   b. Forces from the patient's network
   c. Transference
   d. The therapist's ineffective interventions

2. How do you handle this resistance?
   a. Empathically encourage the patient to do what is expected
   b. Instruct her in detail about how to become assertive
   c. Interpret the fear of assertiveness
   d. Remain silent and wait patiently

VI. A perfectionistic medical student entered therapy for his headaches. They were usually triggered when he was watched by superiors. The therapist recognized that the headaches were related to his interpersonal fears and that a strict focus on the headaches themselves would not be sufficient. The patient experienced headaches not only in the presence of his supervisors but also around colleagues, especially women. The patient, however, wanted only to focus on the headaches themselves and not their interpersonal triggers.

1. The source of this resistance is:
   a. Lack of knowledge about how to change
   b. Forces from the patient's network
   c. Fear of pattern search
   d. The therapist's ineffective intervention

2. How do you handle this resistance?
   a. Empathically encourage the patient to seek the more comprehensive goals
   b. Discuss the reasons for more comprehensive goals
   c. Interpret the patient's avoidance of the comprehensive goals as a need to make the therapist feel powerless
   d. Remain silent and wait patiently

VII. A 38-year-old male patient entered psychotherapy for his anxiety. The therapist was a 26-year-old woman. As he sat down during their first interview, the patient said: "I expected to see an older person. I never expected a young girl to treat me. How long have you been doing psychotherapy?"

1. The source of this resistance is:
   a. Lack of information about the contract and ground rules of psychotherapy
   b. Fears of seeking help from the psychotherapist
   c. Dysfunctional patterns demonstrated
   d. Transference

2. How do you handle this resistance?
   a. Empathically encourage the patient to do what is expected
   b. Explain the reason for the therapist's being so young
   c. Interpret the patient's concern about the therapist not having enough experience to help him
   d. Remain silent and wait patiently

FORM 21
Resistance Case Vignettes

Name_____   Date_____

The case vignettes show patient resistance. Each case vignette is followed by two questions: (1) What is the source (s) of the resistance? and (2) How do you handle this resistance? There are four possible answers (a, b, c, and d) for each of these questions, but only one is the best. Please circle the answer you think best fits that question. As you answer these questions, please review Table 5–4.

I. A 23-year-old female patient saw a young psychiatrist for her depression. In their first interview, the therapist learned that she had gotten pregnant with her first boyfriend and had an abortion when she was 19. The therapist thought the abortion might have contributed to her depression and insisted on asking her to tell him more about that, although the patient was reluctant to discuss it. The patient came late to the next appointment and seemed to ramble on about irrelevant topics.

1. The source of this resistance is:
   a. Dysfunctional patterns demonstrated
   b. Pessimism about change
   c. The therapist's ineffective techniques
   d. Forces from the patient's social network

2. How do you handle this resistance?
   a. Empathically encourage the patient to discuss the abortion
   b. Discuss the difficulties she is having staying with the topic
   c. Interpret the patient's avoidance of discussing the abortion as her hatred of men
   d. Remain silent and wait patiently

II. A patient entered psychotherapy for his social phobia. He had been avoiding any social contact for almost two years. Patient and therapist developed a good working alliance and the patient was motivated to change. However, he didn't go to his boss' birthday party after he and his therapist worked together on helping him to do. He said that whenever he thought of the party he felt overwhelmed and it was the hardest thing for him to do in the world.

1. The source of this resistance is:
   a. The therapist's ineffective intervention
   b. Transference
   c. Forces from the patient's social network
   d. Fear of pattern search

2. How do you handle this resistance?
   a. Empathically encourage the patient to do what is expected
   b. Define less threatening social situations that the patient is more likely to enter
   c. Interpret his avoidance of going to the party as anger at his boss
   d. Remain silent and wait patiently

III. A 65-year-old depressed man reported that he had repeatedly agreed with his wife's criticism of him. It was always his fault, not hers. He was also very self-critical at work. He became very cautious whenever he considered implementing any change at work, fearing he would not do it well. The therapist requested that the patient record some of his inner dialogues. The patient "forgot."

1. The source (s) of this resistance is:
   a. Pessimism about change

    b. A dysfunctional pattern

    c. The therapist's ineffective intervention

    d. Lack of support from social networks

2. How do you handle this resistance?

    a. Reevaluate the therapist's expectation

    b. Empathically encourage the patient to do what is expected

    c. Remain silent and wait patiently

    d. Interpret his "forgot" as his dysfunctional pattern

IV. A 38-year-old man recently diagnosed with manic-depressive illness had become stabilized on valproic acid. At the end of the first session the therapist quickly requested that he keep a diary of his mood swings. When the patient returned, he had recorded nothing.

1. The source (s) of this resistance is:

    a. A dysfunctional pattern demonstrated

    b. Lack of information about how to do the homework

    c. Transference

    d. Forces from the patient's network

2. How do you handle this resistance?

    a. Empathically encourage the patient do what is expected

    b. Define the details about how to do the homework

    c. Interpret his failure to do the diary as his dysfunctional pattern

    d. Remain silent and wait patiently

V. A 23-year-old female patient saw a 30-year-old male psychiatrist because of bulimia. She had been sexually abused by her father, which she never told anyone. She was ashamed to tell the therapist what her father had done to her, although she wanted to. The therapist thought her evasive speech and silence might come from her erotic transference toward him. He said to her, "You seem to want me to be your lover. Why don't we talk about that?" During the following session, the therapist kept focusing on that subject and the patient stayed silent.

1. The source of resistance is

    a. Fear of change

    b. The therapist's unrealistic expectation

    c. A dysfunctional pattern demonstrated

    d. Forces from the patient's social network

2. How do you handle this resistance?

    a. Reevaluate the therapist's expectation

    b. Explain the reason for discussing erotic transference

    c. Interpret the patient's evasive talking and silence as an evidence of her love for him

    d. Transfer to a female therapist

VI. A woman with manic-depressive illness was being treated with lithium carbonate. The patient kept forgetting to take her lithium. Her mother also was manic-depressive, had been treated with lithium, and had committed suicide.

1. The source of this resistance is:

    a. Therapist ineffective intervention

    b. Faulty inductive reasoning

    c. Transference

    d. Fear of change

2. How do you handle this resistance?
    a. Encourage the patient do take the lithium
    b. Define the details about how to take the lithium
    c. Interpret her failure to take the lithium
    d. Remain silent and wait patiently

VII. A young woman was in the habit of castigating herself severely during sessions. Interpretation, challenging her irrational thoughts, and empathically reflecting her emotions failed to help her modify her pattern. Her husband told the therapist that she regarded herself as a failure and that several previous therapists had worked on this problem with her without any change in her perception of herself.

1. The source of this resistance is:
    a. Pessimism about change
    b. Transference
    c. A dysfunctional pattern
    d. Forces from the patient's social network

2. How do you handle this resistance?
    a. Interpret her failure to change
    b. Encourage her to think herself positively
    c. Keep silent and wait patiently
    d. Paradoxically agree that "she is a failure, that she will never change and she better give up"

VIII. During the first interview, the patient complained to Dr. Z that his previous therapist never gave him any advice Dr. Z began giving the patient a great deal of advice without listening in much detail to the patient's difficulty. Although he arranged another appointment with Dr. Z, he did not keep it.

The source of this resistance is:
    a. A dysfunctional pattern
    b. Lack of information about the contract
    c. Fears of seeking help from psychotherapy
    d. Therapist's ineffective intervention

Developing Psychotherapy Competence—A Guided Inquiry
(Post-module 5)

Name_____   Date_____

1. What was the most important thing that happened in training during past several weeks?

2. What changes are you making in your thinking/feeling about psychotherapy issues as a result of this module?

3. What in this module is *helping you* achieve your desired changes?

4. What aspects/influences *outside* of this module are *helping you* achieve your desired changes?

5. What in this module is *keeping you* from making your desired changes?

6. What aspects/influences *outside* of this module are *keeping you* from making your desired changes?

7. Did you find yourself thinking about topics related to this module between training sessions during past several weeks? If so, what *thoughts have you had?*

8. Are you deriving any *benefits* from this module that you did not expect to happen? If so, what are these benefits?

9. Please state the most *immediate concerns* you are having about your psychotherapy competence.

Reprinted with the permission from Heppner, P. P., & O'Brien, K. M. (1994). Multicultural counselor training: Students' perceptions of helpful and hindering events. *Counselor Education and Supervision, 34,* 4–18.

As you answer the following questions, please try to think about how you will behave as a therapist now (after module 5)

Counseling Self-Estimate Inventory
(Post-module 5)

Name_____   Date_____

This is not a test. There are no right and wrong answers. Rather, it is an inventory that attempts to measure how you feel you will behave as a therapist in a therapy situation. Please respond to the items as honestly as you can so as to most accurately portray how you think you will behave as a therapist. Do not respond with how you wish you could perform each item, rather answer in a way that reflects your actual estimate of how you will perform as a therapist at the present time.

	Strong Disagree	Some Disagree	Little Disagree	Little Agree	Some Agree	Strong Agree
1. When using responses like reflection of feeling, active listening, clarifying, and probing, I am confident I will be concise and to the point.	1	2	3	4	5	6
2. I am likely to impose my values on the patient during the interview.	1	2	3	4	5	6
3. When I initiate the end of a session, I am positive it will be in a manner that is not abrupt or brusque and that I will end the session on time.	1	2	3	4	5	6
4. I am confident that I will respond appropriately to the patient in view of what the patient will express (e.g., my questions will be meaningful and not concerned with trivia and minutiae).	1	2	3	4	5	6
5. I am certain that my interpretation and confrontation responses will be concise and to the point.	1	2	3	4	5	6
6. I am worried that the wording of my responses like reflection of feeling, clarification, and probing may be confusing and hard to understand.	1	2	3	4	5	6
7. I feel that I will not be able to respond to the patient in a non-judgmental way with respect to the patient's values, beliefs, etc.	1	2	3	4	5	6
8. I feel I will respond to the patient in an appropriate length of time (neither interrupting the patient or waiting too long to respond).	1	2	3	4	5	6
9. I am worried that the type of responses I use at a particular time, i.e., reflection of feeling, interpretation, etc., may not be the appropriate response.	1	2	3	4	5	6

	Strong Disagree	Some Disagree	Little Disagree	Little Agree	Some Agree	Strong Agree
10. I am sure that the content of my responses, i.e., reflection of feeling, clarifying, and probing, will be consistent with and not discrepant from what the patient is saying.	1	2	3	4	5	6
11. I feel confident that I will appear confident and earn the respect of my patient.	1	2	3	4	5	6
12. I am confident that my interpretation and confrontation responses will be effective in that they will be validated by the patient's immediate response.	1	2	3	4	5	6
13. I feel confident that I have resolved conflicts in my personal life so that they will not interfere with my therapy abilities.	1	2	3	4	5	6
14. I feel that the content of my interpretation and confrontation responses will be consistent with and not discrepant from what the patient is saying.	1	2	3	4	5	6
15. I feel that I have enough fundamental knowledge to do effective psychotherapy.	1	2	3	4	5	6
16. I may not be able to maintain the intensity and energy level needed to produce patient confidence and active participation.	1	2	3	4	5	6
17. I am confident that the wording of my interpretation and confrontation responses will be clear and easy to understand.	1	2	3	4	5	6
18. I am not sure that in a therapeutic relationship I will express myself in a way that is natural without deliberating over every response or action.	1	2	3	4	5	6
19. I am afraid that I may not understand and properly determine probable meanings of the patient's nonverbal behaviors.	1	2	3	4	5	6
20. I am confident that I will know when to use open or close ended probes, and that these probes will reflect the concerns of the patient and not be trivial.	1	2	3	4	5	6
21. My assessment of patient problems may not be as accurate as I would like it to be.	1	2	3	4	5	6

	Strong Disagree	Some Disagree	Little Disagree	Little Agree	Some Agree	Strong Agree
22. I am uncertain as to whether I will be able to appropriately confront and challenge my patient in therapy.	1	2	3	4	5	6
23. When giving responses, i.e., reflection of feeling, active listening, clarifying, and probing, I am afraid that they may not be effective in that they won't be validated by the patient's immediate response.	1	2	3	4	5	6
24. I don't feel I possess a large enough repertoire of techniques to deal with the different problems my patient may present.	1	2	3	4	5	6
25. I feel competent regarding my abilities to deal with crisis situations which may arise during the therapy sessions—e.g., suicide, alcoholism, abuse, etc.	1	2	3	4	5	6
26. I am uncomfortable about dealing with patients who appear unmotivated to work toward mutually determined goals.	1	2	3	4	5	6
27. I may have difficulty dealing with patients who don't verbalize their thoughts during the therapy session.	1	2	3	4	5	6
28. I am unsure as to how to deal with patients who appear noncommittal and indecisive.	1	2	3	4	5	6
29. When working with ethnic minority patients, I am confident that I will be able to bridge cultural differences in the therapy process.	1	2	3	4	5	6
30. I will be an effective therapist with patients of a different social class.	1	2	3	4	5	6
31. I am worried that my interpretation and confrontation responses may not over time assist the patient to be more specific in defining and clarifying the problem.	1	2	3	4	5	6
32. I am confident that I will be able to conceptualize my patient's problems.	1	2	3	4	5	6
33. I am unsure as to how I will lead my patient toward the development and selection of concrete goals to work toward.	1	2	3	4	5	6
34. I am confident that I can assess my patient's readiness and commitment to change.	1	2	3	4	5	6

	Strong Disagree	Some Disagree	Little Disagree	Little Agree	Some Agree	Strong Agree
35. I feel I may give advice.	1	2	3	4	5	6
36. In working with culturally different patients I may have a difficult time viewing situations from their perspective.	1	2	3	4	5	6
37. I am afraid that I may not be able to effectively relate to someone of lower socioeconomic status than me.	1	2	3	4	5	6

Transference and Countertransference

In this module, we introduce the concepts of transference and countertransference in order to increase trainees' ability to recognize and manage them. The concepts of transference (TX) and countertransference (CTX) have evolved since they were first introduced by Freud in 1905 and 1910. Although these two terms originated from psychoanalysis, TX and CTX inevitably occur at any stage of psychotherapy and exist in psychotherapeutic approaches other than psychodynamic ones. They are common to all psychotherapeutic relationships. Transference and countertransference are often regarded as the most complicated part in psychotherapy because they involve interactions between the therapist and the patient, mix the past with present feelings, interact with each other and with nonTX and nonCTX reactions, and reflect the therapist's and patient's unconscious.

TX and CTX may be regarded as necessary (psychoanalysis) or useless (experiential) in the process of therapy (Greenberg, 1995). In general, psychotherapists recognize that TX and CTX may have beneficial or detrimental effects on the course of therapy, depending on the situation, such as the therapist's willingness and ability to recognize and deal with them. Understanding TX and CTX not only allows therapists to prevent and heal breaches in the therapeutic relationship, but also provides them with means to understand themselves and improve their ability to self-observe.

DEFINITIONS OF TRANSFERENCE AND COUNTERTRANSFERENCE

Transference and countertransference refer to attempts by either patient or therapist to elicit responses from the other that fit unconsciously desired role relationships. Psychotherapy requires the development of a working alliance in which the patient seeks self-change through the assistance of the therapist. Any deviations from this role relationship model edge toward transference and countertransference. Therefore, in order to identify transference and countertransference, the therapist must have a clear idea about the boundaries of psychotherapy roles. With clear knowledge of what constitutes psychotherapy role expectations, deviations can be readily identified.

In most interpersonal relationships, individuals attempt to elicit desired responses from others. However, others may not necessarily respond in the desired ways. In life outside therapy, transference and countertransference are not easily identified unless the conscious role relationships are clearly outlined. Outside of psychotherapy, there is also no requirement that individuals involved in transference and countertransference distortions discuss them. In psychotherapy, however, the relationship between therapist and patient can be a fruitful area of investigation.

Transference

Freud (1905) defined transference as "new additions or facsimiles of the impulse and phantasies which are aroused and made conscious during the progress of the analysis; but they have this peculiarity, which is characteristic for their species, that they replace some earlier person by the person of the physician. To put it another way, a whole series of psychological experiences is revived, not as belonging to the past, but as applying to the person of the physician at the present moment" (pp. 116).

For Freud, TX essentially constituted a repetition of past significant relationships in a new context—relationship with the therapist. He neglected the influence of patients' current interpersonal relationships and current life circumstances, as well as the influence of the personality, techniques, and role of the therapist on TX. Subsequent therapists have developed, clarified, modified, and added to the classical concept of TX. Now a broader concept of transference can be defined: *The patient reacts to the therapist with wishes and intentions developed with past and/or current significant others.*

Countertransference

The meaning of countertransference has been debated since it was first used by Freud in 1910. Freud (1910) defined countertransference as the emotional reaction of the analyst to a patient's transference; he viewed countertransference as interfering with the process of therapy. He proposed that analysts undergo analysis themselves in order to minimize the unresolved conflicts that leave them vulnerable to the effects of their patients' transference.

Over the years, other clinicians have recognized that the CTX can be turned to useful clinical purpose (Berman, 1949; Heimann, 1950; Winnicott, 1947). Now, countertransference is recognized as a rich source of information and a vehicle of understanding. It is also viewed as involving potential reciprocal influence of the therapist on patient and patient on the therapist. Singer, Sincoff, and Kolligian (1987) outlined the definitional controversy and claimed that there are three apparent uses of the term countertransference, which are summarized here.

First, the term countertransference refers to all feelings the therapist experiences toward his or her patient. Such feelings may include mild curiosity, political or religious disagreement, deep sympathy when hearing of the patient's traumas, as well as feelings aroused by the therapist's misconceptions or misattributions of the patient.

Second, the term countertransference refers to the therapist's specific reactions to the transference of a given patient, Freud's original use of the term. The specific reactions might include feeling flattered and pleased when the patient regards the therapist as a lover or parent.

Finally, the term countertransference refers to the therapist's transference toward a given patient. Such a transference evolves from the patient's interpersonal effects on the therapist as well as the interpersonal influences of others in therapist's life, including family of origin and current social network. Extreme liking for the patient, including romantic fantasies and possibly sexual attraction, a growing dislike or distortion of the patient can originate primarily from the patient, primarily from the therapist, or from some combination of the two sources.

We prefer the third definition of countertransference, which emphasizes the therapist's transference toward a patient. The first definition seems too broad to indicate the label "countertransference," and the second definition seems too limited. The third definition is balanced between these two extremes and is practical.

CLASSIFICATION OF TRANSFERENCE AND COUNTERTRANSFERENCE

Transference

Transference can be divided into three categories according to its source: patient-originated transference, therapist-originated transference, and interactive transference. Patient-originated transference refers to the patient's attempts to have the therapist conform to his or her wishes and intentions and to respond him or her as significant others did in the past. In other words, the patient attempts to influence the therapist to enter into a role consistent with relationship models developed with others.

Therapist-originated TX refers to triggering of the patient's TX by the therapist's own needs, wishes, and unresolved conflicts. In other words, the therapist's own psychological problems cause, facilitate, and initiate the patient's distorted and unrealistic wishes and intentions toward the therapist. For example, the patient's overdependence on the therapist might originate from the therapist's fear of being abandoned by others; the patient's sexual feeling toward the therapist might come from the therapist's need to feel sexually attractive. Thus, therapist-originated TX generally is countertransference-based and involves the patient's adaptation to the therapist's interpersonal wishes.

The third TX form is relatively rare; it involves an ongoing interaction between the therapist's interpersonal needs and the patient's interpersonal needs. In other words, each contributes some transference-countertransference elements to the relationship and together they form a unique interaction. While the transference reaction of a specific individual may appear quite similar across different therapeutic relationships, the interactive transference-countertransference seems to represent a unique blend of both participants' difficulties and needs. Such unique interactions can persuade the participants that they are each involved with something special and in this way derail the psychotherapeutic relationship.

TX also can be classified as positive or negative. Freud (1912) uses positive TX and negative TX to "affectionate" and "hostile" feelings, respectively. The current, broader concept of positive transference includes the patient's distorted and unrealistic positive feelings toward the therapist, such as love, adoration, sexual fantasies, excessive gratification from the relationship, excessive caring and concern, overdependence and intense intimacy.

Negative TX generally refers to the patient's negatively distorted and unrealistic responses to the therapist, such as aggression, envy, hostility, or devaluation. Therapists tend to focus on negative transference and ignore positive TX, because the former obviously interferes with the process of therapy, while the latter may meet the therapist's own needs and wishes. For example, when the patient does not trust the therapist, the therapist may want to explore why and then to interpret the distrust in order to move the process of therapy. When the patient is overly dependent on, or expresses love for, the therapist, he or she may enjoy this attention and admiration and have little motivation to explore these feelings. Although mild positive transference may facilate working alliance, it doesn't always have a positive impact on therapy; sometimes it may be more destructive than negative transference because it is neglected by the therapist.

Countertransference

It is necessary for trainees to have a reasonably clear intellectual understanding of the types of countertransference responses in order to identify and use them. As with transference, countertransference can be categorized into three types according to source: patient-originated CTX, therapist-originated CTX and interactive CTX (see Figure 6–1).

Patient-originated CTX refers to distorted reactions on the part of the therapist that were initiated mainly by the patient's wishes and intentions. Thus, it is the therapist's reaction to the patient's transference. Patients attempt to "pull" from therapists responses that fit their conscious and unconscious interpersonal needs. Because these

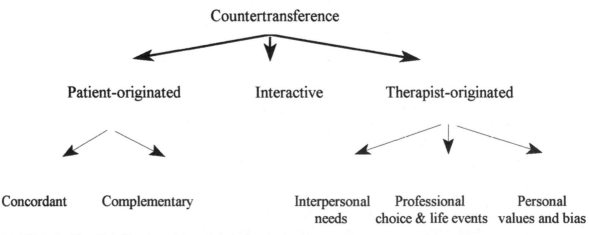

FIGURE 6–1 The Classification of Countertransference

efforts are often subtle and outside of awareness, and because they strike sensitive personal notes in therapists, their sources may be difficult for therapists to pinpoint.

Patient-originated CTX can be divided into concordant and complementary countertransference. In *concordant countertransference,* the therapist experiences a core affect that resembles or is identical to the patient's current experiences. The patient unconsciously communicates to the therapist what he or she is experiencing in a way that circumvents the therapist's awareness. This kind of communication appears mysterious, at first, because neither participant is acting intentionally and yet the patient communicates a hidden experience and the therapist receives it without being aware, initially, of having received it from the patient. Instead the therapist discovers lurking within an unfamiliar set of feelings or thoughts or images. Racker (1968) contended that concordant identification can develop out of the therapist's empathy in accurately reflecting and reproducing the the patient's psychic state. Concordant countertransference may be understood as "unconscious empathy." The patient's ongoing current experience is the primary source of concordant identification. For example, a therapist who suddenly feels extraordinarily sad may be experiencing a feeling hidden behind the patient's apparently unemotional presentation.

In *complementary countertransference,* the therapist feels impelled to assume a role that corresponds with the patient's interpersonal intentions. In other words, the patient attempts to influence the therapist to join in a specific role relationship. The patient is generally unaware of what he or she intends or wishes for from the therapist. For example, a therapist who feels demeaned, ineffective, and inconsequential may be filling a role created by a controlling, arrogant patient.

Like the patient, the therapist enters a psychotherapeutic relationship with his or her interpersonal difficulties, unresolved conflicts, and life stresses, and as well as a theoretical and technical bias. These factors can negatively influence the therapist's conduct in therapy, unless the therapist is willing to explore and observe them consciously and purposively. Therapist-originated countertransference has many sources:

Interpersonal Needs.   The therapist's interpersonal needs, wishes, and intentions may lead to countertransference reactions. For example, a recently divorced 50-year-old therapist may experience a normal interpersonal need for closeness and concern. If he or she attempts to satisfy these needs with a patient, then interpersonal needs are leading to countertransference. The therapist's past psychological difficulties also can be the source of countertransference. The patient may simply resemble someone from the therapist's past. This resemblance may lead the therapist to attempt to influence the patient to behave in ways that mimic the role relationship of the resembled other. Patient appearance and behavior may evoke therapist response patterns connected to earlier significant others, including not only parents, but also siblings, aunts, uncles, and cousins.

Professional Choices and Life Events.   Many of the choices and events associated with professional activities have countertransference implications because they influence the therapist's conduct. The choice of therapeutic school could also reflect therapist CTX. For instance, some therapists are attracted to psychoanalysis because they seek intense, long-term, intimate relationships. If therapists wish to hold people in long-term therapy when it is not of benefit to them, this may be a manifestation of countertransference. On the other hand, some therapists seem to wish to avoid long-term contacts and therefore choose brief therapy (Beitman, 1983).

The common culture and biological events in the therapist's life often have a tremendous impact on personal and professional relationships. However, the therapist may not be completely aware of their effect on therapy. If this effect goes unnoticed, therapy can be impeded. The death of a grandparent, for example, can strongly influence the objective evaluation of a person the grandparent's age. The therapist's extramarital affair may allow him to overidentify with a patient who is also currently involved in an extramarital affair.

Personal Values, View of the World, and Cultural Bias.   Therapists have their own cultural values and bias. When they see a patient from a different culture or racial background, they may have to monitor the emergence in their own mind of the criticisms carried by their culture or race against those of the patient. Therapists are members of cultures; cultures contain values; therapists, therefore, carry these values. For example, a Chinese therapist might dislike an American patient because the patient refuses to take responsibility for his aging parents. For most Chinese it is not acceptable to ignore the needs of one's parents. If a therapist grew up with an alcoholic parent, the therapist might feel excessively angry at any alcoholic patients who are neglecting or abusing their children.

Interactive CTX is found not simply in the therapist's past interpersonal patterns or in the typical pattern evoked in others by the patient, but from the interaction between the therapist and the patient. It results in the creation of shared feelings and fantasies that are at least partly independent of previous patterns. Some feelings and behaviors are reinforced by the interaction, leading to a modified, nonprofessional relationship.

In practice, no countertransference reaction falls exclusively into one of these three categories, since therapists are potentially susceptible to their own personal vulnerabilities as they are triggered by different patients. The three general classes of countertransference reactions can only be differentiated by degree (see Figures 6–1 and 6–2).

SIGNS OF TRANSFERENCE AND COUNTERTRANSFERENCE

Transference

An intense, unexpected response to a therapist's comment by the patient may suggest the emergence of transference and call for a transference investigation. Generally, the patient's excessive hurt, anger, silence, hostility, or untrustworthiness, as well as some positive feelings, such as excessive concern, appreciation, or erotic attraction, may be signals of transference reactions. Behavioral expressions of transference include coming late to appointments, asking to reduce fee or pay late, quit-

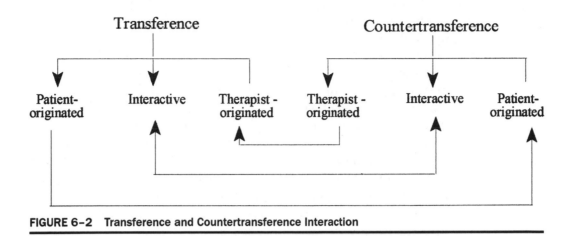

FIGURE 6–2   Transference and Countertransference Interaction

ting therapy abruptly, calling the therapist at home, asking to see the therapist between the sessions, requesting the therapist's home phone number, asking for a hug, sending a special gift, sending unarranged e-mail, excessively criticizing the therapist, writing a love letter or expressing one's love directly in the session. When therapists suspect transference, they should ask:

1. Is the patient experiencing excessive emotion toward me?
2. Does the patient want to terminate with me before we are reasonably finished?
3. Does the patient want to see me outside the office?
4. Does the patient distort our relationship?
5. Does the patient have an excessive desire to see me?
6. Does the patient feel jealous, hostile, or angry toward me?
7. Does the patient feel bored with the therapy? Does he or she find it useless and want to terminate?

Countertransference

Recognition of CTX is harder than recognition of transference, because the former requires the therapist's willingness and courage to introspect. CTX is signaled in the therapist by a deviation from expected responses to the patient(s). The key to recognizing CTX is the signal. Identifying the signal means first understanding the generally expected role responses of the therapist and knowing what is standard good therapy; otherwise, deviations will not be noticed.

Countertransference feelings enter into the therapist's consciousness as they become strong enough to be recognized. The therapist recognizes a feeling as countertransference when the feeling (or thought or behavior) seems excessive, inappropriate, and exaggerated, or does not seem "to belong to me." Signs of countertransference often include impatience with the length of a session or resentment at having to terminate it, dreaming about the patient, arranging an opportunity to socialize with the patient, sexual fantasies about the patient, and unexplained anger at the patient. It is necessary for the therapist to self-examine these feelings throughout the course of therapy in order to increase sensitivity to them. Once they are recognized, the therapist must attempt to categorize the source of the feelings. However, not all these responses are countertransference; in fact, they are fairly common among therapists. For example, some therapists remember many of their dreams and find that patients frenquently enter their dreams. Others find that patients rarely enter their dreams; when they do, it is a surprise. For the first group, dreaming about a patient may have little significance, while for the second group it suggests the necessity of taking a closer look at the therapeutic relationship.

Countertransferential sexual feelings require immediate examination, because sexual involvement can be devastating to both participants. If a therapist notices sexual feelings in response to a patient, several possible sources should be considered: (1) concordant countertransference—the therapist is tuning in so closely to the patient's experience that the patient's sexual feelings have entered the therapist's conscious field; (2) complementary CTX—the patient, through the voice tone, direct statements, mannerisms, and/or dress, behaves in ways that would create a sexual response in many people; and (3) therapist-originated—the therapist is simply sexually interested in this person without any provocation by the patient.

Wolberg (1988) suggested that the therapist ask the following questions in order to become sensitized to CTX manifestations:

1. How do I feel about the patient?
2. Do I look forward to seeing the patient?
3. Do I overidentify with or feel excessively sorry for the patient?
4. Do I feel any resentment or jealousy toward the patient?
5. Do I get extreme pleasure out of seeing the patient?
6. Do I feel bored with the patient?
7. Am I fearful of the patient?
8. Do I want to protect, reject, or punish the patient?
9. Am I impressed by the patient?

The signs listed Table 6–1 are common ones. We cannot describe the signs completely because they vary with patients, therapists, and the dynamic interaction between them.

NONTRANSFERENTIAL AND NONCOUNTERTRANSFERENTIAL REACTIONS

Greenson (1965, 1971) suggests that the therapeutic relationship includes three parts—working alliance, real relationship, and transference-countertransference. Working alliance is defined as relatively nonneurotic, rational rapport the patient has with his therapist. It is essentially realistic, rational, and reasonable, more or less synthetic and artificial, and largely based on the patient's partial identification with the therapist's helpful intentions. Real relationship means the human relationship developing between the therapist and the patient. It also consists of some repetitions from the past, but differs from transference-countertransference in that it is selective and discriminating in terms of what is repeated and modified by internal and

TABLE 6-1 Signs of Transference and Countertransference

	Transference	Countertransference
Signs	Inappropriate or excessive: *Feelings,* such as anger, hostility, hurt, envy, distrust, excessive appreciation, concern, and erotic attraction. *Behaviors,* such as calling the therapist at home, asking to see the therapist outside the office, asking the therapist for excessive personal information, writing a love letter to the therapist, or excessively criticizing the therapist. *Thoughts and fantasies,* such as fantasy to have a family and children with the therapist, become a colleague of the therapist, dream about the therapist. *Resistance reactions* (see module 5), any of which may suggest transference.	Inappropriate or excessive: *Feelings,* such as anger, irritation, anxiety, guilt, fear, sexual stimulation, disappointment, shame, helplessness, envy, boredom, awe, and excessive pride in the patient's accomplishment, high anticipation about seeing the patient, resentment at having to see a patient or, on the other hand, having to terminate therapy. *Behaviors,* such as arranging an opportunity to socialize with the patient, criticizing or excessively reassuring patient, bragging to other therapists about a patient's success, making fun of the patient, asking favors of the patient, trying to impress the patient, keeping excessively silent, reducing or not charging the fee, avoiding discussion of the patient's boundary violations. *Thoughts and fantasies,* such as fantasies of sexual involvement, of romance, of being best friends, of taking a trip together, dreaming about the patient.

external worlds. It is genuine and not inappropriate or fantasy-based. When people meet and work together they develop positive and negative responses to each other. In the extreme these responses merge into transference and countertransference, which can interfere with the working alliance. On the other hand, positive transference reactions among colleagues can imbue relationships with a pleasant familiarity that adds to the work environment. This affection need not be the subject of psychotherapeutic scrutiny.

In actual practice, there are no clear demarcations between Greenson's three elements. For example: some transference-countertransference components may be helpful in establishing a working alliance; if liking in the real relationship is exaggerated, inappropriate, and excessive, it may become CTX; if the therapist becomes too empathic and cannot withdraw from experiencing the patient's emotions to become detached and observant, then the crucial working alliance function of empathy has become countertransference (overidentification is common among empathic beginners). The question becomes: How does the therapist determine whether a particular reaction relates to transference-countertransference or is realistic? Sometimes, the therapist confuses transference-countertransference with both the patient's total relationship with the therapist and with nontransference. It is important for the therapist to monitor himself and the patient's communications for transference-countertransference and nontransferential expressions. The therapist needs to ascertain the valid versus distorted, realistic versus fantasied, components of himself and of the patient's communications. In practice, the distinction between the TX and nonTX is based on the therapist's judgment of reality, including the patient's behaviors, the current situation, and the dynamic interaction between them. However, making the distinction is still a big challenge for therapists, especially for beginners. For example, if a patient tells the therapist he does not want to discuss a specific content area, how does the therapist know whether that signals a problem in the working alliance or transference? If the patient's reasons for wanting to terminate are based in reality, it is probably the working alliance; otherwise, it is likely transference.

Some reponses of the patient based of the working alliance and real relationship should be regarded as nontransferential. These include realistic gratification from contact with the therapist, satisfaction, respect and liking, trust, expectation of understanding and sympathy, dependence, and so on. Thus, nontransference elements consist of those components of the patient's reactions to the therapist or therapeutic situation that are appropriate to the realistic conditions.

Therapists are likely to identify patient negative reactions as transference without considering reality precipitants and possible therapist participation. Actually, some patients' negative reactions, such as being disappointed, discouraged, upset, unhappy, and even angry, might be appropriate in response to inappropriate interventions by the therapist.

Nor are all of the therapist's reactions countertransference. The therapist's appropriate and realistic responses to the patient, based on professional roles and human responses, embody his or her noncountertransference reactions. They help to create the conditions that enable the patient to achieve the desired change. Noncountertransference reactions are the undistorted expression of the therapist's professional role and interpersonal helping abilities; they include sympathetic listening, empathy, rapport, intuitive understanding, urge to learn more about psychotherapy and the human mind, as well as patience, tolerance, acceptance, liking, concern, reassurance, and sense of professional responsibility. Some negative feelings toward the patient may not be countertransference; for example, most people might react with anger and/or fear to a patient who, for no apparent reason, starts screaming at the therapist and begins breaking pictures on the wall. The therapist's fear or anger becomes countertransference if he then attacks the patient.

TX, CTX, nontransference, and noncountertransference constitute important interactive processes in the therapeutic situation (Figure 6–3). It is the working

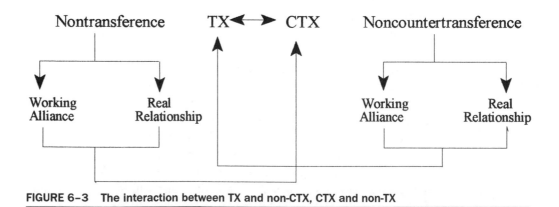

FIGURE 6–3   The interaction between TX and non-CTX, CTX and non-TX

alliance that enables the patient and the therapist to work effectively and maintain a therapeutic relationship with the desired outcome.

THE USE OF TRANSFERENCE AND COUNTERTRANSFERENCE

TX and CTX can be used in a therapeutic way if they are recognized and treated appropriately by the therapist; on the other hand, if they are not recognized or are handled inappropriately, they can destroy the therapeutic relationship.

Transference

Because TX reflects the patient's past or current interpersonal attitudes, wishes, intentions and unresolved conflicts, it provides a way for the therapist to observe, understand, and even experience the patient's problems, as well as the reactions others might be having to the patient. With this understanding, the therapist can help the patient step back to observe his or her transferential dysfunctional patterns. This increases the patient's self-understanding and insight. Alexander (1954) also stressed "corrective emotional experience," in which the patient has an opportunity to encounter old conflicts under new circumstances in the therapeutic relationship.

Countertransference

Once therapists recognize that their own distorted (neurotic) feelings being activated, especially when they know the feelings are coming mainly from within, they may look into them. Analysis of CTX can help therapists to explore their unresolved conflicts, wishes, needs, and interpersonal difficulties; to improve self-awareness and sensitivity to their thoughts, feelings and behaviors; and to expand the ability to self-observe, self-examine, and self-control. The ultimate aim of psychotherapy is to enable the patient's personal growth; however, helping other people grow depends on the growth of oneself. Analysis of CTX may be a good way to encourage the therapist's personal growth. Also, if the therapist is a prime instrument of change, examination of CTX leads to sharpening of the self as therapist and improvement in therapeutic outcomes.

Countertransference can be a tool for understanding the mental processes of the patient. Awareness of it not only helps therapists look into themselves, but also helps them look into neurotic needs in the patient that are activated in his or her other interpersonal relationships. Patient-originated countertransference enables the therapist to experience how others react to the patient, that is, the feelings, thoughts, and behaviors that the patient's interaction patterns arouse in others. This understanding can be used to point out to the patient how he affects the therapist and, presumably, others.

THE MANAGEMENT OF TRANSFERENCE AND COUNTERTRANSFERENCE

Management of TX and CTX requires that self-observation be strengthened and applied to these responses in each participant. In this way, both become participant-observers of the therapeutic process.

Transference

To address the patient's transference, the therapist needs to obtain enough evidence to confirm the existence of TX. If the therapist talks about the patient's transference with no evidence, the relationship could be harmed. For example, a beginning psychotherapist, uncomfortable with a patient's dependence on him, said, "You must think I am like your father." The patient became confused, did not know what the therapist was talking about and quit therapy. Keeping in mind that the transference signs are very different from patient to patient, good management of transference depends on the therapist's ability to judge its existence. The following procedures may help therapist to deal with transference:

1. The therapist notices a sign or several signs of a non-ordinary response from the patient.
2. The therapist needs to think about how much of this response is reality-based and reasonable, as well as how much it deviates from the standard of patient behavior.
3. If the non-ordinary responses from the patient are not reality-based, the therapist can think about how much of these responses comes from the patient's past or current psychological difficulties, and how much is being initiated by the therapist's interaction patterns.
4. Once the therapist answers these questions clearly, he or she can decide whether addressing the transference will be useful. One reason to address transference is to avoid premature termination. Another is to help the patient accomplish therapeutic goals. Not all transference needs to be addressed. Some mildly positive transference reactions seem to aid the process of change.
5. If the therapist decides that addressing the transference will be useful, the next task is to encourage the patient to step back from his or her transference reactions and observe them together with the therapist. The therapist can help the patient to develop his or her observing self by allowing the patient to engage in the same questioning as the therapist did, asking, "Are my responses to the therapist excessive or out of the ordinary?" "Where do these responses come from?" "Do I have the same responses to other people in the past or in the present?"
6. Because transference may be expressed by patients' (or therapists') boundary violations, it is important for the therapist to maintain boundaries when transference reactions occur. Boundary violations shift transference reactions from the arena of examination to that of "acting out," where they are more difficult to discuss.

Countertransference

Instances of countertransference must be addressed immediately if therapy is to be successful. Some experienced therapists recognize their countertransference reactions quickly and have the ability to control and restrain them. For most beginners, however, it will take some time to recognize CTX. Sometimes they are not aware of it until they see their supervisor or talk with their colleagues. The therapist's willingness to examine his or her own responses to the therapeutic relationship plays a key role in managing CTX. Unless they are willing to track usual and expected responses to patients, therapists will lack sensitivity to deviations from the expected.

As we mentioned previously, the observing self helps to manage CTX. Following is a more explicit description of how this is done:

1. The observing self notices a signal of a non-ordinary response to a patient, such as persistent irritability, boredom, anger, extraordinary interest in or attraction to a patient. For example, the therapist notices intense anger at a patient. The observing self notes: "My experiencing self appears excessively angry at this person." The observing self should then carefully observe the intensity and nature of this feeling: "What kind of anger is this? What other feelings are involved? Why is it so strong?"

2. Once the observing self recognizes and confirms the existence of an intense reaction to the patient, the observing self asks, "How much of this anger is contributed by my own personal difficulties? How much is being triggered in me by the patient?" "Would most people react to this person this way at this time or is my reaction peculiar to me?" "Do I have these feelings with other people, including other patients?" "Are these feelings new or recurrent; if recurrent, when, where, and with whom have I felt them?" The answers to these important questions influence what the therapist does next.

3. The observing self acts:

   (a) Patient-originated CTX: Since this reaction is likely to be triggered by some characteristics of the patient, the therapist must observe the patient's behavior carefully and seek a source for it. Perhaps the patient is angry at the therapist or angry generally (concordant countertransference); then the therapist might "hold on," "contain," or "tolerate" CTX for a while in order to obtain more information about the patient's internal world and use that information to help the patient change. (If the therapist simply says to the patient, "I must be feeling what you are feeling. Is that right?" the patient probably will not be able to acknowledge his contributions to the therapist's feelings. "Timing" is difficult to teach, but a fundamental rule is to act in the patient's best interest, waiting until the patient is ready to hear and possibly accept the intervention.)

   (b) Therapist-originated CTX: Since this response is initiated by the therapist's own personal difficulties, the therapist needs to think about whether he or she can continue to see the patient and keep the relationship on the right track. That requires self-examination for the sources of this reaction. The therapist might ask, "Is frustration with our lack of progress, some sense of helplessness, making me feel irritated? Does the patient remind me of someone with whom I am frustrated or have been frustrated?" The therapist may need to request supervision or consult with the colleagues. If the therapist is unable to handle this response, he or she needs to consider transferring the patient to another therapist.

Transference and countertransference are common aspects of human relationships. Thus, observing one's thoughts, feelings, and behaviors toward others, as well as the dynamic interactional patterns with others during daily life, offers a good way for the therapist to increase the professional ability for self-observation and the ability to help patients observe themselves. Not only therapists but also administrators, salesmen, and organizational leaders can benefit from understanding transference reactions people have toward them.

SESSIONS

The goal of module 6 is to understand transference and countertransference through the use of your observing self. The following tools are used in this module:

1. Videotape vignettes of Dr. Beitman's session with J, and Dr. Beitman's report of his reactions to W.
2. Standard CCRT Category (Luborsky & Crits-Christoph, 1990) (Form 22)
3. Relationship Episodes—Practice (Form 23)
4. Relationship Episodes—Homework (Form 24)
5. Questions about "Sex, Love and Psychotherapy" (Form 25)
6. Analysis of Your Reactions to Other People (Form 26)
7. Transcripts of borderline patients (Form 27)
8. TX and CTX case vignettes (Form 28)
9. Transcripts of transference (Form 29)
10. Appendix IV: Sex, Love and Psychotherapy

Session 1

1. The seminar leader discusses transference and countertransference with the group.
2. Homework: Read module 6 text.

Session 2

1. Continue to review the text.
2. Homework: Read module 6 text.

Session 3

1. The seminar leader goes through the Standard CCRT Categories (Form 22) with the group.
2. The seminar leader introduces CCRT (Core Conflict Relationship Theme), and the group uses CCRT to discuss Form 23.
3. Homework: Trainees use Standard CCRT Categories and their own words to rate the relationship episodes in Form 24.

Session 4

1. Using their completed Form 24, trainees report their rating for each relationship episode. The group discusses the ratings.
2. Homework: Trainees are asked to read Appendix IV, "Sex, Love and Psychotherapy," and complete Form 25.

Session 5

The group discusses "Sex, Love and Psychotherapy" and Form 25.

Session 6

1. The group watches videotape vignettes that demonstrate transference and countertransference.

2. Homework: Trainees are asked to complete Form 26. They are asked to chose a patient and one significant other with whom they have many chances to interact (such as one's boss, wife or husband, or a colleague). They analyze their reactions to these people based on the Form 26.

Session 7

1. Trainees discuss patterns with the patient and a significant other, as revealed in Form 26.

2. Homework: Complete Form 27 (transcripts of borderline patients).

Session 8

1. The group discusses Form 27.

2. Homework: Complete Form 28 (case vignettes of transference and countertransference), from which trainees are asked to recognize the different types of TX and CTX.

Session 9

1. The group discusses the homework from Session 8.

2. Homework: Trainees are asked to read transcripts in Form 29, which show the patient's transference and how the therapist might discuss it with the patient. Answer the questions following each transcript.

Session 10

Discuss the Form 29.

Session 11

1. Trainees complete COSE (Post-module 6) and Guided Inquiry (GI, Post-module 6) during the session.

2. The seminar leader discusses the posttraining and reviews the training program experience.

Sex, Love and Psychotherapy

Bernard D. Beitman, M.D.

Psychotherapists are vulnerable to the seductions of their patients. Beginners are at greater risk than more experienced therapists because of their lesser experience in understanding the patient's influence on the person of the therapist, because their sexual drives are generally higher, and because they are less likely to be involved in committed relationships.

Psychotherapists do have sex with their patients. In a national survey of 1,423 psychiatrists, 7% of the male psychiatrists and 3% of the female psychiatrists acknowledged sexual contact with their patients (Gartrell, Herman, Olarte, et al., 1986). A survey of psychiatric residents suggested that 1% had sexual contact with their patients (Gartrell, Herman, Olarte, et al., 1988). A crucial unknown in these surveys is the number of who are consciously, purposely exploiting their patients compared to those who are drawn in by their own vulnerabilities. The distinction is partly drawn by separating repeaters from those therapists who cross the line only once.

Sex with patients is always wrong, always unethical. Why? Because sexual involvement destroys the therapeutic relationship. How? By compromising the therapist's objective perspective and by altering the patient's and therapist's expectations of the relationship. Sexual involvement has so many potentially different meanings to each person that clarification and resolution of these meanings become impossible once the physical acts have begun.

Why does it happen, then? The question must be divided into subcategories: serial offenders versus onetime offenders. Serial offenders force psychotherapists to recognize that persons with very serious problems and what should be called evil intent are part of our practice. They are vicious, cruel, self-justifying exploiters of vulnerable, help-seeking people. For a detailed description of one patient's therapeutic odyssey with such a man, see *Sex in the Therapy Hour* (Bates & Brodsky, 1989). The coauthor of this volume finally was able to confront the therapist perpetrator and to discover the many other women who were tricked and coerced into having sex with him during many sessions as "part of treatment." Despite overwhelming evidence of his harmful behavior and protracted legal battles, this man was still practicing psychotherapy as the story ended.

The focus here is on the more common problem of sexual and loving feelings between patient and therapist. These precious interpersonal experiences induce participants to act on them, sometimes leading to harmful contacts outside the office. Beginners must learn quickly that these powerful emotions may, like energies of all kinds, be turned from bad to good outcome. Freud, when confronted with adoring and sexually inviting patients, was first puzzled by these responses and then turned them into the fulcrum of psychoanalytic changes—analysis of the transference. Modern therapists need not follow his silent, slow model of response. Instead, psychoanalytic ideas coupled with contributions from other schools may help accelerate the change lying latent in these troubling therapeutic experiences. But first, knowing better, why do therapists wish to give in to these seductive impulses?

THERAPIST VULNERABILITY

Like parents who perpetuate their abuse by passing it on to their children, psychotherapists who have been sexually abused may enact similar scenes with their patients. In addition to being exploited as a child, therapists may have been seduced by trusted teachers taking advantage of the power differential between them. A survey of women gaining doctorates in clinical psychology found that 22% reported that they had been sexually involved with their professors (Glaser & Thorpe, 1986). In addition, therapists who participate in other experiences that violate cultural norms (excessive drug or alcohol use, extramarital affairs, unethical business practices) may also be predisposed to justify their exploitation of patients.

Most world cultures view male sexuality as inevitable, unstoppable, and therefore somehow acceptable. This male-centered perspective has, over the years, provided laws permitting men to barter, beat, and own their wives—and implicitly their patients or anyone else under their control. Some men have not yielded to more egalitarian concepts and therefore feel free to choose from their patients someone who might fit their desires. Loneliness and fear of making social contacts in other ways may make some therapists vulnerable. A poor marital relationship, anger at a spouse, boredom, and depression are among the many other possible explanations for sexual involvement.

Some therapists are drawn into sexual liaisons out of a perverted drive to assist. Somehow they wish to rescue their helpless patients by entering into their lives to release them from their psychological bondage. A woman therapist may wish to cook and care for a male patient, show him how it feels to be loved. Sex may be part of that demonstration. Or she may wish to use sex to show him what real love can be so he will stop flitting through a series of brief affairs. Male therapists may become sexually excited by their patient's helplessness and ride their genitals to the rescue. Or they may be sexually excited by their patients' direct sexually seductive maneuvers. The manner in which one human being excites another sexually is a combination of words, voice tone, bodily movements, and who knows what else. Therapists must be prepared to recognize the signals and categorize them in order to place them aside for inspection.

RECOGNIZING SEXUAL STIMULATION

To recognize sexual stimulation by a patient is to know oneself sexually. A suddenly erect penis or engorged clitoris is a good hint. Fantasies at night or during the day are other clues. Or perhaps a desire to rescue the person from an awful life situation may represent a screen fantasy for sexual involvement.

Next comes the most important countertransference question: How much is it me and how much is the patient inducing this response in me? Some patients are remarkably adept at stimulating certain others to feel sexually excited. How? A very good question. Is it clothes? Certain glances? Tone of voice? Certain smells entering unconsciously into our brains? Unnamed sexual energies? Hard questions. How much is the therapist reading his/her own wishes into the patient's self-presentation? Does the therapist make up most of this or is the patient contributing most of the means?

Deviations in standard methods of care seem to occur quite frequently before the final act of sexual involvement. These deviations should also provide hints that the relationship is being improperly distorted. These deviations may include: (1) social discussions rather than problem focused discussions, (2) therapist talking about personal problems that have no relevance to the patient's difficulties, (3) failure to consult when countertransference is very strong, (4) missing a diagnosis that might be medication responsive, (5) drinking alcohol with patient during sessions (Simon, 1991).

BEGINNER MISTAKES

Beginners and untrained therapists have trouble recognizing sexualized transference responses because no one has told them that they exist. Yes, newspapers and movies report incidents of sexual possibilities between patient and therapist, but that, think many beginners, never could happen to me. And yet, it can, and without much thought. Sexualized transference and countertransference require much thought. Consider the following true stories:

> A 28-year-old psychotherapist in private practice had received minimal training in psychotherapy. He considered himself a dream therapist because his personal therapist had analyzed his dreams. After several months of weekly sessions, a woman his age declared simply and forthrightly: "I am in love with you. I've been trying to tell you that, but you don't seem to get the idea, so I'm telling you directly." A little startled, he replied, "No you're not. Tell me your dreams." She was hurt and angry, told him some dreams, and finally decided to terminate.

> A first year psychotherapist was confronted in therapy with the most beautiful woman he had ever seen. She was distraught about a relationship that had recently ended. He cut the session short, asked her to dinner— eventually married her. Divorce took place six months later. During the following two years she was psychiatrically hospitalized several times. She did not trust therapists.

A third-year psychiatric resident was attempting to help a distressed 24-year-old through a series of troubling relationships. She was very gratified by his constant concern, his empathic resonance with her struggles, and his eagerness to support her. As with men before, she expressed her appreciation through a helpless dependence that was sexually tinged. She liked him and found him attractive. However, he could not believe that he might be sexually attractive. Her affections made him anxious. Believing that the anxiety was coming from her, he prescribed Valium for her. She was perplexed, but took the pills any. She became sedated and questioned his therapeutic skill (Langs, 1973). He was correct; someone in the relationship was anxious. He had picked the wrong one.

Poor training about transference may also create problems, as suggested by the following unfortunate incident:

A psychotherapist in a psychoanalytically oriented training program was seeing a 26-year-old woman with depressive symptoms. His supervisor inquired about sexualized transference responses, of which there was little evidence. Nevertheless, the supervisor could see indications, he thought, in much the psychotherapist was reporting. Dutifully, the psychotherapist marched into the 20th session and announced shortly after its beginning: "You are in love with me. We need to talk about it." The patient, surprised, replied: "I am not. I simply came here for help for my sadness and difficulties. Why are you saying that?" He fumbled for an answer but had no clear evidence. Therapy stumbled to a halt.

To bring up transference issues with a patient requires the therapist to gather several lines of evidence. First, if the therapist is experiencing sexual stimulation, the therapist must be confident that these sexual responses are largely being induced by the patient. Second, the therapist must be able to describe specific, mutually confirmable behavior by the patient that suggests sexual and/or romantic interest. Some patients will not discuss transference at all. Some do not wish to address their desire because it reduces the possibility of its coming true. Others simply do not want to admit it. Therapists may not wish to bring it up either, sometimes because discussion will diminish the flattery inherent in someone's attraction to them.

Another beginning mistake is to react to discussion of sexualized therapeutic relationships by running away from psychotherapy. Oh, no, some might think, this is too hard. But beginners need not flee or abandon their patients. First, sexualized relationships are uncommon. Second, they provide the fulcrum of much self-knowledge for both participants.

A TRANSFERENCE DIALOGUE

Miss M is an attractive 23-year-old sales representative who came into therapy because she was repeatedly hurt by her interactions with her perfectionist father. She is also confused by her relationship with men. The therapist is a 36-year-old psychiatrist.

She saw the therapist over a nine-month period. The primary focus was her multiple involvements with men, over which she felt she had no control. She loved men and hated how she felt with them. As the therapy began, she was involved with a married man 15 years older than she. During therapy she began to study her negative responses to her father, to notice how easily she felt hurt by him when he might have inadvertently been insensitive to her. He was quite self-centered, but he did care for her and wanted the best for her. She began to see him as a troubled person who was struggling to maintain his second marriage. Sometimes he just did not know what he was doing. This stepping back helped her to separate from him, to be able to confront him more gently about his insensitive behavior, and to accept him as who he was, not as who she wanted him to be.

There were several clues that a strong transference reaction had taken place in their relationship.

1. From the very beginning, the therapist experienced almost involuntary sexual fantasies about her. These fantasies were vivid and compelling. The therapist talked with several colleagues in order to separate his own feelings from ones she might have been inducing in him.
2. With most men she developed rapid, intense sexual involvement, suggesting that the therapist's experience with her was part of a familiar pattern.
3. As therapy progressed, she made some important improvements in her relationship with her father, and then asked the therapist to come to a concert in which she was playing.
4. As they talked about termination, she became quite sad and anxious.

These clues motivated the therapist to address her thoughts and feelings about him as they entered the termination stage. The therapist was anxious, not really knowing if she would join him in looking at herself. He had difficulty believing that she had actually found him sexually attractive. Following are parts of their dialogue during the last five sessions of therapy. The therapist had not addressed her feelings and thoughts about him before this time.

First Transference Session

M: On my way over here, I forgot your name. That's strange. I was trying to figure out how to do for myself what you have done for me.

T: Strange reactions like that suggest perhaps we should discuss your reactions to me. The reason being that your responses to me seem to reflect your responses to important other people in your life. What do you think?

M: (*Somewhat shaken by the idea*) I don't know. Yes. Maybe. What am I supposed to say?

T: We're talking about termination, and some of your difficulties in relationships may be repeated here with me.

M: I think I know what you mean. But, I don't know what to say.

T: For example, you said you were trying to figure out how to do for yourself what I have done for you. You seem to be giving me credit for your changes. Is that what you mean?

M: No. I know that's not true. I only said that because you were listening. I've thought a lot about this. You've helped by listening and guiding my thinking. I've done a lot of this myself.

T: We have to examine that part of your mind that thinks and talks in ways you know are not true. Why then did this part of your mind give me more credit than you know I deserve?

M: I act as if my self-opinion were dependent upon what others think of me. I am what other people think I am. I get into relationships by being what the other person wants me to be, and then when I get away from that person, I hate who I've become. Then I break up with that person.

T: What made you give me the power over your changes?

M: If you thought I needed you, then you wouldn't leave me. That's how I hold onto people. I do what they want me to be, and give them power over me, so they will see that I need them, and they won't leave me. I hate that I do that, but I do.

T: What expectations of mine have you tried to live up to?

M: I can't say what your expectations were, I can only say what I think they were.

T: Good. Yes, you are right.

M: You wanted me to be strong, take care of myself, more supportive of women's independence and women's rights, do well in school, and be interesting and attractive. You wanted me to be what I wanted for myself.

T: I can agree with some of that. Is there anything else that I wanted from you that you did?

M: I don't know (*pausing*). I can't think of anything.

T: Remember "femme fatale" when you spent the summer having sex with many different men? I was worried about your getting pregnant.

M: Yes.

T: About your becoming an alcoholic.

M: Yes.

T: Were you aware of being seductive with me for the first four sessions we had before you went away for the summer and then after you returned?

(In fact, he had reacted very intensely to her seductiveness with sexual fantasies and sexual arousal. These feelings were also somewhat irritating because of their intensity, as if he were being forced to feel them beyond his own wishes. He spoke with colleagues about his reactions, trying to understand and use them. In therapy, he addressed her behavior indirectly by commenting on her seductiveness with other men (having simply assumed that what she did with him, she did with others). They examined how these actions of hers got her into trouble with men. Finally, he asked if she was seductive with her father. After some thought she was able to say that she was not. After these discussions, she was no longer stimulating him in a sexual way nor was she jumping quickly into bed with newly met men. From her reports, she had dropped that sexy role almost entirely and begun to concentrate on her work.)

M: Oh yes. I knew I was trying to seduce you. Isn't that what all men want? For women to be fully sexual with them?

She began to laugh almost uncontrollably. She tried to describe her feelings and thoughts. They came out in short bursts.

M: What a great accomplishment. Would prove my power. Get my shrink to have sex with me. Not good for me. I came for help. You've got a family. Where would I be? But, great. So what. Amazing thing to do. Not impossible. Could happen. Couldn't it?

T: [He felt a voice welling up in me saying, "I want to." He kept silent.]

M: It would scare me silly if you said you want to.

T: It's getting close to the end of the session. How do you think you will feel when you leave here?

M: I don't know, but I feel queasy right now.

T: We are not finished with this. Do you want to continue this? Do you think it will help you?

M: Oh, yes. If I can work out these problems with men with you right here, then I don't have to do them out there.

T: Let's set our next appointment.

Second Transference Session

Plan for this session: the therapist wanted to keep her to the transference discussion, needed to wait for the opportunity, and did not want to push it hard.

M: I don't want to be here. I've had lots of trouble this week, and talking to you can only make it worse. When I feel good, I seem to always mess myself up, and I did it again.

T: Would you prefer to leave?

M: No. But I might start crying again, and. . . . I don't know.

T: What happened this week?

M: I overspent my checking account. I've spent the last few days trying to borrow money from my ex-husband, from Danny (her current man friend), and my father. I just wanted to get this outfit, but I also have to pay the rent. And, then there's this guy at work who's been really interested in me. His name is Chris. We went out with some other people, had a few drinks, and went over to his place to watch his VCR. We started fooling around a little, and then we had sex. Danny didn't know. Trouble was, I didn't use any protection. Maybe I'm pregnant. I don't know, but I'm going to get a pregnancy test. I just feel awful.

T: How did you feel about our last session?

M: Weird. I feel weird looking at you now. I hardly remember it.

T: Weren't you the one who said that you wanted to have sex with your psychiatrist?

M: That was me, yes. I guess. But, what am I supposed to say about it? Makes me feel strange.

T: You are supposed to talk about it, about what you think about it.

M: I wonder, I guess, what you thought about it.

T: I'm glad you were able to say that you were trying to be seductive with me. I was afraid that you would not be aware of it or would not admit it.

M: I don't mean that. I mean how you reacted to my flirting with you. I like the word "flirting" better than "seductive."

T: Oh. Well, I think it is more important for you to describe how you think I reacted. We are looking at how you view all this.

M: You reacted kinda, you seemed to notice, maybe interested, like you were . . . kind of positive?

T: You mean I seemed interested in you sexually?

M: Not exactly, like you would say, "Hey, I want you in bed." But, nicely responding.

T: What in particular did you notice?

M: The way you looked at me and talked to me. Nothing specific. Kind of normal. The way many men react to me when I am flirting with them. (*Pause*) Oh, I hate this. I hate this analysis. Always examining myself. (*Pause, she begins to sob.*) I know this has something to do with my father. I know it. I have this feeling, deep inside me, I can't explain it, I can't remember it. Like I've been sexually abused somehow, but I don't know an incident. I hate him for doing this to me, but I don't know what he did. Should I know?

T: That may be very important to recover those possible memories. I think it is most important to change in the present.

M: So much energy goes into what I do with men, trying to get their approval by having them smile at me when I flirt with them. I can't get that approval from myself. Got to come from them. What's wrong with me? (*She cries and remains silent for a few minutes.*) I feel better. Kind of cleared out and relieved. I've never said that about my father before. I have trouble talking like this. You know all about me, and I know so little about you. I talk about my reactions to you, and I get vulnerable. You might hurt me. My friend Amy was in therapy with a man who took advantage of her fears and her sexiness by going out with her. He never touched her, but she wanted him sexually, and knew it would be bad for her.

T: Yes. You will have to learn to trust me. That I will not take advantage of you. That I am here for your best interests. The more you learn to trust me and become vulnerable to me, the more you will learn to trust yourself.

M: I notice that I am able to ask you for help when I think I need it, and I don't worry so much about your motives since I think, I believe, that you are interested in what is best for me. Yes. I think that trust is building.

T: It is getting time to stop. I do not wish to push you hard in discussing your reactions to me. I know it is difficult for you, but I also believe it is helpful for you. You can see how this is helpful for you. You unearth mucky stuff that you did not know was there. Perhaps you will liberate yourself from the compulsion to flirt with so many men, and find a different way to relate to them.

M: I am more convinced of that.

Third Transference Session

Plan: Again, the therapist wanted to wait for opportunities to discuss transference with her. She came in full of exuberance.

M: I got the job promotion. I love it. Everything is going great. Chris is a lot of fun. We've been seeing a lot of each other. He wants me to go to Kansas City with him to see a concert. We're going to stay with his parents. I like him. Over the weekend, I went to a bar with some friends of mine and met this guy named Dave. He's got a virgin/whore complex. Any girl he sleeps with he thinks is a whore. I was just being myself, talking, laughing, and he tried to find out about me. I could tell he had a girlfriend now, but he asked me to go home with him. I could tell he was just testing me to say "no." He says his girlfriend will do anything he asks, and I know that is the kiss of death. I said "no" because I thought that would have ruined things with him and anyway he had a girlfriend, and I didn't want to go. Everybody said I was cocky then. I was just feeling good myself. I was having fun.

T: You're cocky in here today, too. (*She was happy, looking directly at him instead of away, emitting happy energy with a little sexual energy mixed in.*)

M: I'm feeling good. Yes. But this is when I have to watch myself. When I'm feeling good, I do things to hurt myself.

T: Perhaps that relates to some of what we have discussed the past few weeks.

M: You know, it's not good to trust someone completely, implicitly, fully. I don't like it when someone does that with me.

T: Giving one's trust fully to another gives that other person complete power over you. You become a doormat like Dave's girlfriend who will do anything for him. Perhaps you are doing that with me. You've given yourself fully over to others and gotten hurt and angry by it.

M: I can see that I might be looking like I'm giving it all to you.

T: Let's look at the loss of control you experience when you are feeling good as you do now. What happens?

M: (She describes several instances in which she felt good and got involved with several different men. Now she was starting with Chris, and possibilities with Dave, and still had lingering feelings about Tom from last year.)

T: You like sex very much. You have a strong sexual energy to which men are attracted. It is a blessing and a curse.

M: Yes, I do love sex. But how is it a curse?

T: Sex means different things to different people. You say you want sex to be a casual thing.

M: That's the way it is with Chris and me. Two friends who mess around.

T: For Dave, it means you are a whore. For others, it means you have to get married.

M: I wish it wasn't so complicated. It is too much fun.

T: You also have a responsibility with your sexual power, your ability to attract men.

M: I don't do it on purpose.

T: You do it somehow, on purpose or not.

M: I've got this friend, Jill. She is beautiful, with a beautiful body. Guys just love her and chase her. She hates it because all they want is sex with her. She had this one guy who really liked her, was real sincere with her, and didn't have sex with her. She got bored with him and went back to the guys who used her. I could see that she was expecting them to act this way toward her and was doing things to make them respond to her sexually. She was angry about it, yet she perpetuated it. I was like that, I can see that now.

T: You seem to be able to step back from yourself and see yourself now.

M: I just want to have sex be casual. But the trouble with Chris is that I never know where I stand with him. What if he becomes important to me?

T: Sex then may have a different meaning to you, perhaps more like Jill's platonic boyfriend.

M: I guess I'll have to see how he reacts. If he doesn't go along with my changes, perhaps the relationship isn't working. I'll just have to see it then.

T: You seem to need to find a way out of the difficult complications that sex can bring: pregnancy fears, marriage, love, commitment, competing sex partners.

Fourth Transference Session

Plan: The therapist wanted to have Miss M discuss what would have happened if he had responded to her seductiveness. He wanted her to live out in her mind what she thought she wanted.

M: I feel good, really good. Everything is going very well.

T: Uh, oh. Trouble.

M: No, not really.

T: When things go well for you, then trouble starts. I wasn't sure that you understood how you get yourself in trouble from our discussion last time.

M: The worst thing I could do is get pregnant and have to get married and have my life stopped before it started like my friend Susan. No life, just family and an unhappy marriage. After I left here last time, I had unprotected sex with Chris. I've done that plenty of times, but this time I knew just what I was doing. I was watching myself do it. I took the risk, a calculated risk because my period had just ended and went ahead. After that I realized that I don't have to do that anymore. I got some sponges (I hate condoms), and I've used them ever since. The risk isn't worth it. I don't have to do that to myself anymore.

T: How do you feel about yourself when you see yourself making a decision like that? [Note: in 1989 when this interchange took place, STDs and AIDS were not the problem they have since become, so the potential for these diseases to disrupt her life were not addressed by the therapist.]

M: Great. I feel that I am maturing, that I don't have to play hurtful games with myself like that anymore. With Chris I feel more separate, more myself when I am with him. We have been together almost every day, but it's not like with other guys. Before, I just threw myself into their lives. What is he doing, who is he with, is he thinking about me? With Chris, instead of snowballing it is progressing. I like him more, and we are talking about it, but it's not pressured. What if he sleeps with someone else? I'm not sure how I'll react, but I'll wait until it happens. I'm finding new solutions to old problems.

T: Last time you were flirting with another guy in the bar. You thought about the possibility of seeing him, of sleeping with him.

M: But Chris and I have been together a lot since then. I must admit that although I talk about sex with many guys, I prefer one at a time.

T: As termination has proceeded, we have talked about your responses to me, how you wanted to have sex with your psychiatrist. I don't think we are finished with that.

M: Yuk! No! I don't want to talk about that. I'm feeling good now. I don't want to get into that mucky stuff.

T: What if I had responded to you as you seemed to want?

M: It would have been awful, terrible. At one time it would have scared me to death. If it had happened early, I would have just gotten rid of you. I never would have gone into therapy again either, and just tried to work it out on my own.

T: By flirting with me, then, what were you trying to accomplish?

M: I didn't want you to do anything, but I was trying to get you to. I don't know. I guess, yes, I was testing you. I wanted to see if you were truly loyal to your family, to your children (*gesturing to the pictures of his children on the wall*) and to your wife, to your marriage. I wanted to see. . . . Oh, just like my father. He was having an affair while he was married to my mother. I wish my Mom wouldn't have told me so much about it. I was only eight, and she was using me to confide in. My father left us, his family, his wife, for another woman. If you would have taken me up on this, then I would have been right. All men only want sex. They aren't loyal to their wives. I didn't want to be right, but I thought I was.

T: What do you think about what you've just said?

M: Coming on sexually and getting a sexual response, it is a self-fulfilling prophecy. Like my friend Jill, she thinks men only want sex and acts sexy with them, and then gets upset when that's all they want. I used to be like that.

T: What about your father and your flirting with me?

M: Thank you for not doing it.

T: I think, by the way you say that, that you mean it very sincerely.

M: I do. If you had said yes to me, then I would have gone around having sex with married men for a long time just to prove over and over that I was right and men were terrible and not to be trusted.

T: That's the negative. Anything positive?

M: Oh, yes. I know that I am in control of the responses I am getting from men. I know that I can influence how they respond to me. I also know that I am responsible for the way I respond to them. I don't have to react in any typical way. I'm just waiting to see how I'll react if Chris sleeps with someone else. I am freer. More separate.

T: I also hope that I may prove the exception to your rule that all men want sex and are not loyal to their families.

M: I don't know about that. Possibly.

T: Before you thought there were none. Now there is at least one. Maybe more.

M: I'm not sure that I will get married ever. I hold the idea too strongly. I just don't know.

T: We can leave it at that. Perhaps I have added a doubt to your certainty about men.

M: Perhaps.

T: You have matured. Before, I could experience your sexual energy, and now I can experience your maturity.

M: Other people tell me the same thing, how I've changed. I feel so much better, separate and on my own.

T: This is termination talk. How should we do it?

M: One more session in two weeks, and then "check-ups" every six months or so.

T: Good idea. Then you can see how much you've changed each time you come back.

M: I know I'll have some problems that I could have done better, and I'd like to talk them over.

Fifth (last) Transference Session

M: I don't know how to say this, but I've been trying to figure out how to help myself without you, and I realized that I think about what we are going to talk about before I come in here, and now I'm able to put things together myself. I need to be able to stop and let myself be with myself and think things through and come up with what I need to know. I can put things together myself. You say that it is me that makes the changes, and I say it is you that made them happen. That's all wrong. We did this; we did this together. I've got a friend, Jason. We work together, and sometimes we sit and talk together. He has a girlfriend to whom he is really committed. And we talk. I'm not trying to get him to like me. I just am able to talk with him and listen to him. He is a man I can trust. I can see that there are men out there that I can trust. Am I making sense?

T: You are describing things that people who are completing a helpful therapy often describe. You are able to do for yourself what you and I have been doing together. And, you are able to develop a trusting relationship with a man whom you respect.

M: Last night, I had an experience that is really hard to explain, really hard. Chris had been out of town for a week. He never called me. I didn't like not hearing from him. I knew things were changing with him. Last night I was with Tom. I used to love Tom last year, and in some ways I still do. We had sex. Jason says having quick sex before getting to know someone is the easy way. The harder way is to let them get to know you slowly. I'm getting to think that Jason is right. Before Tom and I had sex, I realized that I did not bring any protection, but the big problem before in situations like this is that I did not say anything, and just went along and took the big chance. This time I said something. And Tom said he had some protection, and he used it. It was good. But afterwards I felt drained, numb inside. I took a hot bath. And then the threads of my experience began to come together. I started to cry, to sob, couldn't stop it. I was happy and sad at the same time. Women have been told that the reason they have sex is for the security of being held, for closeness, because they have low self-esteem, and they want some reassurance. I knew that didn't fit for me, but I didn't know how. Then, last night I saw it. All those guys I had sex with were no good. The didn't deserve my love. None of them. I didn't respect them. And the reason I had sex with them was to prove that they didn't deserve my love. They were just there for the sex for me. They didn't deserve what I had to give them. Just like my Dad. He didn't deserve it either. Now I see how men must feel when a woman wants to have more than just sex. They kind of sneer inside and wonder what's going on. They don't respect the women, they just want to use them for sex and prove that is all they're good for. They don't respect women.

Now I can feel love because there are men out there like Jason and others who I can respect. There are plenty of no good men and women out there, but some can be respected. My Dad and I are getting along really well. I can love him despite his faults. As you said, he didn't love me the way I wanted or I needed, but he loved me some, and I can accept his limitations. He keeps asking me is there something more I'm hiding from him because we are getting along so well.

I talked to Chris this morning, and told him I didn't want to have sex with him anymore. He is like all the other men, too. He is there only for sex for me. I said we are friends who just fool around. But, I don't respect him. He wanted our relationship to go further, but now I don't. He's leaving town in a few months, and I know we are going nowhere. So, I wanted to stop it before it went any further down a dead end.

(*She pauses and looks at him quizzically.*) I feel you are going to say that I'm talking nonsense, and that I need to stay in therapy for a long, long time.

T: That's absurd. Not true. Quite the opposite. We have to look at what makes you say that.

M: I don't know why. Maybe I was trying to get feedback from you.

T: Then you could have asked directly for feedback. I believe that was one of the multiple meanings in what you said, but not the only one.

M: Here I am again, opening the door for you to tell me what to do.

T: Not exactly. You are telling me to tell you to stay in therapy for a long time. I know that we both know that you are ready to leave, but there is a part of you saying something else here.

M: Well, I think everyone should have a trained person with whom to talk. Sometimes your friends give just awful advice.

T: So everyone should have a therapist forever?

M: Well, no. It is too expensive.

T: This is our last session. Perhaps you are having trouble saying good-bye.

M: Isn't that natural?

T: Of course it is. I am only trying to get you to say it directly.

M: Oh (*she tries to stifle sobs*). . . . You mean now I have to say the sappy stuff?

T: I think it is there, and it needs to be said, yes.

M: This has been so important to me. Changed my life. (*She begins to cry.*) You've helped me so much. I feel freed from so much. I knew I could love, but I had so many stumbling blocks in my way, what I put there. I feel like so many of them are removed. I think I had that experience last night, crying, happy coming together of myself because this is our last meeting. I was so happy to feel those threads of my life come together.

T: I wonder if there is any more to say.

M: I hate good-byes.

T: Why?

M: They mean something terrible has happened. That's why people say good-bye.

T: Like . . .

M: When I break up with guys . . . my father leaving. What about you? How do you feel about saying good-bye to me?

T: Oh, now it's my turn. This is a good-bye for me. You have progressed very well and very far. I've learned a good deal from you, including your answer to the question about who is responsible for you changing. Not you alone, not me, but we are responsible. I like learning that answer since no one ever told me that. I won't miss you very much. The person who came in here looking for help, needing help, is no longer here. You have matured and can function on your own. I believe if I would have seen you several years earlier in my career, I would have been more deeply involved with you and not helped you see the separation between us as much.

M: I'm glad I saw you now and not before.

ADORATION TRANSFERENCE

Patients may fall in love with their therapists—place them on pedestals, idealize them, attribute to them the greatest power and the most wonderful qualities. This adoration is seductive, too. How pleasing to be considered the most ideal of human beings whose every word and gesture paints a picture of perfection!

Pronounced one patient: "How intelligent and attractive you are. Everything you do is just right. I wish I could be like you. I do want to be with you, do for you, help you. Just being with you is what I want." This admission came after some probing questions, since patients do not usually offer speeches of love without a little introduction.

If the speaker is attractive to the therapist, these sweet words may induce the therapist to yearn for an alteration in their roles. What reality could stop this from proceeding? Any therapist who chooses to step into the role imagined by such patients should be warned that the expectations will be impossible to fulfill. Furthermore, the patient wants an impossible somebody of whom the patient is undeserving. Anyone who might love the patient is by definition imperfect, and would have trouble convincing the ex-patient, now lover, that the now ex-therapist's love is true.

SOME PATIENTS WILL NOT TAKE "NO!"
FOR AN ANSWER

Occasionally, patients will not discuss their sexualized and loving reactions to therapists. They do not wish to acknowledge the restraints inherent in the therapeutic relationship. They simply want the therapist, body and soul, and will settle for nothing else. Said one such person: "I take 50% of the responsibility. I will sign a contract to that effect. Whatever will make you feel comfortable. I love you. I want to be with you. I will leave my husband for you. I hope we will be married." She knew what she wanted. As Freud (1915) suggested about these patients, termination and possible transfer to another therapist are the only possibilities.

In those cases where patients have sued therapists for "undue familiarity," a term for sexual and romantic involvement, a large percentage of these legal actions were initiated after the therapist terminated the relationship (Slovenko, 1991). It was saying "no!" that triggered the fury. The patient quoted in the previous paragraph made a mild suicide attempt when she realized that nothing was going to come of her requests. An outside-the-office involvement would have been more disastrous.

UNDUE FAMILIARITY AND THE LAW

Laws reflect social values. Current law makes therapist-patient sex equivalent to rape and incest based on the psychoanalytic idea that patients transfer feelings towards parents onto the person of the therapist. However, transference is a common phenomenon in many human relationships. Doctors of all specialties, lawyers, administrators, leaders and authorities of all types are the objects of transference distortions. Do therapists who have sex with their patients always deserve to be classified as rapists when their level of transference intensity may be little different from that of other common relationships? This legal thrust is particularly paradoxical since lawyers in the state of Illinois are, according to a ruling by an appellate court, permitted to have sex with their clients.

Therapists and patients will continue to be attracted to each other and want to see each other outside of the clinical situation. Legal punishment should be based upon the degree of damage done to the patient when it does happen during the psychotherapeutic relationship. Is there a right way to have such relationships when both people decide? Perhaps. Some have suggested that consultation with colleagues and a one-year waiting period without contact of any kind might provide for an equitable compromise (Appelbaum & Jorgenson, 1991). For any therapist embarking on such a relationship, there is much danger both personally and professionally. Some laws clearly state: Once a patient, always a patient. Any sexual contact anytime during or after therapy is punishable by law.

FORM 22
Standard CCRT Categories

WISHES, NEEDS, INTENTIONS

1. TO BE UNDERSTOOD;	To be comprehended; to be empathized with; to be seen accurately
2. TO BE ACCEPTED;	To be approved of; to not be judged; to be affirmed
3. TO BE RESPECTED;	To be valued; to be treated fairly; to be important to others
4. TO ACCEPT OTHERS;	To be receptive to others
5. TO RESPECT OTHERS;	To value others
6. TO HAVE TRUST;	Others to be honest; others to be genuine
7. TO BE LIKED;	Others to be interested in me
8. TO BE OPENED UP TO;	To be responded to; to be talked to
9. TO BE OPEN;	To express myself; to communicate
10. TO BE DISTANT FROM OTHERS;	To not express myself / my feelings; to be left alone
11. TO BE CLOSE TO OTHERS;	To be included; to not be alone; to be friends
12. TO HELP OTHERS;	To nurture others; to give to others
13. TO BE HELPED;	To be nurtured; to be given support; to be given something valuable; to be protected
14. TO NOT BE HURT;	To avoid pain and aggravation; to avoid rejection; to protect/defend myself
15. TO BE HURT;	To be punished; to be treated badly; to be injured
16. TO HURT OTHERS;	To get revenge; to reject others; to express anger at others
17. TO AVOID CONFLICT;	To compromise; to not anger others; to get along; to be flexible
18. TO OPPOSE OTHERS;	To resist domination; to compete against others
19. TO HAVE CONTROL OVER OTHERS;	To dominate; to have power; to have things my own way
20. TO BE CONTROLLED BY OTHERS;	To be submissive; to be dependent; to be passive; to be given direction
21. TO HAVE SELF-CONTROL;	To be consistent; to be rational
22. TO ACHIEVE;	To be competent; to do well; to win
23. TO BE INDEPENDENT;	To be self-sufficient; to be self-reliant; to be autonomous
24. TO FEEL GOOD ABOUT MYSELF;	To be self-confident; to accept myself; to have a sense of well-being

25. TO BETTER MYSELF;	To improve; to get well
26. TO BE GOOD;	To do the right thing; to be perfect; to be correct
27. TO BE LIKE OTHER;	To identify with other; to be similar to other; to model after other
28. TO BE MY OWN PERSON;	To not conform; to be unique
29. TO NOT BE RESPONSIBLE OR OBLIGATED;	To be free; to not be constrained
30. TO BE STABLE;	To be secure/ to have structure
31. TO FEEL COMFORTABLE;	To relax; to not feel bad
32. TO FEEL HAPPY;	To have fun; to enjoy; to feel good
33. TO BE LOVED;	To be romantically involved
34. TO ASSERT MYSELF;	To compel recognition of one's rights
35. TO COMPETE WITH SOMEONE FOR ANOTHER PERSON'S AFFECTION;	

RESPONSES FROM OTHERS

1. ARE UNDERSTANDING;	Are empathic; are sympathetic; see me accurately
2. ARE NOT UNDERSTANDING;	Are not empathic; are unsympathetic; are inconsiderate
3. ARE ACCEPTING;	Are not rejecting; approve of me; include me
4. ARE REJECTING;	Are disapproving; are critical
5. RESPECT ME;	Treat me fairly; value me; admire me
6. DON'T RESPECT ME;	Don't treat me fairly; don't value me; don't admire me
7. DON'T TRUST ME;	Don't believe me; are suspicious of me
8. ARE NOT TRUSTWORTHY;	Betray me; are deceitful; are dishonest
9. LIKE ME;	Are interested in me
10. DISLIKE ME;	Are not interested in me
11. ARE OPEN;	Are expressive; are disclosing; are available
12. ARE DISTANT;	Are unresponsive; are unavailable
13. ARE HELPFUL;	Are supportive; give to me; explain
14. ARE UNHELPFUL;	Are not comforting; are not reassuring; are not supportive
15. HURT ME;	Are violent; treat me badly; are punishing
16. ARE HURT;	Are pained; are injured; are wounded
17. OPPOSE ME;	Are competitive, deny/block my wishes; go against me

18. ARE COOPERATIVE;	Are agreeable
19. ARE OUT OF CONTROL;	Are unreliable; are not dependable; are irresponsible
20. ARE CONTROLLING;	Are dominating; are intimidating; are aggressive; take charge
21. GIVE ME INDEPENDENCE;	Give me autonomy; encourage self-direction
22. ARE DEPENDENT;	Are influenced by me; are submissive
23. ARE INDEPENDENT;	Are self-directed; are not conforming; are autonomous
24. ARE STRONG;	Are superior; are responsible; are important
25. ARE BAD;	Are wrong; are guilty; are at fault
26. ARE STRICT;	Are rigid; are stern; are severe
27. ARE ANGRY;	Are irritable; are resentful; are frustrated
28. ARE ANXIOUS;	Are scared; are worried; are nervous
29. ARE HAPPY;	Are fun; are glad; enjoy
30. LOVES ME;	Is romantically interested in me

RESPONSES OF SELF

1. UNDERSTAND;	Comprehend; realize; see accurately
2. DON'T UNDERSTAND;	Am confused; am surprised; have poor self-understanding
3. FEEL ACCEPTED;	Feel approved of
4. FEEL RESPECTED;	Feel valued; feel admired
5. LIKE OTHERS;	Am friendly
6. DISLIKE OTHERS;	Hate others
7. AM OPEN;	Express myself
8. AM NOT OPEN;	Am inhibited; am not expressive; am distant
9. AM HELPFUL;	Am supportive; try to please others; am giving
10. HURT OTHERS;	Am violent; act hostile
11. OPPOSE OTHERS;	Am competitive; refuse /deny others conflict with others
12. AM CONTROLLING;	Am dominating; am influential; manipulate others; am assertive; am aggressive
13. AM OUT OF CONTROL;	Am irresponsible; am impulsive; am unreliable
14. AM SELF-CONTROLLED;	Am responsible
15. AM INDEPENDENT;	Make my own decisions; am self-directed; am autonomous

16. AM DEPENDENT;	Am submissive; am passive
17. AM HELPLESS;	Am incompetent; am inadequate
18. FEEL SELF-CONFIDENT;	Am or feel successful; feel proud; feel self-assured
19. AM UNCERTAIN;	Feel torn; am ambivalent; feel conflict
20. FEEL DISAPPOINTED;	Am not satisfied; feel displeased; feel unfulfilled
21. FEEL ANGRY;	Feel resentful; feel irritated; feel frustrated
22. FEEL DEPRESSED;	Feel hopeless; feel sad; feel bad
23. FEEL UNLOVED;	Feel alone; feel rejected
24. FEEL JEALOUS;	Feel envious
25. FEEL GUILTY;	Blame myself; feel wrong; feel at fault
26. FEEL ASHAMED;	Am embarrassed; feel abashed
27. FEEL ANXIOUS;	Feel scared; feel worried; feel nervous
28. FEEL COMFORTABLE;	Feel safe; am or feel satisfied; feel secure
29. FEEL HAPPY;	Feel excited; feel good; feel joy; feel elated
30. FEEL LOVED;	
31. SOMATIC SYMPTOMS;	Headache; rash; pain

Reprinted with permission from Luborsky, L., & Crits-Christoph, P. (1990). *Understanding transference* (pp. 45–49). New York: Basic Books.

FORM 23
Relationship Episodes—Class Practice

Name _____   Date_____

The following pages contain several relationship episodes. Slashes (//) mark the beginning and the end of a thought unit. W means wish, RO means response from others, and RS means response of self. Please use the "tailor-made system" (i.e., use your own words) to judge the patient's transference and write it down at the left margin. And then try to find two numbers from the standard CCRT category which best, and second best, match your judgment, and put those two numbers in the parentheses. The first segment illustrates how to do this.

CCRT Scoring

Relationship Episodes (RE: RE defined as the patient's explicit narratives about the relationships. In each relationship episode a main person with whom the patient is interacting is identified.)

RE# 2: Ex-employers

RO: Rejecting (4, 14)
RO: Rejecting (4, 14)
RO: Give no help (14, 4)
RO: Rejecting (4, 14)
RS: Out of a job (20, 19)
RS: Anger (21, 20)
RS: Have no job; nothing (20, 17)
RS: Horrible state (20, 17)
W: I want a job (help) (13, 26)
RO: Rejecting (4, 14)
RS: Helpless (17, 19)
RS: Discouraged (22, 23)

//^{RO}And then the other job was ah, they didn't even give me a chance.// I was supposed to work on this computer and the computer wasn't hooked up and they said well you don't have to work it. //^{RO, RO} We're replacing you with somebody else.//^{RO, RS} So I was replaced with somebody else. ^{RS}//It really pissed me off //(pause) ^{RS}because I gave up another job to get this job and I ended up with nothing at all, no unemployment, no nothing. // ^{RS} It's horrible. //(pause). . .^WI call them everyday, // ^{RO}but they always say we don't have anything.// It's just terrible. // ^{RS}Because I don't know what I'm going to do. // ^{RS}(pause) It's really discouraging. It's so hard to get out and—get the door slammed in my face constantly.//

CCRT Scoring

Relationship Episodes from Ms. Smyth, Session 3

RE #3: Brother and his wife

1. W: _____

2. RO: _____
3. RS: _____
4. W: _____

5. RS: _____

6. RO: _____
7. RO: _____

8. RS: _____

//Anyway, ^WI want to move out of Bob and Jane's (brother and sister-in-law) house as soon as possible. //
^{RO}Treated like a second-rate citizen there.// ^{RS}It's not very good for my self-esteem.// Like they're both addicts and they have the personality of addicts. // (pause) ^WI guess—I, I much rather be around sober people. //. . . Yeah. The old tapes start running // and ^{RS}it's just real bad. I mean I start thinking negatively as soon as I'm around them, because they're both negative. // ^{RO}They're dishonest. // ^{RO}They're acting like they're doing me a big favor, but I'm paying half the rent there, for their apartment // and I have this tiny little room, no closet, and their junk's in the room and I have to work around their lives. // (pause) ^{RS}So, I just can't stand them.//

RE# 4: Boyfriend

1. W: _____
2. RO: _____
3. RS: _____
4. RO: _____

5. RO: _____
6. RS: _____
7. RS: _____
8. RS: _____
9. RS: _____
10. RS: _____
11. W: _____
12. RS: _____
13. W: _____
14. RS: _____

15. RS: _____
16. RO: _____

17. RO: _____
18. RO: _____

//Yeah ^{W}I've, and I've stopped speaking to that married guy // because ^{RO} he got to be a real asshole. // I ^{RS}mean I'm not taking any shit from anybody this year—for the rest of my life // and uh,^{RO} he just sort of stopped talking to me and uh, he didn't contact me, // he didn't even—where was I going to move to this week. // ^{RO}He didn't contact me // so ^{RS}screw him, //^{RS} I'm not going to

contact him not at all either. . .// ^{RS}it just makes me mad. // ^{RS}I really don't want anything at all to do with him.// $^{RS, W}$

Never again will I—Christmas Eve I spent alone in church crying my eyes out // because $^{RS, W}$ it was an intensely lonely feeling // and I said no way am I ever gonna feel that bad again. No way. // ^{RS}I'm isolated from my friend and family because of this guy I wanted—this married guy.// It's just a conflict between honesty and dishonesty. // ^{RS}I just ah, he pissed me off. // ^{RO}All my other friends gave me all kinds of moral support, even some financial support for this horrible dilemma I'm in right now. // ^{RO}He didn't do shit. . . // ^{RO}He didn't buy me a Christmas present or a card, or a birthday. //

RE# 5: Father

1. RO: _____

2. RO: _____

3. RO: _____
4. RO: _____

5. RO: _____
6. RS: _____

7. W: _____
8. RO: _____
9. W: _____
10. RS: _____
11. W: _____
12. RO: _____
13. RO: _____

//^{RO} I mean he's just acting like a asshole. // I mean, to him I think my grandmother was always a pain in the ass. // ^{RO}That's how he treated his children too. // That's why he's just a total asshole. // A couple of years ago she was sick and she had a sister that lived out in California. // He wanted ^{RO}to ship her out there so he wouldn't have to deal with her and all. // It was horrible. And ^{RO}that's what—and soon after that when I found out how he treated his mother, I realized how (sniff) he felt about me, and the rest of my sisters. // ^{RO}Like he didn't give a shit. // ^{RS}It was just a matter of a

couple of weeks. (Pause) You know, I saw what he's really like. // ^{W}I went to xxx to see him at Christmas time, New Year's and I went hoping to get money, //^{RO}I didn't get any . . . (laughing) ^{W}and I needed it at the time. // ^{RS}I felt sort of

like a whore but I needed money. . . // (pause) ^{W}I just want him out of my life. // ^{RO} He denied that he was a bastard and an asshole // ^{RO}but then I saw right through his face what he really is. // I didn't want to know that I had a father that was a big asshole. I found out he was. Just devastated me. (pause) You know—definitely a dysfunctional family.

RE# 6: Boss

1. RO: _____

2. RS: _____

P: // But ROthese people I work for are very nice. // (pause)
Yeah, RSI feel lucky to have a boss like my boss.//

T: mmh.

P: I was down in town with her, her husband and me.

3. RO: _____

4. RS: _____

//ROWent to see a trade show this week and he drove and
we were out together.// RSIt was nice. // There's a lot of
them.

T: They included you with them?

P: Yeah.

T: And you just started working there?

5. RO: _____

P: Yeah. //ROShe followed me last week. My first week on
the job when the car broke down, to make sure my car
started. She followed me down there to my house //

6. RO: _____

ROwhich is like an hour out of her way.

T: Ha!

7. RO: _____

8. W: _____

P: //RO, WAnd she was concerned about like, you know, about

9. RO: _____

10. RO: _____

11. RO: _____

12. RS: _____

me, //ROhow I was feeling about grandmother dying. // She
ROlet me leave early. // (pause) // ROVery nice lady. // RSI feel
blessed.//

Reprinted with permission from Luborsky, L., & Crits-Christoph. P. (1990). *Understanding transference* (pp. 55–58). New York: Basic Books.

FORM 24

Relationship Episodes—Homework

Name _____ Date_____

The following pages contain several relationship episodes. Slashes (//) mark the beginning and the end of a thought unit. W means wish, RO means response from others, and RS means response of self. Please use the "tailor-made system" (i.e., use your own words) to judge the patient's transference and write it down at the left margin. And then try to find two numbers from the standard CCRT category which best, and second best, match your judgment, and put those two numbers in the parentheses.

- -

CCRT Scoring

RO: _____
W: _____
W: _____
RO: _____
RO: _____
RS: _____
RS: _____

RO: _____
RO: _____
W: _____
RO: _____
RO: _____

RS: _____
RS: _____
RS: _____
RS: _____
RO: _____
RO: _____
RS: _____

W: _____
RS: _____
RO: _____
RS: _____

RS: _____
W: _____
RO: _____

Relationship Episodes (RE)

From Mr. Howard, Age 20, Session 3

RE# 1: Mother

This might have been a dream. // ROMother says it didn't happen. // W, W, RO Up until we moved, when I had questions about sex, mother would explain. // RO When we moved to——, one day I asked and she said sorry we can't talk about that. You're getting to that age. // RS, RS Bothered me because my young sister, age 9 or 10, laughed.//

RE# 2: Mother

// ROAnother incident mother said never happened. // RO We, brother and I before sister was born—when it was really cold, would sleep with parents.//W, RO, RO Parents took my brother in bed with them and they wouldn't take me.//

RE# 3: Therapist

T: What's happening now?
P: //RS I feel generally unresponsive. // RS, RS I'm getting a headache, tense,// RS thinking all week about relating all this stuff to what I was 10 years ago (sigh) and not getting any—I mean, nothing comes out // . . . RO like groups of guys who have embarrassing moments of silence.// RO It proves no perfect rapport exists. // RS I feel blank.

RE# 4: Mother

// W, RS Before I went to school I always used to kiss my mother. // I'm not sure it was a big thing, but it was a big thing when it stopped. // RO She made a big thing about how I didn't want to kiss her anymore. //RS I was suddenly out in the cold again.//

RE# 5: Girlfriend

//RS I'm beginning to feel a lot of resentment to E (girlfriend). // W, RO I went with her for a couple of years. It's just been severed. //

RS: _____

RO: _____

RS: _____

CCTR Scoring

W: _____

RO: _____

RS: _____

W: _____

RO: _____

RO: _____

RS: _____

W: _____

W: _____

RO: _____

W: _____

RO: _____

RS: _____

W: _____

W: _____

RO: _____

RO: _____

W: _____

RO: _____

RS: _____

RS: _____

W: _____

RO: _____

RS: _____

//[RS] I'm fearful of seeing her and feeling something for her. // [RO] He just doesn't give a damn. // [RS]Bothers me I used to be so screwed up about her.//

Relationship Episodes.

From Mr. Howard, Age 20, Session 8

RE# 1: Therapist

Things going well but I feel I have to give up my girlfriend. // [W, RO, RS] I resent you because I have to give up things to get close to you.//

Dream A: Trainers

// War. [W] I enlisted as soldier on our side. // [RO] The trainers of the soldiers had superior strength. // [RO, RS] You (therapist) will smile—I only got into the entertainment troops.//

RE# 2: Boyfriend

// In preschool, [W, W] I wanted to trust someone. // [RO] I confided in (boyfriend) but he could screw me.//

Dream B: Store

// [W] I was going into candy store with other kids. // //[RO] The place is floating in ice cream. // [RS] I got sick and repelled by it.//

Dream C: Store owner

// [W] I was going into a store. // [W] I was naked. // [RO]Two young ladies said "Tsk, tsk" // [RO] I had to escape from the proprietor.//

RE# 3: Therapist

// [W] I felt bad because of distrusting our relationship.// [RO] I saw an article that makes me distrust you. // [RS, RS] I realize that I distrust everybody. //

RE# 4: Father

// [W] I wrote to father for money. // [RO] It is not all right with him to send me it. // [RS] I lose trust.

Reprinted with permission from Luborsky, L. & Crits-Christoph. P. (1990). *Understanding transference* (pp. 55–58). New York: Basic Books.

FORM 25

Questions about "Sex, Love and Psychotherapy"

Name (optional)_____   Date_____

After you read "Sex, Love and Psychotherapy," please answer the following questions:

- -

1. Which type of the transference does the patient have?
   (Pick one best answer)
   a. Patient-originated transference
   b. Therapist-originated transference
   c. Interactive transference

2. What are the signs of the patient's transference?
   (Pick one best answer)
   a. Feeling sad about termination
   b. Asking for social contact with the therapist
   c. Feeling anger, hostility, and envy
   d. Concern about the therapist

3. What are the signs of the therapist's countertransfernece?
   (Pick one best answer)
   a. Sexual fantasies about the patient
   b. Feeling anger and guilt toward the patient
   c. Avoiding discussion of the patient's boundary violation
   d. Dreaming about the patient

4. What is the predominant type of the countertransference the therapist has?
   (Pick one best answer)
   a. Patient-originated countertransference—concordant countertransference
   b. Patient-originated countertransference—complementary countertransference
   c. Therapist-originated countertransference
   d. Interactive countertransference

5. What do you think the therapist's management of transference and countertransference?
   a. Very good
   b. Good
   c. Neutral
   d. Bad
   e. Very bad

6. If you were the therapist for this specific patient, what attitudes and feelings would you have in the session?

   _____

   _____

   _____

   _____

   _____

7. Do you ever have sexual feelings toward your patients? If yes, where do these feelings come from?

_____

_____

_____

_____

_____

8. Do you ever experience a very strong desire to nurture or rescue patients? If yes, what is the origin of these feelings?

_____

_____

_____

_____

_____

FORM 26

Analysis of Your Reactions to Other People

Name (optional)_____   Date_____

This is not a test. Rather it is a way to learn how to objectively observe and then to analyze your subjective reactions to other people, including patients. Please choose a colleague (boss, supervisor, or colleague) or a relative (husband, wife, child, or a parent) for the first part (A) and a patient to whom you have some strong reaction for the second (B), and then answer the following questions.

- -

A

Questions	_____ Colleague Or _____ Relative
How do I feel about him or her? (such as like or dislike him/her, easily trust him/her, feel dependent on him/her, feel uncomfortable if getting close, afraid of being criticized, want to be cared for, feel hostility toward him/her, adore or despise him/her, and so on)	
How strong is this feeling? (1 mild, 5 excessively strong) Does it bother you?	
Is this feeling reasonable? If not, why? If yes, why?	
Where does this feeling come from? Does this feeling originate from him/her, you or your unique interaction?	
If this feeling mainly originated from you, which factor(s) initiated this feelings? (your current interpersonal difficulties, your past experiences, or your life or professional events)	
To which other people do you react similarly?	

B

Questions	Patient
How do I feel about this specific patient? (such as like or dislike, look forward to seeing the patient, over identify with the patient, feel sorry for the patient, feel resentment or jealousy toward the patient, get extreme pleasure out of the patient, feel fearful of the patient, want to care, protect, reject or punish the patient, feel sexually attracted to the patient and so on)	
How strong is this feeling? (1 mild, 5 excessively strong)	
Is this feeling reasonable? If not, why? If yes, why?	
Where does this feeling come from? Is this feeling patient-originated, therapist-originated or interactive ?	
Is this feeling related to past interpersonal or intrapsychic conflicts, your current interpersonal difficulties, your choice of professions or current events in your life?	
To which other patients do you react similarly ?	
What is the similarity between your reaction to your patient and your colleague or relative?	

FORM 27

Transcripts of Borderline Patients

Name (optional)_____   Date_____

This is not a test. Rather it is a way to help you examine your possible countertransference reactions to different patients. On the following pages there are several transcripts. Please project yourself into the role of the therapist as you read these transcripts. Then answer the questions.

- -

1. Ms. W telling Dr. D that she would not go back to the hospital unit at the end of the session.

Ms. W: There's nothing for me on the unit. Nobody likes me there. Nobody has ever liked me. What's wrong with me, Dr. D? Why has no one ever liked me? It seems so hopeless. It's never going to change. Why should I go on?

Dr. D: Right now you feel hopeless. You sound like you're on the verge of despair. You need to be in a protected environment.

Ms. W: How is that going to help me? I've been this way for 10 years. How will being in the hospital unit over the weekend help me? Nothing's going to change.

Dr. D: For one thing, it may help you avoid harming yourself.

Ms. W: I don't think I need to be in a hospital.

Dr. D: Do you feel like killing yourself now?

Ms. W: (Angrily) Why are you asking me that? What a stupid question! I've felt like killing myself for 10 years. There's never a day when I don't feel like killing myself.

Dr. D: Why are you getting so nasty with me now? You know I only asked because I'm concerned about your safety.

Ms. W: (Crying) Now you think I'm nasty! See? No one likes me. Even you think I'm bad. Why shouldn't I kill myself? Nobody likes me. What's wrong with me?

Dr. D: I probably shouldn't have used the word nasty. What I was reacting to is how angry you got at me for expressing concern about your hurting yourself.

Ms. W: No. It's true. I am nasty. That's why everybody hates me. You feel the same way everybody else does toward me. I might as well die. It's so painful to go on living.

Dr. D: I still would like to know if you have any plans to kill yourself. I know it makes you angry for me to ask, but I am concerned, and I need to know how you're feeling.

What are your reactions as you read what the patient said? _____

_____

_____

How would most of your colleagues react to this patient? _____

_____

_____

What personal vulnerabilities in you might this patient trigger? _____

_____

_____

2. Ms. Y entered Dr. B's office for her first session and stared for a moment or two at her therapist. She looked disappointed and even irritated.

Dr. B: I take it that I don't look like what you expected.

Ms. Y: No! I wanted someone older. Someone to mother me. Someone like Ellen, my last therapist. (*Ms. Y begins to cry.*) You look younger than I am. I know you are! Ellen gave me this necklace I'm wearing. It used to be hers.

Dr. B: So you feel like she's with you.

Ms. Y: She was like a mother to me for two years. Now I'm not with her because my husband had to change jobs and move here. I sold my collection of rare stamps so I could be in therapy with Ellen. Those stamps were the most valuable things we owned. But I sold them because Ellen was my life. I was in and out of hospitals for a while, and most of the doctors wouldn't okay passes for me to go to Ellen's office for therapy. They thought I would kill myself. But not as long as I was with Ellen! I would never do that as long as I was with her. A doctor during one of my hospitalizations let me go to Ellen's office. Once I was there, I couldn't leave. I wouldn't leave. It became a bit of a problem. (*Still gasping for air between sobs*) Ellen knows me so well. We are like mother and child. She rearranged the furniture in her office so I would be comfortable. She used to say she's keeping all of the parts of me, and then one day we'll put it all back together. Now I'm here, and she has all of me back there!

Dr. B: You are here, and yet you're not here.

Ms. Y: Ellen is so wonderful. There's no way for me to tell you all that she knows. I could never tell you what I've told her. She knows about my mother, my husband, and my fear of people. Ellen said she'd be there for me always. If I could be with her, everything would be okay.

Dr. B: Have you written to her?

Ms. Y: No! I'm angry with her for referring me to you! She said she couldn't help me any more. She said she'd always be there, and she left me! If she left me, that means other people can do it too! I don't even know your name. I can't remember. I know your first name. Can I call you that?

Dr. B: I prefer to be called "Dr. B." There are about 10 minutes left. I wasn't sure if you wanted to comment on our talk so far or talk about what comes next.

Ms. Y: You seem awful young. Younger than me. I equate youth with inexperience. Ellen was more experienced than you. She taught at the medical school.

Dr. B: What you know of me is what you see, and you're uncertain what I have inside of me.

Ms. Y: Yes, you are young. I know it.

Dr. B: (*Slightly ruffled and a bit annoyed*) You have yet to become familiar with who I am on the inside.

What are your reactions as you read what the patient said? _____

_____

_____

How would most of your colleagues react to this patient? _____

_____

_____

What personal vulnerabilities in you might this patient trigger? _____

_____

_____

3. Ms. U was seeing Dr. F. She became angry at Dr. F, whom she regarded as "all good" a few minutes ago.

Ms. U: I want Bill so badly. I think he was quiet and distant when he saw me at the bar with Mark (her long-time boyfriend) because he really is attracted to me. I'm sure of it. The way he looks at me tells me that he wants me. I could have him if I wanted him. I know I could. He knows I'm jealous of Jane.

As Ms. U went on and on about how Bill was secretly attracted to her, Dr. F became rather bored and realized that he had not been listening to what she was saying. When he realized that his attention had become distracted, he blinked and refocused on the patient's words.

Ms. U: (*shouting*) I'm boring you! You really don't care!

Dr. F: You suddenly shifted gears.

Ms. U: You blinked! (*Now more seriously and angrily*) This therapy isn't working! You don't care. This is obviously not a good match. You don't give me insight. You don't talk about my envy! I can't develop a relationship with you. It's no use to keep at this!

Dr. F: A few minutes ago you wanted me to hold you. I haven't changed. Something inside of you has changed.

Ms. U: No it hasn't. I don't think this can work. You don't give me insights. You don't talk about my jealousy. I can't develop a relationship with you.

Dr. F: I think you were trying to connect with me by telling me about the men in your life, and you felt rejected when I blinked.

Ms. U: Yes. I did! You don't talk about my fears. You don't care about me!

Dr. F: You seem very sensitive to being rejected. Rather than considering the variety of reasons why I might blink, you assume I'm rejecting you.

Ms. U: You seem pretty together. You're well educated, you're attractive, you dress well, and you're happily married, I'm sure. I have none of those things. I could have them if I didn't have such problems. I think you know what's wrong with me, but you're not telling me. How can I possibly manage better when I don't even know what's wrong?

Dr. F: For what reason should I withhold important information from you?

Ms. U: Oh, you're not withholding? Then you don't know, do you? That's even worse! Oh, my God, what's going to happen to me? You're only guessing! I'm lost. You're lost, too. We're both lost.

What are your reactions as you read what the patient said? _____

_____

_____

How would most of your colleagues react to this patient? _____

_____

_____

How would most of your colleagues react to this patient? _____

_____

_____

Reprinted with the permission from Gabbard, G., & Wilkinson, S. (1994). *Management of countertransference with borderline patients* (pp. 26–31, 71–72, 91–93). Washington: American Psychiatric Press, Inc.

FORM 28

Case Vignettes of Transference and Countertransference

Name _____   Date_____

On the following pages there are case vignettes. Please read and categorize the types of transference and countertransference in each case vignette. There may be several types of transference and countertransference in each case vignette; try to select the most prevalent types.

----

1. A 28-year-old man was depressed about his marriage and his failure to complete his Ph.D. thesis. Although he appeared insightful, he spoke incessantly and became very irritated whenever the therapist interrupted him. When he was confronted with his use of speech as a barrier to communication, he felt reproached. He became frightened that he might never be able to speak again. He revealed that his mother and maternal grandmother had used words to fight with others. Any disagreement carried the threat that one person might be annihilated. If he lost, he would become extinguished. He became immobilized with this unresolvable dilemma and simply kept talking to the therapist to avoid disagreements that might extinguish one or the other of them. (Source: Bruch, 1974, pp. 136–137)

   _____ Patient-originated transference

   _____ Therapist-originated transference

   _____ Interactive transference

2. The patient has sought help to limit the bitterness she felt whenever friends moved away. Most pertinent to her history was the manner of her father's death 2½ years earlier. During the last few days of his life, he enveloped himself in a silent curtain that the patient could not penetrate. At first the therapist accepted the patient's need to be silent, but during session 21 to 25, he became anxious to bring therapy "to life." He saw this desire as recapitulation of the patient's efforts to bring her father back from his dead silence. The patient had induced him to sit with her silence as she had to sit with the silence of her father. The therapist described this role reversal to the patient. A few sessions after the interpretation, the patient agreed. Subsequently, she experienced greater personal independence and was able to commit herself to a heterosexual relationship. (Source: Morgenstern, 1980, pp. 252–255)

   _____ Patient-originated transference   _____ Patient-originated countertransference

   _____ Therapist-originated transference   _____ Concordant Countertransference

   _____ Interactive transference   _____ Complementary Countertransference

3. A 30-year-old male therapist had seen a 38-year-old, depressed, homosexual man for five sessions. The patient was uncomfortable and irritable during the sixth session; he was talking about termination. The therapist interpreted his desire to leave therapy as a fear of coming too close to another man, despite the patient's claims to the contrary. There were, however, some realistic reasons for the patient's discomfort with the therapist. First, the patient was being charged a fee although he was a member of a health plan permitting him free access to any of the hospital's services. Second, the therapist had quickly asked the patient if he was sexually attracted to him, thereby demonstrating his ignorance of homosexual attractions. (The patient had replied, "Are you sexually attracted to all women?") (Source: Beitman, 1987, pp. 159)

   _____ Patient-originated transference   _____ Patient-originated countertransference

   _____ Therapist-originated transference   _____ Concordant countertransference

   _____ Interactive transference   _____ Complementary countertransference

_____ Therapist-originated countertransference

_____ Interactive countertransference

4. A 30-year-old woman therapist was treating a 60-year-old depressed man who had prostate cancer. She had difficulty with his statements about liking younger women and was confused by his mild but persistent sexual advances toward her. She was afraid to confront him on his sexual interest in her, fearing that he would terminate therapy. On the other hand, she knew she needed to confront him in order to keep therapy moving. She remained paralyzed by these contradictory injunctions and, eventually, the patient slipped away from therapy, never to return. In discussing this case with a colleague, the therapist realized that although she knew that this man in some way resembled her deceased father who was seductive toward her and had died of prostate cancer, she had not realized how much the similarity had paralyzed her. Among the possible interpretations was her wish for sexual contact and her fear of being reminded of his death. (Source: Beitman, 1983, pp. 85)

_____ Patient-originated countertransference

_____ Concordant countertransference

_____ Complementary countertransference

_____ Therapist-originated countertransference

_____ Interactive countertransference

5. A financially troubled therapist had engaged a 28-year-old woman who was supported by investments made by her wealthy father. The therapist envied this woman's financial freedom and failed to address her complaints that therapy was too expensive, although the patient easily took spur-of-the moment airplane trips to distant cities and purchased expensive clothing on a whim. (Source: Beitman, 1987, pp. 164)

_____ Patient-originated countertransference

_____ Concordant countertransference

_____ Complementary countertransference

_____ Therapist-originated countertransference

_____ Interactive countertransference

6. A 28-year-old therapist was attempting to understand the personality pattern of her 24-year-old woman patient who was aspiring to become a psychotherapist as well. The patient repetitively badgered her therapist. "You are cold, you are unfeminine, no man could ever want you, you aren't helping me at all. I met someone just like you and I didn't like her." The therapist began to withdraw and had to reassure herself that men did like her and that she was trying to help and that she was trying to care. Nevertheless, their relationship took a fixed form in which the patient criticized and the therapist responded meekly. The therapist tried to break the deadlock by saying: "You seem to be trying to make me angry at you." The patient responded: "You don't have it together enough to become angry." During supervision, the therapist expressed her intense rage and helplessness. As she became more objective about her own reaction, she was able to see how frightened the patient was about revealing herself. Confrontation of this fear of developing a self-observer alliance broke the stalemate. (Source: Beitman, 1987, pp. 167)

_____ Patient-originated transference   _____ Patient-originated countertransference

_____ Therapist-originated transference   _____ Concordant countertransference

_____ Interactive transference   _____ Complementary countertransference

_____ Therapist-originated countertransference

_____ Interactive countertransference

7. A 45-year-old manic-depressive woman at first refused to accept lithium treatment until she had been deeply depressed twice more after the therapist's initial evaluation. Her character style during the engagement was rapid, flippant, "gamey" sexuality by which she attempted to avoid self-revelation. After numerous confrontations on her "games," she initiated more subtle ones. When she finally accepted lithium treatment some 12 months later, her avoidance manipulations were dramatically reduced. In fact, she felt herself as "empty," with nothing underneath those attractive, socially effective facades. She complained about how her deceased husband had controlled her, how she felt empty and worthless without a man, although she ran her own business reasonably well. She described how at 16 her father had tried to stop her from marrying, but she persisted in entering the relationship. She was beaten and then deserted. Years later while in psychotherapy, she entered a new relationship that most of her friends told her would be destructive. She cast the therapist in the role of her friend, encouraging the therapist to tell her that she should stay away from the man, who did jilt her. She took an overdose of diazepam supplied by her primary care physician. At the time of the overdose, the therapist had not yet seen that he was being placed in the role of her father, who had tried to stop her marrying at age 16. She became involved with another man, who assumed the role of lay therapist for her manic-depressive illness, and induced him to suggest that she stop therapy. The therapist's jealousy and competitive feelings signaled again her attempt at repetition of the adolescent triangle. (Source: Beitman, 1987, pp. 152)

_____ Patient-originated transference

_____ Therapist-originated transference

_____ Interactive transference

_____ Patient-originated countertransference

_____ Concordant countertransference

_____ Complementary countertransference

_____ Therapist-originated countertransference

_____ Interactive countertransference

8. A 32-year-old woman was unable to relax during the first psychotherapy session with her new therapist. After the therapist confronted her anxiety, she recognized the problem. Her previous therapist had hypnotized her and made sexual advances toward her while she was in a trance. (Source: Beitman, 1987, pp. 156)

_____ Patient-originated transference

_____ Therapist-originated transference

_____ Interactive transference

9. The 18-year-old woman entered therapy with multiple shifting somatic symptoms, uncontrollable laughter and crying, and unremitting abdominal pain, all of which began shortly after she left home to attend college. She was considered a "problem child"; all developmental stages had been stormy. Within the first three weeks of therapy with a psychiatric resident, her somatic symptoms disappeared. The transference was very positive, eroticized, and intense. The patient expressed a desire to displace all of the therapist's other patients.

During the first several months, the patient displayed a wide variety of antisocial symptoms, but gradually it became apparent that she genuinely wanted to be "good" in order to gain the love of the therapist. In time she decided that being "good" included having a steady job, not having indiscriminate sex or taking illicit drugs, and only being "appropriately rebellious." During the ensuing months, she looked "as if" she were any other young adult female secretary in a metropolitan office. The transference relationship continued on in an intense, positive, and deeply dependent basis. Gradually she revealed her wish to merge with the therapist through the following fantasy: she wished to be physically attached to the therapist, perhaps with epoxy cement, and carried about with him forever.

In part, the therapist's own omnipotent fantasies were coming true. This very disturbed person had made a startling recovery and no overt psychotic thinking or behavior could be observed outside the transference. The therapist decided to encourage the patient to date and offered to ask her family to fix her up with nice men. In retrospect, the therapist was reacting against the deep enmeshment he experienced with the patient.

Although she responded positively to the suggestion, in the next interview she was overtly depressed. She became circumstantial, tangential, and rambling. She then made a suicide gesture and was readmitted to the hospital, at which time she was grossly psychotic. The patient subsequently made it clear that she felt the therapist's discussion about dating was an attempt to get rid of her. She then demanded physical affection (hugging) from the therapist and, when this was not forthcoming, made another suicide gesture in her therapist's office. (Source: Stone, 1971, pp. 22–24)

_____ Patient-originated transference   _____ Patient-originated countertransference

_____ Therapist-originated transference   _____ Concordant countertransference

_____ Interactive transference   _____ Complementary countertransference

                                                          _____ Therapist-originated countertransference

                                                           _____ Interactive countertransference

10. A 24-year-old man began his videotaped 16th session with a first-year psychiatric resident by talking about a party at his house and how "I always manage to get myself in the center of attention." (He may have been referring to the camera and its potential audience.) He then said that he did not like being on stage and that he was going to stop seeing his woman companion (Linda). He ended the session by saying that he would not return to therapy. Therefore, Linda appears to have been an analogue for the therapist. The therapist reported that he had been very directive with the patient, "He was one of my favorites, I was like his guru." Further evidence for the Linda-therapist analogue had come when the patient had stated his reasons for not seeing her. "It's negative experience walking with her because she doesn't walk with you. . . . She'll just choose to cross the street at a point which I would not choose to cross the street. . . . She's very domineering in the way she walks. . . . One time it was like she dragging me through the street, you know, by the hair." (Both Linda and the therapist were highly directive.) A little later, the patient had stated that the only reason he went to her house that day was to get some marijuana. (He was also receiving medications from the therapist.) The patient had followed that possible parallel with a description of the relationship he hoped to have with Linda (and his therapist?): "When you establish a relationship with someone, I imagine that there is some work to be done and something to be accomplished, a mutual complement of one another's growth, especially in a relationship as intimate as the one I thought I may have had with Linda." (Source: Beitman, 1987, pp. 161)

_____ Patient-originated transference

_____ Therapist-originated transference

_____ Interactive transference

11. A 34-year-old junior high English teacher was referred with the diagnosis pedophilia made by a previous psychiatrist. He was unable to continue seeing that psychiatrist after four sessions because the patient's girlfriend was also in therapy with that psychiatrist for a longstanding character problem. The patient belonged to a fundamentalist religion that taught sex before marriage was sinful. Although the patient had not engaged in intercourse with his girlfriend, he felt guilty for having experimented with naked sexual contact with her, his first such contact with any woman. His reason for entering therapy in the first

place and continuing on with the second therapist was his fear of being caught caressing children. He found that they were often attracted to him and liked to play wrestling games with him. Sometimes he found himself getting an erection, which to him was wrong and frightening. Four years previously he had roomed with an 8-year-old boy during a church retreat and impulsively went over to the sleeping child and stroked his penis to erection. He did nothing more and the child was not awakened but he was greatly frightened by this lack of self-control. He was afraid that his reputation would be ruined if he were discovered. He was also disturbed by his failure to find a wife since getting married and having a family was his fondest dream.

During therapy he began dating a woman who showed interest in him. As the relationship evolved during therapy, his rules for "marriageable" women began to emerge. If someone liked him, he had to run from her. If she did not want him, he could chase her knowing that he could not have her. Was this new date a friend or was she more than a friend? When he went to her house with her he wondered what he was expected to do, should he go in, should he touch her, should he kiss her?

He scanned her every movement, trying to interpret the meaning of her gestures, her tone, her words. In therapy, while the patient was obsessively reviewing his attempts at interpersonal analysis, the therapist suddenly saw an image of a dentate vagina and was momentarily thrust back into his own frightening experiences with girls and women. His feelings during premature ejaculations washed over him. Now he could label those feelings! He was afraid! Coming out of his reverie he could see that these were also his patient's feelings now. He was frightened of women, frightened of what they could do to him. (Source: Beitman, 1987, pp. 165)

_____ Patient-originated countertransference

_____ Concordant countertransference

_____ Complementary countertransference

_____ Therapist-originated countertransference

_____ Interactive countertransference

12. A therapist assumed that his psychotic patient needed information about his grieving for a loved one because of her shaky reality testing. He believed she must have noticed his changed demeanor. Therefore, he told her some details. The patient experienced the therapist's revelation as an overwhelming demand that she care for him, an experience that recapitulated her major childhood relationships. The revelation derailed therapy and led to a premature termination. The therapist later realized that he had needed to be cared for and had also wanted to deflect her rage at his emotional unavailability. (Source: Gilvelber & Simon, 1981, pp. 144)

_____ Patient-originated countertransference

_____ Concordant countertransference

_____ Complementary countertransference

_____ Therapist-originated countertransference

_____ Interactive countertransference

13. A 26-year-old woman was making the transition from severely disturbed borderline character to narcissistic-neurotic one. As she was making the transition, she took a position as a secretary in the therapist's psychiatry department in a different hospital, moved to an apartment near his home (the address of which she knew), and began a romantic relationship with a trainee who was one of the therapist's friends. As the therapist reviewed these behaviors with her, he blurted out in a therapy hour, "I feel like a caged mouse being stalked by a lion." This metaphor did not seem to touch the patient, but he gave it

considerable thought. In a previous intense relationship, his woman friend had declared her desire to cage and study him. He interpreted his remarks as suggesting his own fear of giving in to her advances. The patient was very attractive to him and had fulfilled his therapeutic narcissism by making remarkable therapeutic advances. Much later in therapy she was able to state how, indeed, she was looking for any clues he might give her that he might be vulnerable to her affection and be willing to step outside his therapeutic stance. Because he was caught up in his own difficulties, he was not able to perceive clearly how accurate his spontaneous remark had been in describing her intention toward him. (Source: Beitman, 1987, pp. 166)

_____ Patient-originated transference   _____ Patient-originated countertransference

_____ Therapist-originated transference   _____ Concordant countertransference

_____ Interactive transference   _____ Complementary countertransference

   _____ Therapist-originated countertransference

   _____ Interactive countertransference

14. An analyst needed an analytic "control" case to fulfill the requirements of his psychoanalytic training so, after 18 months, he asked a patient to increase the frequency of their sessions from two to three times per week and to lie on the couch. He needed her to excel as an analytic patient, and she felt this pressure from him. When she deteriorated after his vacation, she struggled to ease the pain of his distress over her dysfunction by complying with his suggestion for an increase in session frequency. As she improved, she indirectly expressed her fears that the therapist could not tolerate her separation from him. He acknowledged to his supervisor that termination would be humiliating and shameful for him. A critical point of therapy involved the therapist's ability to point out to the patient her compulsion to fulfill the therapist's needs because she feared that he would retaliate if she failed to do so. (Source: Beitman, 1987, pp. 168)

_____ Patient-originated transference   _____ Patient-originated countertransference

_____ Therapist-originated transference   _____ Concordant countertransference

_____ Interactive transference   _____ Complementary countertransference

                                                     _____ Therapist-originated countertransference

                                                     _____ Interactive countertransference

Excerpts reprinted with the permission from Beitman, B. (1987). _The structure of individual psychotherapy_ (pp. 146–168). New York: Guilford.

FORM 29
Transcripts of Transference

Name _____ Date_____

The following transcripts show the patient's transference. Please read them and think about how you might respond to the patient's transference reaction. Please describe what you would say to the patient.

- -

1.

T: I notice that it is difficult for you to tell me about your problem.

P: (*Obviously in discomfort*) I don't know what to say. I expected that I would see an older person. Have you had much experience with cases like me?

You would say:

_____

_____

_____

_____

2.

T: (*Noting the patient's hesitant speech*) You seem to be upset about something.

P: Why, should I be upset?

T: You might be if I did something you didn't like.

P: (*Pause*) No—I'm afraid, just afraid I'm not doing what I should. I've been here six times and still have that panicky feeling from time to time. Do other patients do better?

T: You seem to be comparing yourself to my other patients.

P: I—I—I guess so. The young man that came before me. He seems so self-confident and cheerful. I guess I felt inferior, that you would find fault with me.

T: Do you think I like him better than I do you?

P: Well, wouldn't you, if he was doing better than I was?

T: That's interesting. Tell me more.

P: I've been that way. My parents, I felt, preferred my older brother. He always came in on top. They were proud of his accomplishments in school.

T: So in a way you feel I should be acting like your parents.

P: I can't help feeling that way.

T: Don't you think this is a pattern that is really self-defeating? We ought to explore this more.

P: (*Emotionally*) Well, I really thought today you were going to send me to another doctor because you were sick of me.

You would say:

_____

_____

_____

_____

3.

T: I notice that it is difficult for you to tell me about your problem.

T: You know sometimes I get the impression that you act with me as if you are walking on eggs. I wonder if you have any feelings toward me you are not talking about.

P: I don't, I don't know. This is one of the disturbing things . . . when I'm all tangled up inside and don't know (*weeps*) . . . don't want to cry . . . I'll wipe my nose . . . don't know why I'm so upset today, really I don't. I felt so much better yesterday.

T: Perhaps it's because I bring up the subject of your feeling toward me.

P: (*Cries*) I feel irritated, just a momentary anger. I haven't been particularly conscious of it. I don't dislike you, just irritated. (*Pause*).

T: Do you want to tell me more about your feelings toward me?

P: I don't want to have feelings for you.

T: You don't want to have feelings for me?

P: No. I don't know why.

T: Perhaps you are afraid of showing emotion?

P: I certainly would be afraid of feeling affectionate.

T: You would?

P: I certainly would.

T: I wonder why?

P: I was thinking of it, as a matter of fact, yesterday. I felt . . . well . . . if I behaved well . . . perhaps you would be good to me . . . fatherly like, I mean.

T: If you behaved affectionately to me you mean?

P: Yes, but I'm afraid.

T: Afraid? Of what?

P: That it would not be taken seriously. Would it?

T: If you felt affectionate toward me, of course I would take your feelings seriously. Perhaps what you're saying is that I might reject you or hurt you in some way?

P: What I mean is that I'd be ashamed of my feelings, that this would be a one-sided relationship. I think I feel you'd ridicule me.

T: Actually, you don't know how I'd act, and yet you behave as if I do ridicule you for your feelings.

P: If I had feelings would they be responded to . . . would they?

T: You mean would I reciprocate with the same kind of feeling?

P: That's it.

T: If I did, this would not be a therapeutic situation for you.

P: I suppose not.

You would say:

_____

_____

_____

_____

4.

T: I notice that you don't want to look at me today.

P: I don't want to like you. I'd rather not like you.

T: I wonder why?

P: I feel I'll be hurt. Liking you will expose me to being hurt.

T: But how do you feel about me?

P: I don't know. I have conflicting emotions about you. Sometimes I like you too much, and sometimes I get mad at you for no reason. I often can't think of you, even picture you.

T: Do you feel that you stop yourself in your feelings toward me?

P: Yes, I don't want to like you. If I do, I won't be able to stop myself. I'll get hurt. But why do I feel or insist that I'm in love with you.

T: Are you?

P: Yes. And I feel so guilty and upset about it. At night I think of you and get sexual feelings and it frightens me.

You would say:

_____

_____

_____

_____

Reprinted with the permission from Wolberg, L. (1988). *The technique of psychotherapy* (pp. 706–708). New York: Grune & Stratton.

Developing Psychotherapy Competence—A Guided Inquiry
(Post-Module 6)

Name _____ Date _____

1. What was the most important thing that happened in training during past several weeks?

2. What changes are you making in your thinking/feeling about psychotherapy issues as a result of this module?

3. What in this module is *helping you* achieve your desired changes?

4. What aspects/influences *outside* of this module are *helping you* achieve your desired changes?

5. What in this module is *keeping you* from making your desired changes?

6. What aspects/influences *outside* of this module are *keeping you* from making your desired changes?

7. Did you find yourself thinking about topics related to this module between training sessions during past several weeks? If so, what *thoughts have you had?*

8. Are you deriving any *benefits* from this module that you did not expect to happen? If so, what are these benefits?

9. Please state the *most immediate concerns* you are having about your psychotherapy competence.

Reprinted with permission from Heppner, P. P. & O'Brien, K. M. (1994). Multicultural counselor training: Students' perceptions of helpful and hindering events. *Counselor Education and Supervision, 34,* 4–18.

As you answer the following questions, please try to think about how you will behave as a therapist now (after Module 6)

Counseling Self-Estimate Inventory
(Post-module 6)

Name_____ Date_____

This is not a test. There are no right and wrong answers. Rather, it is an inventory that attempts to measure how you feel you will behave as a therapist in a therapy situation. Please respond to the items as honestly as you can so as to most accurately portray how you think you will behave as a therapist. Do not respond with how you wish you could perform each item, rather answer in a way that reflects your actual estimate of how you will perform as a therapist at the present time.

	Strong Disagree	Some Disagree	Little Disagree	Little Agree	Some Agree	Strong Agree
1. When using responses like reflection of feeling, active listening, clarifying, and probing, I am confident I will be concise and to the point.	1	2	3	4	5	6
2. I am likely to impose my values on the patient during the interview.	1	2	3	4	5	6
3. When I initiate the end of a session, I am positive it will be in a manner that is not abrupt or brusque and that I will end the session on time.	1	2	3	4	5	6
4. I am confident that I will respond appropriately to the patient in view of what the patient will express (e.g., my questions will be meaningful and not concerned with trivia and minutiae).	1	2	3	4	5	6
5. I am certain that my interpretation and confrontation responses will be concise and to the point.	1	2	3	4	5	6
6. I am worried that the wording of my responses like reflection of feeling, clarification, and probing may be confusing and hard to understand.	1	2	3	4	5	6
7. I feel that I will not be able to respond to the patient in a non-judgmental way with respect to the patient's values, beliefs, etc.	1	2	3	4	5	6
8. I feel I will respond to the patient in an appropriate length of time (neither interrupting the patient or waiting too long to respond).	1	2	3	4	5	6
9. I am worried that the type of responses I use at a particular time, i.e., reflection of feeling, interpretation, etc., may not be the appropriate response.	1	2	3	4	5	6

	Strong Disagree	Some Disagree	Little Disagree	Little Agree	Some Agree	Strong Agree
10. I am sure that the content of my responses, i.e., reflection of feeling, clarifying, and probing, will be consistent with and not discrepant from what the patient is saying.	1	2	3	4	5	6
11. I feel confident that I will appear confident and earn the respect of my patient.	1	2	3	4	5	6
12. I am confident that my interpretation and confrontation responses will be effective in that they will be validated by the patient's immediate response.	1	2	3	4	5	6
13. I feel confident that I have resolved conflicts in my personal life so that they will not interfere with my therapy abilities.	1	2	3	4	5	6
14. I feel that the content of my interpretation and confrontation responses will be consistent with and not discrepant from what the patient is saying.	1	2	3	4	5	6
15. I feel that I have enough fundamental knowledge to do effective psychotherapy.	1	2	3	4	5	6
16. I may not be able to maintain the intensity and energy level needed to produce patient confidence and active participation.	1	2	3	4	5	6
17. I am confident that the wording of my interpretation and confrontation responses will be clear and easy to understand.	1	2	3	4	5	6
18. I am not sure that in a therapeutic relationship I will express myself in a way that is natural without deliberating over every response or action.	1	2	3	4	5	6
19. I am afraid that I may not understand and properly determine probable meanings of the patient's nonverbal behaviors.	1	2	3	4	5	6
20. I am confident that I will know when to use open or close ended probes, and that these probes will reflect the concerns of the patient and not be trivial.	1	2	3	4	5	6
21. My assessment of patient problems may not be as accurate as I would like it to be.	1	2	3	4	5	6

	Strong Disagree	Some Disagree	Little Disagree	Little Agree	Some Agree	Strong Agree
22. I am uncertain as to whether I will be able to appropriately confront and challenge my patient in therapy.	1	2	3	4	5	6
23. When giving responses, i.e., reflection of feeling, active listening, clarifying, and probing, I am afraid that they may not be effective in that they won't be validated by the patient's immediate response.	1	2	3	4	5	6
24. I don't feel I possess a large enough repertoire of techniques to deal with the different problems my patient may present.	1	2	3	4	5	6
25. I feel competent regarding my abilities to deal with crisis situations which may arise during the therapy sessions—e.g., suicide, alcoholism, abuse, etc.	1	2	3	4	5	6
26. I am uncomfortable about dealing with patients who appear unmotivated to work toward mutually determined goals.	1	2	3	4	5	6
27. I may have difficulty dealing with patients who don't verbalize their thoughts during the therapy session.	1	2	3	4	5	6
28. I am unsure as to how to deal with patients who appear noncommittal and indecisive.	1	2	3	4	5	6
29. When working with ethnic minority patients, I am confident that I will be able to bridge cultural differences in the therapy process.	1	2	3	4	5	6
30. I will be an effective therapist with patients of a different social class.	1	2	3	4	5	6
31. I am worried that my interpretation and confrontation responses may not over time assist the patient to be more specific in defining and clarifying the problem.	1	2	3	4	5	6
32. I am confident that I will be able to conceptualize my patient's problems.	1	2	3	4	5	6
33. I am unsure as to how I will lead my patient toward the development and selection of concrete goals to work toward.	1	2	3	4	5	6
34. I am confident that I can assess my patient's readiness and commitment to change.	1	2	3	4	5	6

	Strong Disagree	Some Disagree	Little Disagree	Little Agree	Some Agree	Strong Agree
35. I feel I may give advice.	1	2	3	4	5	6
36. In working with culturally different patients I may have a difficult time viewing situations from their perspective.	1	2	3	4	5	6
37. I am afraid that I may not be able to effectively relate to someone of lower socioeconomic status than me.	1	2	3	4	5	6

The Counseling Self-Estimate Inventory is copyrighted by L. M. Larson, 1990. Reprinted with permission.

Posttraining

During the posttraining period, the trainee produces an audiotape from the third session of each of two psychotherapy relationships to serve as a comparison to pretraining relationships.

Session 1

1. The trainee learns the measures that need to be completed when seeing the two psychotherapy patients. Trainees need to complete the following forms for each patient:

1. One Patient Profile (Form 2)
2. One Working Alliance Inventory-WAI (Form 4-1)
3. One Rating the Therapist's Intentions (Form 6)

Each patient completes:

1. Two TOP questionnaires (Form 3-a, Form 3-b)
2. One Working Alliance Inventory-WAI (Form 4-2)
3. One Session Evaluation Questionnaire (SEQ) (Form 5)
4. One Patient Reaction System form (Form 7)
5. One patient consent form for being audio or videotaped

2. The trainee is required to see two psychotherapy patients for at least three sessions. Session length may vary from 20 minutes to one hour, with 40-45 minutes being preferable. (Note: Ideally the diagnosis and other demographics for the posttraining patients will match the pretraining patients.) The following procedures are identical to the pretraining procedures.

First Session: Before the first session begins the trainee asks the patient to complete the TOP Questionnaire (Form 3-a). The trainee completes the Patient Profile (Form 2) within the first two sessions.

Third session: The third therapy session is videotaped or audiotaped. The consent forms are completed at that time. The patient should also agree to spend an additional hour reviewing the tape with the therapist after the session or at another time. Before the third session starts the patient should fill out the second TOP questionnaire (Form 3-b). Immediately after the session, the patient needs to finish the WAI (Form 4-2) and SEQ (Form 5), and the trainee needs to complete WAI (Form 4-1). Completing Form 6 (Rating the Therapist's Intentions) and Form 7 (Patient Reaction System) generally takes about an hour. We suggest that the therapist and patient set aside another hour to review the tape and finish Form 6 and Form 7. Both of them should try to recall what they felt during the session rather than focusing on what they feel at the time of the review. The tape recorder is stoped after the therapist's each speech turn. A *turn* is defined as any therapist speech act surrounded by two patient speech acts. At each of these points when the tape is stopped, the therapist use Rating the Therapist's Intentions form (Form 6) to record up to five intentions used in each turn. The patient use Patient Reaction System (Form 7) to record reactions to the therapist's interventions.

The same steps are followed with the second patient.

The trainee returns the following forms:

1. Two patient profiles (Form 2).
2. Four TOP questionnaires (Form 3-a, Form 3-b) finished before session 1 and session 3.
3. Two WAI (Form 4-1) done by the therapist after session 3.
4. Two WAI (Form 4-2) done by the patient after session 3.
5. Two SEQs (Form 5) completed by the patient after session 3.
6. Two Rating the Therapist's Intentions forms (Form 6) done by the therapist after session 3.
7. Two Patient Reaction System forms (Form 7) completed by the patient after session 3.
8. Two audiotapes or videotapes of session 3.

Session 2

This session is used to share feedback about psychotherapy experiences.

FORM 2 (POSTTRAINING)

Patient Profile

Name_____   Sex_____(F/M)   Age_____

Date_____(Month/Day/Yr.)   Therapist Name_____

- -

Diagnosis:

Axis I _____

Axis II _____

Axis III _____

Axis IV _____

Axis V _____

Please have your patient complete this form at the beginning of session 1

FORM 3–a (POSTTRAINING)
Treatment Outcome Profile (TOP)

Patient Name_____   Date_____(Month/Day/Yr.)

Your opinion counts in helping us evaluate mental health services. Please take a few moments to complete this short survey about how you have been doing during the last month and about the treatment you received. Just check the appropriate circle.

(The following items concern how you feel about your life in general.)

	Strongly Disagree	Disagree	Neutral	Agree	Strongly Agree
1. I am satisfied with my life.	O	O	O	O	O
2. I feel good about myself.	O	O	O	O	O
3. I am happy with the way I look.	O	O	O	O	O
4. I have a good relationship with my family.	O	O	O	O	O
5. I have supportive friends.	O	O	O	O	O
6. My health is good.	O	O	O	O	O
7. I experience little physical pain.	O	O	O	O	O
8. I have adequate physical strength.	O	O	O	O	O
9. I enjoy my leisure time.	O	O	O	O	O
10. I am happy with my job/work.	O	O	O	O	O

(The following items concern feelings you may have had during the last month)

11. I have feelings of hopelessness about the future.	O	O	O	O	O
12. I feel worthless.	O	O	O	O	O
13. I feel blue.	O	O	O	O	O
14. I feel weak in part of my body.	O	O	O	O	O
15. My heart pounds and races.	O	O	O	O	O
16. I have to avoid certain things, places, or situations because they frighten me.	O	O	O	O	O
17. I feel that people, in general, are unfriendly and dislike me.	O	O	O	O	O
18. I have urges to beat, injure, or harm someone.	O	O	O	O	O
19. I feel that I am being watched or talked about by others.	O	O	O	O	O

(The following items describe difficult or stressful situations you may have experienced during the last month)

20. I have recently had a physical fight with someone.	O	O	O	O	O
21. I have recently tried to harm myself or had a plan to do so.	O	O	O	O	O

	Strongly Disagree	Disagree	Neutral	Agree	Strongly Agree
22. I have recently become upset or angry.	O	O	O	O	O
23. I have recently broken things or destroyed property.	O	O	O	O	O
24. I am able to get around in the community on my own.	O	O	O	O	O
25. I can get help when I need it.	O	O	O	O	O
26. I take care of my home and living space.	O	O	O	O	O
27. I am functioning well at my work/school.	O	O	O	O	O

Reprinted with the permission from Holcomb, W. R., Parker, J. C., & Leong, G. B. (1997). Outcomes of inpatients treated on a VA psychiatry unit and a substance abuse treatment unit. *Psychiatric Services, 48,* 699–704.

Please have your patient complete this form at the beginning of session 1

FORM 3–b (POSTTRAINING)
Treatment Outcome Profile (TOP)

Patient Name_____   Date_____(Month/Day/Yr.)

Your opinion counts in helping us evaluate mental health services. Please take a few moments to complete this short survey about how you have been doing during the last month and about the treatment you received. Just check the appropriate circle.

(The following items concern how you feel about your life in general.)

	Strongly Disagree	Disagree	Neutral	Agree	Strongly Agree
1. I am satisfied with my life.	O	O	O	O	O
2. I feel good about myself.	O	O	O	O	O
3. I am happy with the way I look.	O	O	O	O	O
4. I have a good relationship with my family.	O	O	O	O	O
5. I have supportive friends.	O	O	O	O	O
6. My health is good.	O	O	O	O	O
7. I experience little physical pain.	O	O	O	O	O
8. I have adequate physical strength.	O	O	O	O	O
9. I enjoy my leisure time.	O	O	O	O	O
10. I am happy with my job/work.	O	O	O	O	O

(The following items concern feelings you may have had during the last month)

11. I have feelings of hopelessness about the future.	O	O	O	O	O
12. I feel worthless.	O	O	O	O	O
13. I feel blue.	O	O	O	O	O
14. I feel weak in part of my body.	O	O	O	O	O
15. My heart pounds and races.	O	O	O	O	O
16. I have to avoid certain things, places, or situations because they frighten me.	O	O	O	O	O
17. I feel that people, in general, are unfriendly and dislike me.	O	O	O	O	O
18. I have urges to beat, injure, or harm someone.	O	O	O	O	O
19. I feel that I am being watched or talked about by others.	O	O	O	O	O

(The following items describe difficult or stressful situations you may have experienced during the last month)

20. I have recently had a physical fight with someone.	O	O	O	O	O
21. I have recently tried to harm myself or had a plan to do so.	O	O	O	O	O

	Strongly Disagree	Disagree	Neutral	Agree	Strongly Agree
22. I have recently become upset or angry.	O	O	O	O	O
23. I have recently broken things or destroyed property.	O	O	O	O	O
24. I am able to get around in the community on my own.	O	O	O	O	O
25. I can get help when I need it.	O	O	O	O	O
26. I take care of my home and living space.	O	O	O	O	O
27. I am functioning well at my work/school.	O	O	O	O	O

(The following items ask your opinion about the treatment you received)

	Strongly Disagree	Disagree	Neutral	Agree	Strongly Agree
28. I feel better after receiving treatment.	O	O	O	O	O
29. I am satisfied withe services I received.	O	O	O	O	O
30. I would return for treatment if I needed help.	O	O	O	O	O
31. My diagnosis and treatment were explained to me.	O	O	O	O	O
32. Treatment staff spent enough time with me.	O	O	O	O	O
33. Treatment staff were understanding of my needs.	O	O	O	O	O
34. Rules and procedures were reasonable.	O	O	O	O	O
35. My privacy was respected.	O	O	O	O	O
36. The facilities were comfortable and pleasant in appearance.	O	O	O	O	O

Reprinted with the permission from Holcomb, W. R., Parker, J. C., & Leong, G. B. (1997). Outcomes of inpatients treated on a VA psychiatry unit and a substance abuse treatment unit. *Psychiatric Services, 48,* 699–704.

You (the therapist) need to complete this form immediately after your third session

FORM 4–1 (POSTTRAINING)
Working Alliance Inventory-Form T

Patient's Name_____ Sex _____(F/M) Age_____ Session Number_____

Therapist's Name_____ Date_____(Month/Day/Yr.)

The following sentences describe some of the different ways a person might think or feel about his or her patient. As you read the sentences, mentally insert the name of your patient in place of _____ in the text. If the statement describes the way you always feel (or think), circle the number 7. If it never applies to you circle the number 1. Use the numbers in between to describe the variations between these extremes. Work fast; your first impressions are the best. (Please respond to every item.)

	Never	Rarely	Occasionally	Sometimes	Often	Very Often	Always
1. _____ believes the way we are working with his/her problem is correct.	1	2	3	4	5	6	7
2. We agree on what is important for to _____ work on.	1	2	3	4	5	6	7
3. _____ and I agree about the steps to be taken to improve his/her situation.	1	2	3	4	5	6	7
4. My patient and I both feel confident about the usefulness of our current activity in therapy.	1	2	3	4	5	6	7
5. I believe _____ likes me.	1	2	3	4	5	6	7
6. I am confident in my ability to help _____.	1	2	3	4	5	6	7
7. I appreciate _____ as a person.	1	2	3	4	5	6	7
8. _____ and I have built a mutual trust.	1	2	3	4	5	6	7
9. I have doubts about what we are trying to accomplish in therapy.	1	2	3	4	5	6	7
10. We are working toward mutually agreed upon goals.	1	2	3	4	5	6	7
11. _____ and I have different ideas on what his/her real problems are.	1	2	3	4	5	6	7
12. We have established a good understanding between us of the kind of changes that would be good for _____.	1	2	3	4	5	6	7

Please name three things you did that helped your patient in this session:

1. _____

2. _____

3. _____

Name three things you did that were unhelpful to your patient in this session:

1. _____

2. _____

3. _____

Reprinted with permission from Anna Marie Kokotovic.

Please have your patient complete this form immediately after your third session

FORM 4–2 (POSTTRAINING)
Working Alliance Inventory-Form P

Patient's Name_____ Sex ____(F/M) Age____ Session Number_____

Therapist's Name_____ Date_____(Month/Day/Yr.)

The following sentences describe some of the different ways a person might think or feel about his or her therapist. As you read the sentences, mentally insert the name of your therapist in place of _____ in the text. If the statement describes the way you always feel (or think), circle the number 7. If it never applies to you circle the number 1. Use the numbers in between to describe the variations between these extremes. Work fast; your first impressions are the best. (Please respond to every item.)

	Never	Rarely	Occasionally	Sometimes	Often	Very Often	Always
1. I believe the way we are working with my problem is correct.	1	2	3	4	5	6	7
2. We agree on what is important for me to work on.	1	2	3	4	5	6	7
3. _____ and I agree about the things I will need to do in therapy to help improve my situation.	1	2	3	4	5	6	7
4. What I am doing in therapy gives me new ways of looking at my problems.	1	2	3	4	5	6	7
5. I believe _____ likes me.	1	2	3	4	5	6	7
6. I am confident in _____'s ability to help me.	1	2	3	4	5	6	7
7. I feel that _____ appreciates me.	1	2	3	4	5	6	7
8. _____ and I trust one another.	1	2	3	4	5	6	7
9. _____ does not understand what I am trying to accomplish in therapy.	1	2	3	4	5	6	7
10. _____ and I are working toward mutually agreed upon the goals.	1	2	3	4	5	6	7
11. _____ and I have different ideas on what my problems are.	1	2	3	4	5	6	7
12. We have established a good understanding of the kind of changes that would be good for me.	1	2	3	4	5	6	7

Please name three things the therapist did that helped you in this session:

1. _____

2. _____

3. _____

Name three things the therapist did that were unhelpful in this session:

1. _____

2. _____

3. _____

Please have your patient complete this form immediately after your third session

FORM 5 (POSTTRAINING)
Session Evaluation Questionnaire (SEQ)

Patient Name_____   Therapist Name_____

Session Number_____   Date_____ (Month/Day/Yr.)

Rater_____ (Therapist/Patient)

Please circle the number to show how you feel about this session.

This session was:

1. Bad   Good
   1   2   3   4   5   6   7

2. Safe   Dangerous
   1   2   3   4   5   6   7

3. Difficult   Easy
   1   2   3   4   5   6   7

4. Valuable   Worthless
   1   2   3   4   5   6   7

5. Shallow   Deep
   1   2   3   4   5   6   7

6. Relaxed   Tense
   1   2   3   4   5   6   7

7. Unpleasant   Pleasant
   1   2   3   4   5   6   7

8. Full   Empty
   1   2   3   4   5   6   7

9. Weak   Powerful
   1   2   3   4   5   6   7

10. Special   Ordinary
   1   2   3   4   5   6   7

11. Rough   Smooth
   1   2   3   4   5   6   7

12. Comfortable   Uncomfortable
   1   2   3   4   5   6   7

Reprinted with the permission from Stiles, W. B., & Snow, J. S. (1984). Counseling session impact as viewed by novice counselors and their clients. *Journal of Counseling Psychology, 31,* 3–12.

You (the therapist) need to complete this form after your third session. Please read the instructions first.

FORM 6 (POSTTRAINING)
Rating the Therapist's Intentions

Therapist Name_____   Patient Name_____

Session Number_____   Date_____(Month/Day/Yr.)

To judge intentions, the therapist should review the tape right after the session (if you cannot, try to do it as soon as possible). The therapist should stop the tape after each therapist turn (everything the therapist says between two client speech acts) and indicate as many intentions as apply for that turn. The numbers in the following table indicate the therapist's turn. Put your intention category numbers for each turn in the column titled "the category numbers of therapist intentions." You should strive to remember exactly what was going through your mind right at the time of the intervention and be as honest as possible in reporting what you were actually thinking. Remember that there are no right or wrong answers; the purpose is simply to uncover what you planned to do at that moment. Also remember that you should indicate your intentions only for that immediate intervention, rather than report global strategies for the entire session. In general, the therapist should choose those intentions that best apply, even if all the phrasing is not exactly applicable to the current situation.

List of Therapist Intentions

1. **Set limits:**   To structure, make arrangements, establish goals and objectives of treatment, outline methods to attain goals, correct expectations about treatment, or establish rules or parameters of relationship (e.g., time, fees, cancellation policies, homework).

2. **Get information:**   To find out specific facts about history, client functioning, future plans, relationships, work.

3. **Give Information:**   To educate, give facts, correct misperceptions or misinformation, give reasons for therapist's behavior or procedures.

4. **Support:**   To provide a warm supportive, empathic environment; increase trust and rapport and build relationship; help client feel accepted, understood, comfortable, reassured and less anxious; help establish a person-to-person relationship.

5. **Focus:**   To help client get back on track, change a subject, channel or structure the discussion if he or she is unable to begin or has been diffuse or rambling.

6. **Clarify:**   To provide or solicit more elaboration, emphasis or specification when client or therapist has been vague, incomplete, confusing, contradictory or inaudible.

7. **Hope:**   To convey the expectation that change is possible and likely to occur, convey that the therapist will be able to help the client, restore morale, build up the client's confidence to make changes.

8. **Cathart:**   To promote relief from unwanted feelings, allow the client a chance to talk through feelings and problems.

9. **Cognitions:**   To identify maladaptive, illogical, or irrational thoughts, self-talk, automatic thoughts, attitudes or beliefs.

10. **Behaviors:**   To identify and describe the client's inappropriate or dysfunctional behaviors and/or their consequences, analyze the stimulus-response sequences of dysfunctional behavior, describe dysfunctional interpersonal patterns.

11. *Self-control:* To encourage client to take responsibility or gain a sense of mastery or control over dysfunctional thoughts, feelings, behaviors or impulses, help client become more responsible for interpersonal effects rather than blaming others.

12. *Feelings:* To identify intense feelings and/or enable acceptance of feelings; encourage or provoke the client to become aware of underlying or hidden feelings; to experience feelings at a deeper level.

13. *Insight:* To encourage understanding of the underlying reasons, dynamics, assumptions, motivations, history or meaning of cognition, behaviors, attitudes or feelings. May include an understanding of client's reactions to others' behavior.

14. *Change:* To encourage the development of new and more adaptive skills, behaviors, or cognition in dealing with self and others. May be to offer new, more adaptive assumptive models, frameworks, explanations, views or conceptualizations. May be to offer a new option for behavior or self-view.

15. *Reinforce change:* To offer positive reinforcement or positive feedback about behavioral, cognitive, interpersonal or affective attempts at change to enhance the probability that change will continue or be maintained; encourage risk taking and new ways of behaving. To review new changes to understand the reasons for them in order to increase the likelihood that new change will be maintained.

16. *Resistance:* To overcome obstacles to change or progress by discussing them. May also discuss failure to adhere to therapeutic procedures in the past or to prevent possibility of such failure in the future.

17. *Challenge:* To jolt the client out of a present state; shake up current beliefs or feelings; test validity, reality, or accurateness of beliefs, thoughts, feelings or behaviors; help client question the necessity of maintaining old patterns.

18. *Relationship:* To resolve problems as they arise in the relationship in order to build or maintain a smooth working alliance; to heal ruptures in the alliance; deal with issues appropriate to stage in treatment; identify and resolve distortions in client's thinking about the relationship that are based on past experiences and patterns rather than on current reality.

19. *Therapist needs:* To protect, relieve or defend the person of the therapist; to alleviate therapist's anxiety. May try excessively to persuade, argue, or feel good or superior at the expense of the client. May be done more in the service of the therapist's needs than the client's.

20. *Interpersonal:* To clarify the patient's reactions, attitudes, thoughts, behaviors and feelings to another person and sometimes the other person's reactions to the patient in order to understand the patient's interpersonal schema.

Modified from Hill, C. E., & O'Grady, K. E. (1985). List of therapist intentions illustrated in a case study and with therapists of varying theoretical orientations. *Journal of Counseling Psychology, 32,* 3–22.

The number of therapist speaking turn	The category number(s) of therapist intentions	The number of therapist speaking turn	The category number(s) of therapist intentions	The number of therapist speaking turn	The category number(s) of therapist intentions
1		27		53	
2		28		54	
3		29		55	
4		30		56	
5		31		57	
6		32		58	
7		33		59	
8		34		60	
9		35		61	
10		36		62	
11		37		63	
12		38		64	
13		39		65	
14		40		66	
15		41		67	
16		42		68	
17		43		69	
18		44		70	
19		45		71	
20		46		72	
21		47		73	
22		48		74	
23		49		75	
24		50		76	
25		51		77	
26		52		78	

The number of therapist speaking turn	The category number(s) of therapist intentions	The number of therapist speaking turn	The category number(s) of therapist intentions	The number of therapist speaking turn	The category number(s) of therapist intentions
79		105		131	
80		106		132	
81		107		133	
82		108		134	
83		109		135	
84		110		136	
85		111		137	
86		112		138	
87		113		139	
88		114		140	
89		115		141	
90		116		142	
91		117		143	
92		118		144	
93		119		145	
94		120		146	
95		121		147	
96		122		148	
97		123		149	
98		124		150	
99		125		151	
100		126		152	
101		127		153	
102		128		154	
103		129		155	
104		130		156	

Please have your patient complete this form after your third session

FORM 7 (POSTTRAINING)
Patient Reaction System

Therapist Name_____   Patient Name_____

Session Number_____   Date_____(Month/Day/Yr.)

(To the therapist: The patient rates each therapist turn using this "patient reaction system" while you rate the same turn using Form 6, Rating the Therapist's Intentions)

To the patient: Review the tape immediately after the session. Try to remember what you were experiencing during the session. Stop the tape after each therapist speaking turn and list the numbers of the reactions that you felt when you first heard what the therapist said. Choose those reactions that best describe your experiences, even if every part of the definition does not apply or the phrasing is not exactly accurate.

- -

List of Patient Reactions

Positive Reactions:

1. *Understood:* I felt that my therapist really understood me and knew what I was saying or what was going on with me.

2. *Supported:* I felt accepted, reassured, liked, cared for, or safe. I felt like my therapist was on my side or I came to trust, like, respect, or admire my therapist more. This may have involved a change in my relationship with my therapist, such that we resolved a problem between us.

3. *Hopeful:* I felt confident, encouraged, optimistic, strong, pleased, or happy, and felt like I could change.

4. *Relief:* I felt less depressed, anxious, guilty, angry, or had fewer uncomfortable or painful feelings.

5. *Negative thoughts or behaviors:* I became aware of specific negative thoughts or painful feelings.

6. *Better self-understanding:* I gained new insight about myself, saw new connections, or began to understand why I behaved or felt a certain way. This new understanding helped me accept and like myself.

7. *Clear:* I got more focused about what I was really trying to say, what areas I need to change in my life, what my goals are, or what I want to work on in therapy.

8. *Feelings:* I felt a greater awareness or deepening of feelings or could express my emotion better.

9. *Responsibility:* I accepted my role in events and blamed others less.

10. *Unstuck:* I overcame a block and felt freed up and more involved in what I have to do in therapy.

11. *New perspective:* I gained a new understanding of another person, situation, or the world. I understand why people or things are as they are.

12. *Educated:* I gained greater knowledge or information. I learned something I had not known.

13. *New ways to behave:* I learned specific ideas about what I can do differently to cope with particularly situations or problems. I solved a problem, made a choice or decision, or decided to take a risk.

14. *Challenged:* I felt shook up, forced to question myself, or to look at issues I had been avoiding.

Negative Reactions:

15. *Scared:* I felt overwhelmed, afraid, or wanted to avoid or not admit to having some feeling or problem. I may have felt that my therapist was too pushy or would disapprove of me or would not like me.

16. *Worse:* I felt less hopeful, sicker, out of control, dumb, incompetent, ashamed, or like giving up. Perhaps my therapist ignored me, criticized me, hurt me, pitied me, or treated me as weak and helpless. I may have felt jealous of or competitive with my therapist.

17. *Stuck:* I felt blocked, impatient, or bored. I did not know what to do next or how to get out of the situation. I felt dissatisfied with the progress of therapy or having to go over the same things again.

18. *Lack of direction:* I felt angry or upset that my therapist didn't give me enough guidance or direction.

19. *Confused:* I did not know how I was feeling or felt distracted from what I wanted to say. I was puzzled or could not understand what my therapist was trying to say. I was not sure I agreed with my therapist.

20. *Misunderstood:* I felt that my therapist did not really hear what I was trying to say, misjudged me, or made assumptions about me that were incorrect.

21. *No reaction:* I had no particular reaction. My therapist may have been making social conversation, gathering information, or was unclear.

Reprinted with permission from Hill, C. E., Helm, J. E., Spiegel, S.B., & Tichenor, V. (1988). Development of a system for categorizing client reactions to therapist interventions. *Journal of Counseling Psychology, 35,* 27–36.

The number of therapist speaking turn	The category number(s) of patient reaction system	The number of therapist speaking turn	The category number(s) of patient reaction system	The number of therapist speaking turn	The category number(s) of patient reaction system
1		26		51	
2		27		52	
3		28		53	
4		29		54	
5		30		55	
6		31		56	
7		32		57	
8		33		58	
9		34		59	
10		35		60	
11		36		61	
12		37		62	
13		38		63	
14		39		64	
15		40		65	
16		41		66	
17		42		67	
18		43		68	
19		44		69	
20		45		70	
21		46		71	
22		47		72	
23		48		73	
24		49		74	
25		50		75	

The number of therapist speaking turn	The category number(s) of patient reaction system	The number of therapist speaking turn	The category number(s) of patient reaction system	The number of therapist speaking turn	The category number(s) of patient reaction system
76		101		126	
77		102		127	
78		103		128	
79		104		129	
80		105		130	
81		106		131	
82		107		132	
83		108		133	
84		109		134	
85		110		135	
86		111		136	
87		112		137	
88		113		138	
89		114		139	
90		115		140	
91		116		141	
92		117		142	
93		118		143	
94		119		144	
95		120		145	
96		121		146	
97		122		147	
98		123		148	
99		124		149	
100		125		150	

Afterword

Any book, any course, or any set of videotapes about psychotherapy has limitations, since the field is so broad and so deep. Our limitations are several:

1. The method of teaching through limited reading, much homework, and seminar discussion has many advantages. However, our program does not include other more time-consuming but also valuable approaches, including case conferences and in-depth reading of classical and practical papers and texts.

2. Our approach remains conceptual—practically conceptual but conceptual nevertheless. We do not attempt in-depth training in generic skills, such as empathic reflections and relaxation training, or school specific skills, including interpretation, cognitive restructuring, and role rehearsal. We do not teach trainees how to do these techniques nor do we teach them when to use them.

3. We have not attempted to articulate a theory of normal human development, a theory of normal personality, a theory of psychopathology, and a comprehensive theory of treatment related to the previous theories. Ideally, but perhaps not necessarily, psychotherapy change models should be related to theories of normal and abnormal development.

4. Several content areas that could be useful to all trainees are not covered. These include: assertiveness training, termination, combining pharmacotherapy and psychotherapy, culture and gender issues, and as integrated approaches to a variety of *DSM-IV* diagnostic categories, such as major depression, panic disorder, and substance abuse.

In our opinion, this training program works well as an introduction to school specific approaches. Ideally, these ideas are presented first and then trainees are taught cognitive therapy, interpersonal therapy, psychodynamic therapy, solution-focused therapies, and/or family therapy. Teachers of these and other approaches tend to believe that specific schools should be targeted for specific problems. While significant research evidence suggests that specific approaches treat specific problems, a broader view suggests that cognitive therapy (Lipsey & Wilson, 1993), for example, resembles Prozac and its relatives Paxil and Zoloft (Schatzberg & Nemeroff, 1995), in that each is effective for a variety of diagnoses. Furthermore, practicing clinicians appear to combine what appears to them to be useful from different approaches to fit the perceived needs of their patients (Goldfried & Wolfe, 1996), including pharmacotherapy and psychotherapy (Beitman & Klerman, 1991). We believe that sophisticated psychotherapy integration, based upon the foundation presented here, lies in the future of psychotherapy education and practice.

Finally, we bring you back to the beginning. We believe that psychotherapy training should be fun! You learn about yourself while helping others; you study the human condition while serving humanity; you are involved in helping others find their ways through this confusing life and help resolve some of your own misgivings and fears about living. To bring humor to the consulting room helps all participants. May fun and joy be part of your teaching and learning.

References

Alexander, F. (1954). Some quantitative aspects of psychoanalytic technique. *Journal of the American Psychoanalytic Association, 2,* 685–701.

Alexander, F., & French, T. M. (1946). *Psychoanalytic therapy.* New York: Ronald.

Allen, N. B. (1996). Cognitive psychotherapy. In S. Bloch (Ed.). *An introduction to the psychotherapies* (3rd ed.). (pp. 173–174). New York: Oxford University Press.

Andrews, J. D., Norcross, J. C., & Halgin, R. P. (1992). Training in psychotherapy integration. In J. C. Norcross & M. R. Goldfried (Eds.), *Handbook of psychotherapy integration* (pp. 563). New York: Basic Books.

Appelbaum, P. S., & Jorgenson, L. (1991). Psychotherapist-patient sexual contact after termination of treatment: An analysis and a proposal. *American Journal of Psychiatry, 148,* 1466–1473.

Barlow, D. H. (1990). Long-term outcome for patients with panic disorder treated with cognitive-behavioral therapy. *Journal of Clinical Psychiatry, 51* (Supp. A), 17–23.

Basch, M. F. (1980). *Doing psychotherapy.* New York: Basic Books.

Bates, C. M., & Brodsky, A. M. (1989). *Sex in the therapy hour.* New York: Guilford.

Beck, A. (1995). An interview with a depressed and suicidal patient. In D. Wedding & R. Corsini (Eds.), *Case studies in psychotherapy.* Itasca, IL: Peacock.

Beck, A., Rush, A., Shaw, B., & Emery, G. (1979). *Cognitive therapy of depression.* New York: Guilford.

Beck, A., & Weishaar, M. (1989). *Cognitive therapy.* In A. Freeman, K. Simon, L. Beutler, & H. Arkowitz (Eds.), *Comprehensive handbook of cognitive therapy.* New York: Plenum Press.

Beitman, B. D. (1983). Categories of countertransference. *Journal of Operational Psychiatry, 14,* 82–90.

Beitman, B. D. (1987). *The structure of individual psychotherapy.* New York: Guilford.

Beitman, B. D., & Klerman, G. L. (Eds.). (1991). *Integrating pharmacotherapy and psychotherapy.* Washington, DC: American Psychiatric Press, Inc.

Berman, L. (1949). Countertransference and attitudes of the analyst in the therapeutic process. *Psychiatry, 12,* 159–166.

Beutler, L., & Consoli, A. (1992). Systematic eclectic psychotherapy. In J. Norcross & M. R. Goldfried (Eds.), *Handbook of psychotherapy integration.* New York: Basic Books.

Beutler, L. E., Mohr, D. C., Grawe, K., Engle, D., & MacDonald, R. (1991). Looking for differential psychotherapy efficacy. *Journal of Psychotherapy Integration, 1,* 121–142.

Bordin, E. S. (1979). The generalizability of the psychoanalytic concept of the working alliance. *Psychotherapy: Theory, Research and Practice, 16,* 252–259.

Boscolo, L., Cecchin, G., Hoffman, L., & Penn, P. (1987). *Milan system family therapy.* New York: Basic Books.

Bruch, H. (1974). *Learning psychotherapy.* Boston: Harvard University Press.

Cormier, L. S., & Hackney, H. (1987). *The professional counselor* (pp. 126–127). Englewood Cliffs, NJ: Prentice-Hall.

Corey, R. (1996). *Theory and practice of counseling and psychotherapy.* Pacific Grove, CA: Brooks/Cole.

Deikman, A. (1983). *The observing self.* Boston: Beacon Press.

Ellis, A. (1974). *Growth through reason.* Hollywood: Wilshire Books.

Epstein, R. S., & Simon, R. I. (1990). The Exploitation Index: An early warning indication of boundary violations in psychotherapy. *Bulletin of Menninger Clinic, 54,* 450–465.

Epstein, R. S., & Simon, R. I. (1992). Assessing boundary violations in psychotherapy: Survey results with the Exploitation Index. *Bulletin of Menninger Clinic, 56,* 150–166.

Erikson, E. (1963). *Childhood and society.* New York: Norton.

Foreman, S. A., & Marmar, C. R. (1985). Therapist actions that address initially poor therapeutic alliance in psychotherapy. *American Journal of Psychiatry, 142,* 922–926.

Freeman, A., & White, D. (1989). The treatment of suicidal behavior. In A. Freeman, K. Simon, L. Beutler, & H. Arkowitz (Eds.), *Comprehensive handbook of cognitive therapy.* New York: Plenum Press.

Freud, S. (1905). Fragment of an analysis of a case of hysteria. In J. Strachey (Ed. & Trans.), *The standard edition of the complete psychological works of Sigmund Freud* (Vol. 7, pp. 3–22). New York: Norton. [hereafter the *Standard Edition*].

Freud, S. (1910). The future of prospects for psycho-analytic therapy. *Standard Edition* (Vol. 11, pp. 141–151). New York: Norton.

Freud, S. (1912). The dynamics of transference. *Standard Edition* (Vol. 12, pp. 97–108) New York: Norton.

Freud, S. (1915). Observations on transference-love. *Standard Edition* (Vol. 12, pp. 157–171). New York: Norton.

Fuller, F., & Hill, C. E. (1985). Counselor and helpee perceptions of counselor intentions in relation to outcome in a single counseling session. *Journal of Counseling Psychology, 32,* 329–338.

Gabbard, G., & Wilkinson, S. (1994). *Management of countertransference with borderline patients.* Washington: American Psychiatric Press, Inc.

Garfield, S. L. (1995). *Psychotherapy: An eclectic-integrative approach* (2nd ed.). New York: Wiley.

Gartrell, N., Herman, J., & Olarte, S. (1986). Psychiatrist-patient sexual contact: Results of a national survey, I: Prevalence. *American Journal of Psychiatry, 143,* 1126–1131.

Gartrell, N., Herman J., & Olarte S. (1988). Psychiatric residents sexual contact with educators and patients: Results of a national survey. *American Journal of Psychiatry, 145,* 690–694.

Gelso, C., & Carter, J. A. (1985). The relationship in counseling and psychotherapy: Components, consequences, and theoretical antecedents. *Counseling Psychologist, 13,* 155–243.

Givelber, F., & Simon, B. (1981). A death in the life of a therapist and its impact on the therapy. *Psychiatry, 44,* 141–149.

Glaser, R., & Thorpe, J. (1986). Unethical intimacy: A survey of sexual contact and advances between psychology educators and female graduate students. *American Psychologist, 41,* 43–51.

Goldfried, M. R. (1995). *From cognitive-behavior therapy to psychotherapy integration.* New York: Springer.

Goldfried, M. R., & Davison, G. C. (1976). *Clinical behavior therapy.* New York: Holt, Rinehart and Winston.

Goldfried, M. R., & Padawer, W. (1982). Current status and future directions in psychotherapy. In M. R. Goldfried (Eds.). *Converging themes in psychotherapy: Trends in psychodynamic, humanistic, and behavioral practice* (pp. 203). New York: Springer.

Goldfried, M. R., & Wolfe, B. E. (1996). Psychotherapy practice and research: Repairing a strained alliance. *American Psychologist, 51,* 1007–1017.

Greenberg, L. (1995a). Process experiential psychotherapy. In G. VandenBos, J. Frank-McNeil, J. Norcross, & D. Freedheim (Eds.). *The anatomy of psychotherapy.* Washington, DC: American Psychological Association.

Greenberg, L. (1995b). The therapeutic alliance in psychodynamic, cognitive-behavioral, and experiential therapies. *Journal of Psychotherapy Integration, 5,* 1–26.

Greenberg, L. S., Rice, L. N., & Elliott, R. (1993). *Facilitating emotional change.* New York: Guilford.

Greenson, R. R. (1965). The working alliance and the transference neurosis. *Psychoanalytic Quarterly, 34,* 155–181.

Greenson, R. R. (1967). *The technique and practice of psychoanalysis* (Vol. I). New York: International Universities Press.

Greenson, R. R. (1971). The real relationship between the patient and the psychoanalyst. In M. Kanzer (Eds.), *The unconscious today* (pp. 213–232). New York: International Universities Press.

Griffin, W. A. (1993). *Family therapy.* New York: Brunner/Mazel.

Growe, M. (1996). Couple therapy. In S. Bloch (Eds.). *An introduction to the psychotherapies* (pp. 193–211). New York: Oxford University Press.

Hedges, L. E. (1983). *Listening perspectives in psychotherapy.* New York: Aronson.

Heimann, P. (1950). On countertransference. *International Journal of Psychoanalysis, 31,* 81–84.

Heppner, P. P., & O'Brien, K. M. (1994). Multicultural counselor training: Students' perceptions of helpful and hindering events. *Counselor Education and Supervision, 34,* 4–18.

Hill, C. E. (1982). Counseling process research: Methodological and philosophical issues. *Counseling Psychologist, 10,* 7–19.

Hill, C. E. (1986). An overview of the Hill counselor and client verbal response modes category systems. In L. Greenberg & W. Pinsof (Eds.), *The psychotherapeutic process: A research handbook* (pp.131–159). New York: Guilford.

Hill, C. E., Helm, J. E., Tichenor, V., O'Grady, K. E., & Perry, E. S. (1988). Effect of therapist response modes in brief psychotherapy. *Journal of Counseling Psychology, 35,* 222–233.

Hill, C. E., Helm, J. E., Spiegel, S. B., & Tichenor, V. (1988). Development of a system for categorizing client reactions to therapist interventions. *Journal of Counseling Psychology, 35,* 27–36.

Hill, C. E., & O'Grady, K. E. (1985). List of therapist intentions illustrated in a case study and with therapists of varying theoretical orientations. *Journal of Counseling Psychology, 32,* 3–22.

Holcomb, W. R., Parker, J. C., & Leong, G. B. (1997). Outcomes of inpatients treated on a VA psychiatry unit and a substance abuse treatment unit. *Psychiatric Services, 48,* 699–704.

Horvath, A. O., & Greenberg, L. S. (1989). Development and validation of the working alliance. *Journal of Counseling Psychology, 36,* 223–233.

Horvath, A. O. (1995). The therapeutic relationship: From transference to alliance. *Psychotherapy in Practice, 1,* 7–17.

Horowitz, M. J., Marmar, C., Weiss, D., Dewitt, K. N., & Rosenbaum, R. (1984). Brief psychotherapy of bereavement reactions: The relationship of process to outcome. *Archives of General Psychiatry. 41,* 438–448.

Kabat-Zinn, J. (1990). *Full catastrophe living.* New York: Delta.

Kivlighan, D. M. (1989). Changes in counselor intentions and response modes and in client reactions and session evaluation after training. *Journal of Counseling Psychology, 3,* 471–476.

Kivlighan, D. M. (1990). Relationship between counselor use of intentions and clients perception of working alliance. *Journal of Counseling Psychology, 37,* 27–32.

Kivlighan, D. M., & Schmitz, P. J. (1992). Counselor technical activity in cases with improving working alliances and continuing-poor working alliance. *Journal of Counseling Psychology, 39,* 32–38.

Kleinke, C. L. (1993). *Common principles of psychotherapy.* Pacific Grove, CA: Brooks/Cole.

Klerman, G. L., Weissman, M. M., Markowitz, J. C., Glick, I., Wilner, P. J., Mason, B., & Shear, M. K. (1994). Medication and psychotherapy. In A. E. Bergin, & S. L. Garfield (Eds.), *Handbook of psychotherapy and behavior change* (pp. 734–783). New York: Wiley.

Klerman, G., Weissman, M., Rounsaville, B., & Chevron, E. (1984). *Interpersonal psychotherapy of depression.* New York: Basic Books.

Kramer, J. R. (1985). *Family interfaces: Transgenerational patterns.* New York: Brunner/Mazel.

Lambert, J., & Bergin, A. E. (1994). The effectiveness of psychotherapy. In A. E. Bergin & S. L. Garfield (Eds.), *Handbook of psychotherapy and behavior change* (pp. 143–189). New York: Wiley.

Langs, R. (1973). *The technique of psychoanalytic psychotherapy* (Vol. 1). New York: Jason Aronson.

Larson, L. M., Suzuki, L. A., Gillespie, K. N., Potenza, M. T., Bechtel, M. A., & Toulouse, A. L. (1992). Development and validation of the counseling self-estimate inventory. *Journal of Counseling Psychology, 39,* 105–120.

Lazarus, A. A. (1996). The utility and futility of combining treatments in psychotherapy. *Clinical Psychology—Science & Practice, 3,* 1, 59–68.

Lipsey, M. W., & Wilson, D. B. (1993). The efficacy of psychological, educational, and behavioral treatment: Confirmation from a meta-analysis. *American Psychologist, 48,* 1181–1209.

Luborsky, L., & Crits-Christoph, P. C. (1990). *Understanding transference.* New York: Basic Books.

Merluzzi, T. V., & Boltwood, M. D. (1989). Cognitive assessment. In A. Freeman, K. Simon, L. Beutler, & H. Arkowitz. (Eds.), *Comprehensive handbook of cognitive therapy.* New York: Plenum Press.

Minuchin, S., & Fishman, H. C. (1981). *Family therapy techniques.* Cambridge, MA: Harvard University Press.

Morgenstern, A. (1980). Reliving the last goodbye: The psychotherapy of an almost silent patient. *Psychiatry, 43,* 251–258.

Moras, K., & Strupp. H. H. (1982). Pretherapy interpersonal relations, patient's alliance and outcome of brief therapy. *Achieves of General Psychiatry, 39,* 405–409.

Mosak, H., & Maniacci, M. (1995). The case of Roger. In D. Wedding & R. Corsini (Eds.), *Case studies in pychotherapy.* Itasca, IL: Peacock.

Nichols, M., & Schwartz, R. (1991). *Family therapy.* Boston: Allyn and Bacon.

Norcross, J. C., & Goldfried, M. R. (1992). *Handbook of psychotherapy integration.* New York: Basic Books.

Orlinsky, D. E., & Howard, K. I. (1978). The relation of process to outcome in psychotherapy. In S. L. Garfield & A. E. Bergin (Eds). *Handbook of psychotherapy and behavior change: An empirical analysis.* New York: Wiley.

Papp, P. (1995). The daughter who said no. In D. Wedding & R. Corsini (Eds.), *Case studies in psychotherapy* (pp. 179–180). Itasca, IL: Peacock.

Parlett, M., & Hemming, J. (1996). Gestalt therapy. In W. Dryden (Ed.), *Handbook of individual psychotherapy.* London: Sage.

Racker, H. (1968). *Transference and countertransference.* New York: International Universities Press.

Rice, L. A., & Greenberg, L. S. (1984). *Patterns of change.* New York: Guilford.

Robertson, M. H. (1995). *Psychotherapy education and training: An integrative pespective.* Madison, CT: International Universities Press.

Rockland, L. H. (1989). *Supportive psychotherapy—A psychodynamic approach.* New York: Basic Books.

Rogers, C. R. (1957). The necessary and sufficient conditions of therapeutic personality change. *Journal of Counseling Psychology, 22,* 95–1103.

Schatzberg, A. F., & Nemeroff, C. B. (Eds.). (1995). *The American Psychiatric Press textbook of psychopharmacology.* Washington, DC: American Psychiatric Press.

Sherman, R., Oresky, P., & Rountrees, Y. (1991). *Solving problems in couples and family therapy.* New York: Brunner/Mazel.

Shostrom, E. L. (Producer). (1966). *Three approaches to psychotherapy.* [Film]. (Available from Psychological and Educational Films, Corona Del Mar, CA).

Simon, R. I. (1991). Psychological injury caused by boundary violation precursors to therapist-patient sex. *Psychiatric Annals, 21,* 614–619.

Singer, J. L., Sincoff, J. B., & Kolligian, J. (1987). Countertransference and cognition: Studying the psychotherapist's distortions as consequences of normal information processing. *Psychotherapy, 26,* 344–355.

Sipps, G. J., & Sugden, G. J. (1988). Counselor training level and verbal response type: Their relationship to efficacy and outcome expectations. *Journal of Counseling Psychology, 35,* 397–401.

Slovenko, R. (1991). "Undue familiarity or undue damages?" *Psychiatric Annals, 21,* 598–610.

Small, J. (1984). *Notes on marriage and family therapy.* Unpublished.

Stiles, W. B., & Snow, J. S. (1984). Counseling session impact as viewed by novice counselors and their clients. *Journal of Counseling Psychology, 31,* 3–12.

Stone, A. S. (1971). Suicide precipitated by psychotherapy. *American Journal of Psychotherapy 25,* 18–26.

Strong, S. R. (1968). Counseling: An interpersonal influence process. *Journal of Counseling Psychology, 15,* 215–224.

Strupp, H., & Binder, J. (1984). *Psychotherapy in a new key.* New York: Basic Books.

Sullivan, G. (1996). Behavior therapy. In W. Dryden (Ed.), *Handbook of individual psychotherapy.* London: Sage.

Thompson, A. P. (1986). Changes in counseling skills during graduate and undergraduate study. *Journal of Counseling Psychology, 33,* 65–72.

Thorne, B. (1996). Person-centered therapy. In W. Dryden (Ed.), *Handbook of individual psychotherapy* (pp. 121–145). London: Sage.

Tracey, T. J., Glindden, C. E., & Kokotovic, A. M. (1988). Factor structure of the Counselor Rating Form—Short. *Journal of Counseling Psychology, 35,* 330–335.

Tracey, T. J., Hays, K. A., & Malone, J. (1988). Changes in counselor response as a function of experience. *Journal of Counseling Psychology, 35,* 119–126.

Turner, N. (1994). Nuclear family vs. family of origin: A paradox. In G. Weeks & L. Hof (Eds.), *The marital relationship therapy casebook.* New York: Brunner/Mazel.

Wachtel, E., & Wachtel, P. (1986). *Family dynamics in individual psychotherapy: A guide to clinical strategies.* New York: Guilford.

Walter, J. L., & Peller, J. E. (1992). *Becoming solution-focused in brief therapy.* New York: Brunner/Mazel.

Winnicott, D. W. (1947). Hate in the countertransference. In *Through paediatrics to psychanalysis* (pp. 194–203). London: Hogarth.

Wolberg, L. R. (1988). *The techniques of psychotherapy.* New York: Grune & Stratton.

Yalom, I. (1980). *Existential psychotherapy.* New York: Basic Books.

Index